RESEARCH, WRITING, AND CREATIVE PROCESS IN OPEN AND DISTANCE EDUCATION

Research, Writing, and Creative Process in Open and Distance Education

Tales from the Field

Edited by Dianne Conrad

https://www.openbookpublishers.com

©2023 Dianne Conrad (ed.)

Copyright of individual chapters is maintained by the chapter's authors

This work is licensed under an Attribution-NonCommercial 4.0 International (CC BY-NC 4.0). This license allows you to share, copy, distribute and transmit the text; to adapt the text for non-commercial purposes of the text providing attribution is made to the authors (but not in any way that suggests that they endorse you or your use of the work). Attribution should include the following information:

Dianne Conrad (ed.), *Research, Writing, and Creative Process in Open and Distance Education: Tales from the Field*. Cambridge, UK: Open Book Publishers, 2023, https://doi.org/10.11647/OBP.0356

Copyright and permissions for the reuse of many of the images included in this publication differ from the above. This information is provided in the captions and in the list of illustrations. Every effort has been made to identify and contact copyright holders and any omission or error will be corrected if notification is made to the publisher.

Further details about CC BY-NC licenses are available at
http://creativecommons.org/licenses/by-nc/4.0/

All external links were active at the time of publication unless otherwise stated and have been archived via the Internet Archive Wayback Machine at https://archive.org/web

Any digital material and resources associated with this volume will be available at https://doi.org/10.11647/OBP.0356#resources

ISBN Paperback: 978-1-80511-094-1
ISBN Hardback: 978-1-80511-095-8
ISBN Digital (PDF): 978-1-80511-096-5
ISBN Digital ebook (epub): 978-1-80511-097-2
ISBN XML: 978-1-80511-099-6
ISBN HTML: 978-1-80511-100-9
DOI: 10.11647/OBP.0356

Cover image: Thom Milkovic, 'Vintage Words' (2017), https://unsplash.com/photos/FTNGfpYCpGM

Cover design: Jeevanjot Kaur Nagpal

another book for Ray, who
keeps his words and his process
close to his chest,
preferring instead to exercise
his artistry with paint
and brushes

Contents

Acknowledgement	xi
Contributing Authors	1
Foreword: The Way of Academic Writing *Terry Anderson*	7
1. Introduction and Welcome *Dianne Conrad*	13
2. The Way of Academic Writing: Reflections of a Traveller *David Starr-Glass*	19
3. On Being Written *Jon Dron*	33
4. What Lies Beneath *Pamela Ryan*	47
5. Reminiscences and Reflections: No Regrets *Dianne Conrad*	59
6. Intrinsic Motivation, Agency, and Self-Efficacy: Journeying From "Quasi-University" Student to Steward of the ODE Community *Junhong Xiao*	71
7. 1001 Nights of Research: The Good, Bad, and the Ugly Magic Carpet Ride *Jennifer Roberts*	87
8. Creative Academic Writing and Anatomy of a Scholarly Paper *Aras Bozkurt*	101
9. Writing and Making the World *Catherine Cronin*	119

10. A Collaborative Approach to Research and Writing *D. Randy Garrison*	129
11. Serendipity: Becoming a Specialist in Online Learning *Tony Bates*	141
12. Writing in the Margins: Maintaining a Scholarly Voice as an Executive *Mark Nichols*	155
13. Indigenous, Settler, Diasporic, and Post-colonial: The Identities Woven Through our Academic Writing *Marguerite Koole, Michael Cottrell, Janet Mola Okoko, and Kristine Dreaver-Charles*	173
14. Born Curious and in Trouble: Making Sense of Writing *Paul Prinsloo*	197
15. A Few Words in Conclusion *Dianne Conrad*	213
Index	217

Acknowledgement

With many, many thanks, I would like to acknowledge the supportive guidance of the Open Book Publishers press. From my initial contact with Dr. Alessandra Tosi, to the wonderful work of Lucy Barnes and the production team of designers and copy editors, OBP has been prompt, efficient, and lovely to work with. I am so grateful.

Contributing Authors

Aras Bozkurt is a researcher and faculty member in the Department of Distance Education, Open Education Faculty at Anadolu University, Turkey. He holds MA and PhD degrees in distance education. Aras conducts empirical studies on distance education, open and distance learning, online learning, networked learning, and educational technology to which he applies various critical theories, such as connectivism, rhizomatic learning, and heutagogy. He is also interested in emerging research paradigms, including social network analysis, sentiment analysis, and data mining. He shares his views on his Twitter feed @arasbozkurt.

Catherine Cronin is an independent scholar focusing on critical and social justice approaches in digital, open and higher education. She is co-editor of *Higher Education for Good: Teaching and Learning Futures* (forthcoming with Open Book Publishers, https://doi.org/10.11647/OBP.0363) and was a 2022 Global Open Education Graduate Network (GO-GN) Fellow. Catherine has worked in both the higher education and community education sectors, most recently as Digital and Open Education lead in Ireland's National Forum for the Enhancement of Teaching & Learning in Higher Education. A born New Yorker who has made her home in Ireland, you can find Catherine at https://catherinecronin.net.

David Starr-Glass is a mentor with the International Education (Prague) at SUNY Empire State College. He teaches a range of business and cross-culture courses online and is also a dissertation supervisor for undergraduate dissertations in business and economics. Over the last twenty years, he has published more than 120 book chapters and peer-reviewed articles. He has earned master's degrees in business administration (University of Notre Dame de Namur, California), occupational psychology (Birkbeck College, University of London), and in online education (University of Southern Queensland). When not in Prague, he lives in Jerusalem and teaches economic and business-related courses with a number of local colleges.

Dianne Conrad has spent her post-secondary career firstly in adult education, specializing in prior learning assessment; and after that, in online, open and distance education, with an emphasis on learning, community, and assessment. Since retirement from Athabasca University, she has published five books (including this one) on several topics dear to her heart: online assessment, open learning, online doctoral potential, and seniors' learning in today's digital age. She has taught all manner and levels of distance education courses, published many journal articles, and served as co-editor of the *International Review of Research in Open and Distributed Learning* (IRRODL). She hopes to keep going.

Jennifer Roberts is an associate professor in the Institute for Open Distance Learning (IODL) in the College of Education at the University of South Africa (Unisa). A truly interdisciplinary scholar, she has undergraduate studies in statistics and sociology, and graduate degrees in tourism development and management, and in distance teaching and curriculum design. She is widely published in distance education, discipline in education, metacognition, research trends and staff development and has presented papers around the world. Jennifer was the first South African to be elected to the executive committee of the Open and Distance Learning Association of Australia (ODLAA), where she was vice president and publications officer and has also twice guest-edited the *Distance Education Journal*. In 2021, she was acknowledged by the AD Scientific Index as a member of the top 10,000 influential scientists on the African continent and occupied the number three position in Africa for DE research.

Jon Dron is a full professor at Athabasca University, based in the School of Computing and Information Systems. He has received national and institutional awards for his teaching, is author of various award-winning research papers, and is a regular keynote speaker. His research is cross-disciplinary, including social, pedagogical, technological, systemic and philosophical aspects of technology, learning, and education, about which he has authored three books. Prior to becoming an academic, he sang swing for a living for ten years, before becoming an IT support manager. He has qualifications in philosophy, information systems, university education, and learning technologies.

Junhong Xiao is a professor at the Open University of Shantou (formerly known as Shantou Radio & Television University), China; founding member of the Center for Open Education Research (COER) of the University of Oldenburg; co-editor of *SpringerBriefs in Open and Distance Education* series (https://www.springer.com/series/15238); editor of Section I, History, Theory and Research in ODE, *Handbook of Open, Distance and Digital Education* (https://link.springer.com/referencework/10.1007/978-981-19-0351-9#toc); editorial board member of several journals; co-author of over 250 publications in Chinese and English; and reviewer of numerous journals and conferences. He has been engaged in open and distance education for thirty-five years as a practitioner and researcher.

Marguerite Koole is an associate professor in educational technology and design in the College of Education, University of Saskatchewan. Her PhD thesis, completed in 2013 at Lancaster University, UK, is entitled "Identity Positioning of Doctoral Students in Networked Learning Environments". She holds a Master of Education in Distance Education (MEd) with a focus on mobile learning and a BA in modern languages. She also completed a college diploma in multimedia production with training in web development, audio, video, animation, 3D animation, marketing, and business. Marguerite has been involved in teaching, instructional design, multimedia programming, content management, e-portfolios, and social software. She has designed interactive, online learning activities for various learning purposes and platforms — including print, web, and mobile devices. Email: m.koole@usask.ca

Mark Nichols is, at time of writing, executive director of learning design & development at Open Polytechnic, a subsidiary of Te Pūkenga in New Zealand. Mark is a principal fellow of the Higher Education Academy and a European Distance and e-Learning Network (EDEN)

fellow, and he has served on the executive committees of the Flexible Learning Association of New Zealand (FLANZ), Australasian Society for Computers in Tertiary Education (ASCILITE), and currently the International Council for Open and Distance Education (ICDE). His research work includes outputs related to studying on screen, student retention, indigenous courseware development, teaching and learning models, and open, distance and flexible (ODFL) systems and change. Mark hosts the Leaders & Legends of Online Learning podcast.

Pamela Ryan has retired from full-time academia and now works as an academic consultant helping young academics with their research papers and research funding applications. She also serves as an editor for theses, dissertations and academic books. She was appointed as research fellow at St Edmund's College, University of Cambridge in 2003, and fulfilled this role annually until 2017. Originally from the Department of English Studies, her interests are in Sylvia Plath, modern women's fiction, psychoanalysis, postcolonial studies, open learning, and digital literacy. Pam lives in a small village two hours from Cape Town, South Africa, and spends her time walking, reading, gardening and just generally staring in awe at the mountains.

Paul Prinsloo is a research professor in Open and Distance Learning (ODL) in the Department of Business Management, College of Economic and Management Sciences, University of South Africa (Unisa). He is a visiting professor at the Carl von Ossietzky University of Oldenburg, Germany, a research associate for Contact North/Contact Nord (Canada), a fellow of the European Distance and E-Learning Network (EDEN), member of the Executive Committee for the Society of Learning Analytics Research (SoLAR) and serves on several editorial boards. Paul's recent research focuses on the ethical collection, analysis, and use of student data in learning analytics. He was born curious and in trouble and nothing has changed.

Randy Garrison, professor emeritus at the University of Calgary, has served as dean of extension at the University of Alberta and Director of the Teaching and Learning Centre at the University of Calgary. He has published extensively on teaching and learning in adult, higher and distance education. Randy has authored, co-authored, or edited fifteen books and over 100 refereed articles/chapters. He currently has two books in press: Vaughan, Dell, Cleveland-Innes, and Garrison (2023), *Community of Inquiry: Seven principles of blended learning*; and Cleveland-Innes, Stenbom, and Garrison (eds) (2023), *Community of Inquiry applications: Introduction, design, delivery*.

Tony Bates is a senior advisor at the Chang School of Continuing Education, Ryerson University, Toronto and is also a research associate at Contact North, Ontario. He was chair of the Board of the Canadian Digital Learning Research Association from 2018 to 2022 and is a consultant assisting with the implementation of the British Columbia Institute of Technology's e-Learning Strategy. He is the author of twelve books, including his latest online, open textbook for faculty and instructors, Teaching in a Digital Age, which has been downloaded over one million times and translated into ten languages. He has honorary degrees from two Canadian universities (Laurentian and Athabasca) and four foreign universities for his research into online learning and distance education.

*Using an innovative format in her chapter, Dr Koole included three colleagues in a discussion designed to address chapter themes through several interconnected lenses. Her co-writers' biographical notes are here, also alphabetized by first name:

Janet Mola Okoko is an associate professor in the Department of Educational Administration, College of Education at the University of Saskatchewan in Canada. She holds a Bachelor of Education from Kenyatta University in Kenya, a Master of Education, and a PhD in educational leadership from the University of Calgary. Her research focuses on school leadership preparation and development. She is currently studying how school leaders' capacity to use practitioner-oriented and technology-mediated research to support student learning can be enhanced. Her recent publications report on cross-cultural perspectives on teacher leadership and contextual perspectives of qualitative research methods. Email: janet.okoko@usask.ca

Kristine Dreaver-Charles is a member of the Mistawasis First Nation, and she grew up in Prince Albert, Saskatchewan. Her early career was spent teaching middle years and high school students in northern Saskatchewan. A position teaching online led to a master's degree in instructional media from Wilkes University. Kristine works at the University of Saskatchewan and in 2022 began a new position as an academic innovation specialist with the information and communications technology portfolio. As a PhD candidate, Kristine's areas of interest are decolonization in distance education, Indigenization, and reconciliation in higher education. She also has a related area of interest in Indigenization and internationalization in study abroad — a part of this work includes Indigenous assessment. Email: kristine.dreavercharles@usask.ca; https://orcid.org/0000-0003-2550-163X

Michael Cottrell is associate professor and graduate chair in the department of Educational Administration, College of Education at the University of Saskatchewan. Michael's research and teaching areas include Indigenous-Newcomer relations, Indigenous education, international and comparative education, and Irish diasporic studies. In addition to peer-reviewed scholarship he has conducted a significant body of social-justice oriented applied and advocacy research, frequently on behalf of Indigenous communities. Email: michael.cottrell@usask.ca

Foreword: The Way of Academic Writing

Terry Anderson

A year ago, Dianne Conrad asked me (along with the authors of this text) to write a "reflective chapter" on research. At times in my career, I would have been thrilled to be invited to write and publish in an academic book — especially on a topic that did not require any original data collection. However, I declined as I had officially retired (a great excuse for not committing to projects). But more importantly, I was still getting over a chapter I had recently submitted to an ambitious encyclopedia project. I did not know a great deal about the topic I was asked to write on, but it inspired my curiosity and it was an important development in our field. I thought, well, all I must do for an encyclopedia article is document and try to make sense of the relevant research, which I did. The first draft came back with the reviewers' comments that stated that, among other deficiencies, "the article was rudderless." I am a sailor and I have a managed a boat with a damaged rudder; I was not flattered. Worse, I could see the problem — but I couldn't see a solution. Fortunately, a co-author helped save the day and while we were left with an acceptable, perhaps even a good chapter, I was left with a bruised ego and yet another incident of "Imposter Syndrome." Even after a celebrated career, ten books and over 100 peer-reviewed articles, I felt yet again that I was a phony academic — an imposter. Thus, I declined Dianne's request.

The story did not end there as twelve months later, Dianne asked me to write this foreword. How could I say no twice? Fortunately, this time I had the benefit of being able to read the chapters (standing on the shoulders of real giants) and I gained not only tips and techniques, but, more importantly, insights into the craft and into the personalities of these distinguished academic authors.

The authors have common interests and proven publication records in the swiftly growing field of open and distributed education. From this commonality, one might conclude, based on the notion of "academic tribes," that they would hold common views on writing methodologies, formats, styes, voice, publishing outlets, and writing perspectives. However, after reading the chapters, it became clear that this particular academic tribe is more like an old-fashioned zoo than a homogenous cohort. The animals (authors) on display hail from many countries, come in many academic sizes, and share a common audience; but they have each found a distinct voice in the eclectic world of teaching and learning in ways that extend beyond the classroom. Thus, in this text we find qualitative and quantitative researchers. We find authors for whom issues of racial and social justice are critical and central while others don't go there. We find authors, those who, until this text, have never written an academic paper in the first person; and those who can't imagine writing from any other point of view. This eclectic yet connected context provides a very rich tapestry of knowledge honed by the experience and skill of successful writers.

Even prior to COVID-19 times, the educational world was waking to the reality and need for lifelong education that spanned both geography and time. This sense of opportunity, coupled with a commitment to being a part of something; as well as possession of the skills and, just as importantly, the opportunity to write and research, further defines the animals in this zoo. I hope each reader takes the opportunity, not only to read each chapter closely, but to carefully note which of the approaches, challenges, perspectives and contexts most matches their own. Equally valuable is noting how authors who have many different contexts, styles, and approaches to writing produce a stimulating academic work. Of course, all these authors have multiple products available for scrutiny in the academic press and a trip down a Google Scholar-inspired rabbit hole will provide a deeper context and understanding of these writers. The reader can be confident that exploring and following many of the paths and actual suggestions from the authors will result in both improved writing and likely more success at having their work published. After all, if the authors in this book were not good at these tasks, they would not be included here!

I also assume that readers of this book are engaged in some sort of academic enterprise, and many are likely researchers in open and distance education. Thus, they too have commonalities. All university academics are required to research and share (publicize) the results of their work. Though this is well known and generally perceived to be a reasonable expectation, there are many who come to higher education with neither the desire nor the skills to both conduct research and to disseminate that work which is most often achieved through writing. For them, following Rilke's advice (from Paul Prinsloo's chapter) they must "examine the reasons they write and check whether it reaches its roots into the deepest region of your heart, admit to yourself whether you would die if it should be denied you to write."

For many, publishing means communicating in a language that it is not native to them. For others, it is teaching and mentoring, programming, or researching — and not writing — that inspires and energizes them. Through a careful reading, the chapters in this text will provide comfort, technique, and inspiration for those for whom writing is not an enjoyable activity. Few of us will match the quantity and quality of the writers in this text, but we all can learn. Fortunately, those attracted to the academy are usually good learners and thus most will find this book both useful and very, very interesting. There is also hope in this book — even for those for whom writing deadlines and expectation hang like Damocles' sword waiting to destroy their academic careers — that they will find at least one chapter with sound advice that speaks to them.

In Canada, we are struggling to come to terms and deal with a history of poor treatment of the first inhabitants of this continent. One of the cultural norms we are coming to appreciate is the value of acknowledging and listening to elders. Certainly, and chronologically, many of these authors are old and grey enough to be called "elder." However, Chief Clarence Louis notes that elders become elders not by thinking of themselves as such but by recognition of their unique worth and wisdom by others. Further, an elder is one who has special knowledge — whether of hunting, homemaking, healing, or husbandry. You are thus holding a book of wisdom written by elders, honed by Dianne's considerable editing skills, and forged in the fire of real-world experience of practicing education research. Each of these chapter's authors gives us an elder's wisdom — often a brief chronological overview of the important events, people (mentors, colleagues, and students) and the ideas that inspire and motivate them.

Many of the authors' names and work will be familiar to those working in open and distance learning. Only choosing successful scholars has its advantages in that these authors have had their work revised, edited, copy-edited, and both published and rejected. They've walked the talk. One of the joys (burdens?) of publishing widely is that your name pops up regularly in the reviewer databases. This means that you have a chance to see others' initial efforts, and you are allowed and indeed required to work to not only help the author move to a better work, but also to winnow the crop, sorting the grain from the chaff.

Assuming that readers of this volume are researchers, potential researchers, or those who feel guilty because they are not writing and publishing enough makes me confident that this volume is a useful work. Some of the authors note specific do's and do not's; others narrate what forces and personal idiosyncrasies compel and fuel their research journeys. The remainder celebrate the joys and insights of writing. Or as Jon Dron eloquently expresses it: "Writing for me, personally, is both a cognitive and emotional prosthesis, something that helps to form my identity as much as it emerges from it. I am the maker and the made, the writer and the written." Thus, this work offers tools and tricks for the pragmatic as well as visions and inspiring dreams for the visionary.

Let me end this "blurb" with a comment about the editor herself. Dianne Conrad is a most amazing woman. At what would be the end of very successful career as an administrator, a teacher, researcher, editor, mother, grandmother, and recently wife, Dianne decided to be a be a full-time writer. I recall a comment from the famous Canadian author Margaret Atwood, who commented (while rolling her eyes) about professionals who described their plan to become writers in their retirement, if they could match the skills, training, perseverance, and luck of the many professional authors that Atwood had taught and mentored over her career, not to mention having the skill and tenacity to author the many works of fiction, poetry and essays that Atwood has produced.

In "retirement," Dianne has published five books as well as articles, book chapters, and journal reviews. This volume is perhaps her most important (but knowing Dianne, it is likely not the last) in that it provides the meta-thinking in addition to the nuts and bolts of writing for academic publication. Dianne, along with these chapter authors, teaches us to fish — obviously more useful than selling us a fish. On behalf of all those who dream, plan, and look forward to experiencing the thrill of reading one's own work in press, congratulations, and thanks Dianne!

1. Introduction and Welcome

Dianne Conrad

I embarked on this project with great excitement. The topic of research and the writing process has fascinated me for years and continues to do so; additionally, literature on this topic seems to be much needed. It is well known in academe that doing research and publishing that research are important and necessary activities for advancement and recognition in the field. Our field of open, online, and distance learning (ODL) is multi-faceted, global, and progressive, thanks, in no small measure, to the inclusion of technical functionality and affordances at the heart of what we do.

Over the past many decades of growth in ODL, our field has expanded to include myriad journals hosted by organizations and institutions all over the world. Scholars' initial choices of a few print-based journals have grown to feature a wide range of online and open journals covering micro, meso, and macro levels of research. For the new scholar, challenges to publishing can include a range of decisions, from locating a research topic to choosing an appropriate publication venue. And of course, in between lies the mountainous task of writing.

As I describe in my chapter that follows, I was once a novice writer who anguished for too long over how to get started! And then... I put fingers to keyboard and began. From that point on, I was learning, honing, gathering, and, to the best of my ability, perfecting. Writing is a craft that requires endless skill, labour, and repetition. At times, I look back at a piece published years earlier and realized that I could have written it differently — perhaps better or more concisely. One can always improve.

Much of my writing "know-how" comes from a period of six years when I served as editor of the prestigious *International Review of Research in Open and Distributed Learning* (thank you, Terry Anderson for that precious opportunity and thanks to Rory McGreal for co-editing with me). It was indeed a privilege to be privy to so many scholarly works — so many topics, so many styles. But I must also credit my elementary school education which, in the 1950s, included a rigorous focus on grammar and punctuation. In high school, I studied Latin, French, and Spanish; those pleasant excursions into other languages, especially the dead one, firmed up a strong sense of sentence structure and verb tenses. English was my first undergraduate degree at university, although I do not think it contributed to a sense of "writerly-ness" as the curriculum was all literature and I'm fairly certain that teaching assistants marked my essays in a perfunctory manner, not being too concerned with the mechanics of the work.

There were two occasions in graduate school that I recall as instructional. The first, in my master's programme, involved a professor sitting down with me and attacking my use of punctuation in a paper. "Pull up your socks, Missy" is actually what she said. I was appalled; and I knew the scolding she gave me was not deserved. Her own success with writing was less than superb. Her publications were minimal. From that experience, I learned to have faith in myself and not to invest trust or respect willy-nilly in the professoriate.

The second occasion was more constructive. I was writing my first piece for publication and I passed the paper before the keen eyes of my doctoral supervisor for input. She promptly slashed the first eight pages of the document. "Not necessary!" she barked. Apparently, I had greatly surpassed the appropriate amount of context and history for my argument! That lesson in topic-honing and the resulting humiliation was an important one.

To construct this book, I reached out to many colleagues and scholars with whose work I was familiar and asked them to contribute their stories of creativity, research, and writing process. Some well-respected colleagues were too busy to comply, understandably. But the roster of authors who are contained here is impressive and this book is filled with amazing and humbling stories. The pages herein offer considerable and valuable input from these excellent writers.

On Reflection

It has been my experience that the technique of writing reflectively has either been taken for granted, not exercised well, or perhaps not taught well. I have encountered many doctoral students who had not engaged in reflective writing prior to my asking them to do so. Perhaps, too, the difficulty could be that of language, as is often the case. I, myself, have been puzzled by the occasional reference to *reflexivity* (as regards cognition and thought and not science) as opposed to *reflection*. Even dictionary advice differs (English Language and Usage, n.d.); in the long run, the terms appear to mean essentially the same thing, reflection being the modern and more commonly used term; hence its use here.

Schön has been a primary source for understanding reflection, both *reflection-in-action* and *reflection-on-action*. As is implied by the prepositional use of "in" and "on," the latter refers to thinking back, retrospectively, to actions or practices that have been completed; and trying to make sense out of them in some way — to interpret, to learn, to improve or change.

Not everyone is comfortable writing reflective material and not everyone has the time, either personally or academically (see Prinsloo's chapter for a detailed description of how academic time vis-à-vis writing is measured and valued), to do so. Ellen Rose, in her thoughtful book *On Reflection: An essay on technology, education, and the status of thought in the twenty-first century*, argues that we must reconsider the value of, the meaning, and the practice of reflection in order to halt the technological juggernaut of our times. Slow down, she says, and take the time to "simply stop and think" (2013, p. 108). She suggests that reflection is, or *can* be, a "way of being," a way that we can move forward in our practises with integrity and creativity.

Realizing then, that there is an important and necessary role for pondering one's writing process, I asked contributors to this book to consider the following: background and scholarly training; scholarly interests; reasons and motivation for researching and writing; guiding philosophies; conflicts, barriers, mentors; opportunities, insights, and sorrows. Contributing authors responded to each facet of my request in varying degrees. This, I found fascinating — noting, as I did, the influence of socio-economic, geographical, and political backgrounds, education, and personal choices in their stories, mediated by just plain luck. There is no "one size fits all" here.

A sterling example of authors responding to "place and space," as described above, can be found in Koole's chapter. Taking stock of the history and heritage of their Canadian province, Saskatchewan, Koole invited three colleagues to a guided discussion wherein they addressed my seed questions through each writer's particular lens. The resulting polyvocality demonstrates an intriguing mix of voices in the narrative. Not surprisingly, the chapter is very long, but rivetingly informative.

I also asked for words of wisdom: advice and takeaways. To that end, there is a wonderful collection of tips and advice for novice or struggling writers provided in these pages. Among others, Bozkurt has provided a clear outline of his writing process, certain to be of use to those who are trying to find their own way. In these sections of the chapters, similarities can be noted. I take this as a prized agglomeration of seasoned wisdom from "the folks who know," those whose mentoring is invaluable.

On the topic of mentors, I see this text as a mentoring opportunity not only for me but also for the contributing authors. It takes the passing of years and the accumulation of experience to wake up one morning and realize that one is now equipped — now mature enough — to serve as a mentor to others. At least it did for me! My sense is that this realization creeps up on an individual, perhaps hastened by others asking for advice, guidance, or assistance; perhaps encouraged by a sterling performance review or reflection for a tenure application. Whatever the circumstances, there comes a time for giving back. (For more insight into mentoring and its value, see Starr-Glass's and Roberts' chapters; and see Xiao's chapter for "giving back.")

The contributing authors in this text span a remarkable breadth of experience, history, and geography. I am indebted to each of them for sharing their stories so articulately, so honestly. Each one is unique; many are disarming, even shocking. The scope of approach to the task can be perceived from chapter titles — an interesting balance of functionality and personality. But all are incredibly informative and, in my opinion, extraordinary fodder for novice writers and scholars.

Given the diversity described above, I did not struggle to try to identify themes or likenesses. Each story stands alone, although you will find some of the same hurdles and barriers described as they were experienced by our contributors in diverse ways. And, on the positive side, you might also notice several references to curiosity, passion, and the quest for knowledge. On the negative side, authors enumerate hardships both professional and personal, often in startling detail.

That said, what was of great interest to me, as I think it will be for you, was the variety of ways in which these well-known and celebrated contributors to our field framed the exercises of "looking back" and "giving back" — giving back in the sense of digging deep into their experiences to share insights arising from their own histories and advice based on those histories. To trace the journeys described in several of these chapters (see, for instance, Bates, Garrison, Cronin, Ryan, Dron) has provided humbling reading for me. I have worked with, and know personally, the majority of this book's authors; however, hearing their own thoughts and words on the topic of "self" and the self's relationship to the crafts of research and writing opened up many new portals of information — personal information, philosophical musings and stances, and great dollops of humour. *This* is what these pages are intended to share.

Enjoy these reflections and musings from these colleagues in the field. They are so precious; and perhaps even rare in that many contributors have not written before about their own writing or creative experiences. So many of the authors confessed this to me and, better yet, told me that they had found it a very enjoyable activity, perhaps even liberating. For those revelations, I am extremely grateful.

In the most positive and appreciative sense, I enjoyed reading the stories of early struggles, wrong turns, and barriers. I suffered these myself. I had come to graduate work freshly out of a marriage; my children and I lived in semi-poverty in somewhat less-than-attractive student family housing in a large, strange city. Eventually, my cheques bounced. An early research grant, the proposal designed and submitted by my then boss and mentor, Walter Archer, saved the day. As his research assistant, I happily accepted my share of the funds.

My master's thesis was written at night on an Apple 2e in a dingy kitchen after the kids had gone to bed. My twelve-year-old was entrusted with the care and feeding of his eight-year-old brother while I attended classes. I rode the bus, which made the journey home even longer. The boys fought insufferably; tears all around. (But I am happy to say that they are best friends now, in their maturity.)

Because of my financial situation, I always wore two hats: administrator (day job), and university teaching (part-time-when-available job). I taught, co-taught, tele-taught, video-taught, summer-course-taught... and then, as described in my chapter, I finally began to write. My writing enabled me to consort with "real" academics at conferences, allowed me to be invited to contribute chapters and articles here and there. Other contributors have also described "late" entries into the field, and Brookfield's (1990) description of Imposter Syndrome is also mentioned. Perhaps we have all experienced that.

Occasionally, I regret not taking up an offer to join a faculty as a "real" academic. (See also Nichols' views on this positionality.) Most of the time, however, I am content with my dog-legged journey to retirement. I have been privileged to meet so many inspiring and wonderful people, truly pioneers and innovators in our field. I have enjoyed so many fruitful, exciting conferences and had the opportunity to speak my piece. I have travelled. I have had fun.

Best of all, though, I recently found myself in a position to tell not only my own story, but the stories of many of my colleagues, in this book. I sincerely hope that readers enjoy and benefit from the wealth of experience and honesty contained in these pages.

References

Brookfield, S. D. (1990). *The Skillful Teacher*. Jossey-Bass.

English Language and Usage. (n.d.). Difference between "reflection" and "reflexion"– English Language & Usage Stack Exchange

Rose, E. (2013). *On Reflection: An essay on technology, education, and the status of thought in the twenty-first century*. Canadian Scholars' Press.

Schön, D. (1984). *The Reflective Practitioner: How professionals think in action*. Luria.

2. The Way of Academic Writing: Reflections of a Traveller

David Starr-Glass

> What the Way is to the world, the stream is to the river and the sea.
> Lao Tzu, *Tao Te Chin*, Chapter 32

This chapter touches on many issues, but it has one main purpose — to encourage interested members of academic communities to consider writing and publishing, especially if they have not done so previously.

Writing and publishing are realistic goals for all members of the academic community — for those who are passionate about their disciplinary area, their research, and their teaching. A self-perceived inability to write might deter some, but the greatest blocks to successful writing and publishing are low motivation and a lack of encouragement. Successful scholarly writers must be dedicated, resourceful, and encouraged.

It might be argued that writing only makes sense for those in the early stages of their academic journeys, with writing and publication being seen as necessary prerequisites for a scholarly career. It is certainly advantageous to begin writing early; however, cultivating an interest in writing can be just as rewarding for those who have seen their careers blossom, gained considerable disciplinary knowledge, but who have published little or even not at all.

Before Embarking on the Way

Writing is a craft that requires ongoing effort, focused commitment, and a dedication to refinement. It consumes but does not waste time, especially when the writing explores issues with which we are involved in our professional practice. Academic writing (which in this chapter is considered synonymous with scholarly writing) provides an additional dimension — an expanded and extended dimension — for disciplinary engagement and professional development. Writing is a formal and dedicated practice that can potentially heighten awareness and stimulate deeper reflection about the what, why, and the how of our academic activities.

Some academic writers emphasize the importance of the final *product*: the published manuscript. Others — including the present writer — recognize that it is the *process* of writing that is perhaps of even greater value. The process of creating and communicating new meaning can significantly complement the other areas of our academic lives. It can infuse them with a fresh and synergistic energy and, of course, it can increase our interest, awareness, and satisfaction. Academic writing has inherent value and pragmatic utility, but perhaps its enduring worth is when it is recognized as an extension of self.

This chapter is a personal reflection on practice. I hope that it will be appreciated as a sharing of thoughts that might help and encourage, not as an exercise in self-indulgence or the manifestation of late-onset reminiscence.

A little contextual background might be in order. My areas of academic interest are business, organizational behaviour, and occupational psychology. I have advanced degrees in these areas and a master's in open and distance learning. I identify as an eclectic scholar, a transdisciplinary explorer, and an attentive teacher and mentor. I strive to guide students in their exploration and construction of knowledge. As an academic and researcher, I self-categorized as a bricoleur — bricolage is a recurring theme in my published work (Starr-Glass, 2010; 2019).

Over the last twenty-five years, I have published over 100 peer-reviewed works divided more or less equally between peer-reviewed journal articles and edited book chapters. I have also written dozens of reflections and opinion pieces for academic and non-academic journals and published three non-fiction books. I greatly enjoy writing and have benefitted from it. For me, writing is a challenging but pleasurable experience that provides an opportunity to pause, reflect, and communicate what is important to me and what might be of interest to others. Writing is a voice — my unique voice — and I always understand that what I write is the starting point of a new conversation with the "other."

Early Steps on the Way

Academic writing provides voice for those within the disciplinary area: voice at both a communal and a personal level. Potentially, academic publications contribute to three separate but connected processes:

- Defining and shaping the disciplinary community.
- Defining and shaping the individual, or individuals, within the community who have authored the work.
- Creating bridges between the community and those beyond and outside it — scholars in other disciplines, novices in related fields of practice, and those who are interested in entering or exploring the subject domain.

Each academic discipline develops its own unique norms, culture, language, and modes of communication. Academic disciplines have been perceptively seen as distinctive tribes occupying and defining distinctive territories (Trowler et al., 2012). In some disciplines — and in some institutions of higher education — there is an expectation of communicating research and/or teaching experience: the "publish or perish" imperative. Here, although other facets of writing and publishing are recognized, the prime concern is to expand and consolidate disciplinary territory. Although academic publications certainly shape and strengthen the community, they also provide benefit for the individual author: enhancing professional reputation, facilitating future research grants, and working towards promotion and tenure (Korkeamäki, et al., 2018).

However, in many other disciplinary areas — and especially outside the research university — publications are desired and appreciated but are neither required nor forced. In these settings, writing and publication are viewed as laudable peripheral activities but not at all central to the overall academic enterprise. Significant teaching commitments and academic obligations often leave little time for writing and institutions themselves may provide little by way of reward or recognition for those who publish. Even where academic writing is valued and encouraged, publishing is usually skewed — a small number of prolific writers produce most work, most faculty members publish little and only occasionally (Rørstad & Aksnes, 2015).

Perhaps, in these low-publishing disciplines and institutions, faculty members come to doubt whether they have a voice — whether they have knowledge, experience, or perspectives that are novel or significant enough to communicate. Otherwise, thoughtful and highly competent academics are often prone to what has been termed "Imposter Syndrome," and they may seriously doubt their own competency, professional ability, or scholarly worth. Writing is perceived as the specialized activity of special people. When teaching loads are heavy, time is at a premium, and the work-life balance is significantly out of balance, writing is just not seen as a realistic or viable option.

That was the context within which I worked. I had been teaching undergraduates for many years, but the idea of writing a journal article never occurred to me. Not, that is, until I was teaching a management course in which all of the students happened to be Belgians — a truly international venture: an American college, located in Jerusalem, which (at that time) served a predominantly European student body. My students were bright, articulate, and communicated exceedingly well in English (for most of them, their third language). But there was a problem.

The subject matter was uncomplicated, but it did not resonate with students. The textbook was a well-known American one, but students had difficulty in fully appreciating the nuanced assumptions, values, and beliefs that permeated it. They had difficulty in understanding what "American" businesses did and what preoccupied "American" managers. After much discussion, it emerged that a very real and palpable national cultural divide existed between my students (Belgian) and the learning material (American).

I wrote a short article for a management journal, reflecting on the teaching/learning challenge and outlining how I had attempted to bridge the cultural divide. After many weeks, the reviewers' observations finally arrived (this was in the era prior to email). I read the first page of blistering comments and cringed. I felt that my audacity in submitting a manuscript had been called out. I really had nothing to say and what I had said was patently foolish, or at least ill-advised. I was an imposter and the reviewers had recognized me as such. The review was about four pages long, but I only made it through the first two. I was deflated, chastised, and dejected. I put the reviews aside and resumed my day.

Only later, on re-reading the summarized reviews, I found that the editor had added a short note at the very end: "If you address the minor points raised by our reviewers, we would be pleased to publish your work in our next edition." I read the reviews again but could not reconcile them with the editor's optimistic note. Of course, I took the editor's advice, rewriting the manuscript and carefully addressing each "failing" raised by the reviewers. The revision was accepted without comment and my first published article saw the light of day. In the process, I learned something very important about peer-reviews, peer-reviewers, and editors. This was my first somewhat shaky step on the way and I was in my late forties (Starr-Glass, 1996).

Thoughts Along the Way

There is an extensive literature on the purpose of academic writing: what it is considered to do, how it can be recognized, and how it might be evaluated (Boyer, 1990; 1996; Glassick et al., 1997; Tight, 2018). It might be a good idea for the prospective academic writer to review this literature. However, it should be appreciated that much of this work centres on the creation of academic writing in newly established disciplinary areas (such as the Scholarship of Teaching and Learning) and the intent of these authors is to utilize writing and publication as a means of advancing and consolidating these new disciplinary domains.

There is a much more limited literature on how to *produce* academic writing. The present chapter is not intended to be an extensive or comprehensive how-to manual; nevertheless, the following points — gained from personal experience and ongoing involvement — might be of use for those contemplating academic writing and publishing.

Consider Content

Writing for publication only materializes if there is content. There are two obviously linked issues. First, the writing — what appears on the printed page — must contain ideas, concepts, and observations that are accessible and potentially useful to the reader. This content is created by the writer, but it is ultimately identified and utilized by the reader. Content is what the reader decodes, recognizes, and remembers. Content, in this sense, is what the reader engages with and considers — it is from the content presented that the reader will construct his or her own narrative and new understanding.

But this public *presented content* is grounded in a second domain: the unique and personal *content of the writer*. This content is the writer's inner reservoir of knowledge, appreciation, reflection, and expression. It is the existence of this internal content that initiates communication, even if that communication is only with the self. In order to write there needs to be *something* to write about — something in the writer's interiority that is capable of identifying itself and demanding articulation.

Communication is not simply about the transmission of a message. It begins with the writer who encodes the message, which is considered significant, and ends with the reader who attempts to decode this and bring it into his or her world. Communication always involves people and is always personal. In the academic world, writing for publication is often narrowly considered to be "appropriate" when it is impersonal, judiciously sterile, and remote from the human source of its origin. Academic writing may well be a place for distance, detachment, and objectivity; however, it cannot avoid being a place for personal connection and human communication. That connection is with *you*, the writer. That content is from *you*. Search within you for things that are important to you. Search for your authentic voice. Find it and engage with it. Ensure that your distinctiveness permeates what you write.

Reflect on Experience

Academic writing seeks to convey knowledge: new consideration of theory, novel applications of principles, and consolidations of what is currently known. Knowledge is a fluid and personal construction.

Experience is the process through which knowledge becomes recognized, tested, and understood to be relevant at both a personal and disciplinary level. Schön (1991) distinguishes between two complementary reflective practices: *reflection-in-action* (which takes place as we are actively engaged in the practice) and *reflection-on-action* (which is a retrospective reflection on what has been done). It is through reflection both in and on our practice — and the articulation and communication of those reflections — that new knowledge is created, affirmed, and revised (Eraut, 1985).

All academic writing is implicitly a reflection on experience. Be willing to share your own reflections, not just on knowledge but on practice. The two are always contested — they are in a process of dynamic evolution, not of static certitude. Your writing will contribute to the process of disciplinary vigour and evolution, just as it will contribute to your own growth.

Be Mindful of the Journey

When you read a published article, you are engaging with a final product. In a metaphorical sense, this was the writer's destination. Destinations, however, are only part of the journey. As a writer, it is the whole journey with which you will be preoccupied. You have to know where you want to go, but you also need to appreciate that there is no clear and obvious way of reaching that place. Structure the journey: know where you are going. Tentatively map out the journey: know how you will reach your destination.

Set out and do not be afraid to explore the territory: you might find that it is simply not shown or not accurately depicted on your map. Some pathways will quickly appear but then prove to be dead ends; other routes may suggest themselves slowly but be more productive. The published article shows no trace of these explorations. It shows no sign of the way in which the journey was changed, the multiple drafts that were created, or the continual reiterations and refinements that are part of the article's literary history. All of these remain with the writer but are not evident to the reader.

Personally, when starting to write a new academic work, my destination is usually somewhat vague and covered in shifting mists of possibility. Over time, there is a growing sense of where I want to go and then a tentative idea of the way in which that destination might be reached. For me, this process takes time and ongoing reconsideration. It cannot be rushed but — usually in a rather sudden and unexpected manner — things begin to crystallize and pathways become visible. This crystallization usually begins with a title that seems to encapsulate the central idea of the work: my titles are conceived first, just as my abstracts and introductions are always written last.

The process is undoubtedly different and unique for other writers, but the point is that all academic works are actively constructed and reshaped: they do not magically materialize. Some writers of academic works might claim that their final articles "wrote themselves." Many more acknowledge that the art and craft of the writer lies in a process of construction and reconstruction: the final publishable article takes shape gradually; it does not appear in an instant. Acceptance of this at the outset might be particularly valuable for new writers, focusing them more on the journey that lies ahead rather than the destination.

Mine the Unknown

There is a common adage that you should write about what you know. This seems intuitive and makes a great deal of sense, especially in academic writing. Readers of academic works want to be informed, not necessarily entertained. For the writer, however, there can be advantages and pleasure in learning about a new topic — a topic about which little or nothing is presently known — through the process of writing. As scholars and practitioners, we are constantly involved in creating and absorbing new knowledge. One of the tests of whether new knowledge has been acquired is whether you can successfully explain it to someone else, especially to someone familiar and competent with the general subject matter of the disciplinary area.

You might want to consider writing as part of your learning experience. Through writing you have not only attempted to inform your reader but, in doing so, you will also be challenged to acquire a greater understanding about something that was previously little known to you. To do this, immerse yourself in the unknown material, construct your own knowledge from it, and learn more in order to anticipate and answer the questions that your reader will have. Continue to exploit that double learning-feedback loop until you believe that you have acquired some degree of competency with the subject matter.

Share your growing understanding of the subject with interested colleagues and knowledgeable peers. Continue to read extensively and eclectically. Reflect on what you are learning and on how you are beginning to form new outlooks, perspectives, and connections. At this stage, you might like to communicate your new understanding by writing an article, or book chapter, from which your readers can, in turn, gain a deeper understanding of the topic. Academic writing is a powerful process through which the presently unknown is mined, brought to the surface, and shared with others who might have a nascent interest in the subject but who have not themselves become miners.

Target Journals

It might seem logical to write what you considered a stellar manuscript and then seek a publisher. That can work, but it is often more effective and rewarding to think backwards — first target the journal that seems like a good vehicle for the work before writing. Start by researching outlets that seem relevant and appealing. Look for a journal in which you would be happy to be published. Check the journal's scope, its intended readership, the composition of its editorial board, the kinds of people who are published, and manuscript submission requirements.

You may aspire to publish only in high-impact journals with impressive disciplinary profiles and citation rates: many people do. But, as you contemplate writing your first few manuscripts, keep in mind that these journals are aggressively competitive, receiving large volumes of submissions and rejecting most (perhaps more than 90%). Citation rates are important and impact factors have a place, but they do not exclusively define a journal and may not provide you with the outcomes that you really desire in publishing.

Select three or four journals that attract you. Browse content, read editorials, and see who is publishing what. Is there a fit between you, your proposed manuscript, and this publication? Would you be pleased to see your work in this journal alongside the works of these other scholars? Keep in mind that the acceptance rate for high-quality journals is traditionally maintained at about 15%. Assiduously avoid journals that have higher acceptance rates, "expedited publishing pathways," or which require publishing or open access fees. Remember that when you are published, your work (and you as the author) will be forever connected with this journal — its quality, reputation, and standing in the academic world. There are many people desperate to be published and there are also many predatory publishing houses only too happy to profit from their desperation or their vanity.

Submit for Acceptance

Once the best outlet has been selected — write and submit. When overworked editors receive a hundred new manuscripts, they do not select the best thirty for subsequent peer review: they reject the least promising seventy, and they do so very quickly. Many "ifs" come into play: *if* the subject matter is inappropriate for the journal, *if* the length is excessively long or short, *if* there are five references in a 7000-word literature review, *if* the English usage is obscure or problematic, *if* the submission requirements stipulated APA but the manuscript is crafted in exemplary MLA style, *if* the manuscript lacks any coherent structure, etc.

Any one of these points does not guarantee automatic rejection, but it significantly increases the chance of the manuscript ending in the larger pile. Your strategy — your responsibility as an author seeking publication — is to ensure that none of these "ifs" apply to your submission. Never submit to be rejected. Never contest an editor's decision to reject. If your manuscript is rejected, always learn lessons from that rejection. If your work does happen to be rejected by the first targeted journal, submit to the next one on your list.

Never simultaneously submit the same manuscript to multiple journals — it only underscores a lack of confidence, commitment, and determination to allow the submission to your targeted journal to be successful. Simultaneous submissions may make a great deal of sense for writers, but they are frowned upon by the publishing world, consume unnecessary and pointless reviewer time, and are explicitly forbidden by most academic journals.

Appreciate Criticism

Your manuscript will be reviewed. Reviewers are expected to provide critical feedback about the *manuscript*; it is not an assault on *you as a person*, although it can sometimes feel that way. Reviewers gauge the academic quality of the manuscript, the level of the author's subject area competence, and the appropriateness and integrity of research methodology. I review manuscripts for about a dozen journals and book proposals for a number of publishers. I anticipate that reviewers will be thoughtful, critical, and competent. They should be able to assess whether a manuscript can be published or whether it might be reworked in ways that will benefit the author, the journal, and the readership. If reviewers see potential, they should be constructive and supportive.

Unfortunately, some reviewers fall short of these expectations. Some are novices, who have not acquired these skills; others present themselves as overburdened, jaded, and sourly cynical. Yet all reviewers — even the less agreeable and the less than competent — can help you see things that were previously unseen and prompt you to communicate more effectively.

Never argue with reviewers — make the effort to appreciate their comments and respond constructively to them in your revised manuscript. In the past twenty-five years, I have only challenged a single reviewer (via the editor). The reviewer summarily rejected my manuscript and advised me to have a native English-speaker help me in the future. It turned out that she was a graduate student, performing her first review. She had assumed that, given the international context and setting of the paper, I was a "foreigner." Her characterizations were unreasonable and incorrect. It was clear that she had not actually read the manuscript — or if she had, her reading was distorted by her initial stereotyping. I had published previously with that journal and knew the editor. I objected to the review and she, somewhat embarrassed and apologetic, reassigned the manuscript to several other reviewers. A few minor changes were requested and the manuscript was subsequently published.

Think about Book Chapters

Academic writing is not restricted to peer-reviewed journals; it also encompasses chapters in edited books. There are numerous calls for such chapters and these calls require the submission of a chapter proposal. The focus and scope of the book are clearly stated in the call, as is the chapter format. Writing a book chapter is a satisfying way of reviewing subject matter in depth, engaging with the literature, consolidating prior knowledge, exploring new areas of interest, and producing a novel perspective and understanding. If the chapter proposal is a good fit with the book's purpose, the odds of acceptance are high. If the first review of the submitted chapter is positive, publication is almost guaranteed.

Over the years, I have come to appreciate the wide scope and flexibility associated with chapter writing. Characteristically, book chapters are usually longer than peer-reviewed journal articles and this length allows for a more extensive, creative, and compelling narrative.

Writing a book chapter is always an option, but it can be particularly valuable at two points in the academic writer's career: beginning and maturity. At the beginning, the chapter can be a wonderful way of exploring new academic territory and providing a relatively low-risk entrée into academic writing. For the mature writer, book chapters provide a valuable vehicle for integrating and consolidating accumulated knowledge, experience, and practice. There is a caveat. Book chapters generally have a much lower readership and citation rate than journal articles. They may be helpful in starting your writing and publishing trajectory, but they will make little significant impact on your citation metrics (h-index, i-10 index, etc.).

Considering the Way

The way of academic writing passes through two continuously alternating territories: one located within the writer, the other in the external world where the writing is consumed. If you want to enter the world of academic writing, you will retrieve fragments of your knowledge and communicate excerpts of your experience to those who are interested in learning. You will undoubtedly contribute to the shared understanding and practice of your disciplinary area.

If you contemplate the way of academic writing, you will be compelled to reach into the reservoirs of your knowledge, experience, and professional passion. You will be challenged to communicate these to an external readership that is usually familiar with your academic discipline. Sometimes, you will attempt to enlarge and expand the disciplinary world with which you identify; other times, you will seek to challenge and reshape these worlds.

Those who are on the way of academic writing come to appreciate that they have been changed and enriched by it. They also come to realize that they have — to some degree — enriched their disciplinary area and strengthened their professional practice. It is difficult, perhaps unnecessary, to measure the extent of that enrichment. The point is that you — as a scholarly writer — have elected to participate actively in your disciplinary community, to contribute to its growth and development, and to enhance your personal and professional growth. You will also be able to enjoy the craft of writing and the pleasure of your literary creations.

The way is open to all within the academic world. Faculty members are sometimes coerced by supervisors, peers, and circumstance to travel the way. They may be knowledgeable and demonstrate their scholarly competence. Sometimes, however, academics arrive on the way by choice. They too may be knowledgeable and competent travellers on that way, but — in my own experience — those who have elected to write, to connect, and to share voluntarily tend to enjoy the journey more than those who had academic writing thrust upon them.

At the outset, this chapter laid out its main purpose — to encourage interested members of academic communities to consider writing and publishing, especially if they have not done so previously. Hopefully, that encouragement permeated the chapter and helped you to reach this point. It is with encouragement that the chapter ends. It is for you to consider what the next chapter should be.

References

Boyer, E. L. (1990). *Scholarship Reconsidered: Priorities of the professoriate*. Carnegie Foundation for the Advancement of Teaching.

Boyer, E. L. (1996). From scholarship reconsidered to scholarship assessed. *Quest, 48*(2), 129–39. https://doi.org/10.1080/00336297.1996.10484184

Eraut, M. (1985). Knowledge creation and knowledge use in professional contexts. *Studies in Higher Education, 10*(2), 117–33. https://doi.org/10.1080/03075078512331378549

Glassick, C. E., Huber, M. T., & Maeroff, G. I. (1997). *Scholarship Assessed: Evaluation of the professoriate*. Jossey-Bass.

Korkeamäki, T., Sihvonen, J., & Vähämaa, S. (2018). Evaluating publications across business disciplines: Inferring interdisciplinary "exchange rates" from intradisciplinary author rankings. *Journal of Business Research, 84*, 220–32. https://doi.org/10.1016/j.jbusres.2017.11.024

Rørstad, K., & Aksnes, D. W. (2015). Publication rate expressed by age, gender and academic position – A large-scale analysis of Norwegian academic staff. *Journal of Informetrics, 9*(2), 317–33. https://doi.org/10.1016/j.joi.2015.02.003

Schön, D. (1983). *The Reflective Practitioner*. Basic Books.

Starr-Glass, D. (1996). Development of cross-cultural sensitivity in business courses: The Culturelog. *Journal of Teaching in International Business, 7*(3), 61–69. https://doi.org/10.1300/J066v07n03_05

Starr-Glass, D. (2010). Wild pansies, Trojan horses, and Others: International teaching and learning as bricolage. *International Journal for the Scholarship of Teaching and Learning, 4*(2), Article 24. Available at https://digitalcommons.georgiasouthern.edu/cgi/viewcontent.cgi?article=1244&context=ij-sotl

Starr-Glass, D. (2019). Bricolage: Excursions into transdisciplinary territory. In V. C. X. Wang (Ed.), *Handbook of Research on Transdisciplinary Knowledge generation* (pp. 216–30). IGI-Global. https://doi.org/10.4018/978-1-5225-9531-1.ch016

Tight, M. (2018). Tracking the scholarship of teaching and learning. *Policy Reviews in Higher Education, 2*(1), 61–78. https://doi.org/10.1080/23322969.2017.1390690

Trowler, P., Saunders, M., & Bamber, V. (2012). *Tribes and Territories in the 21st Century: Rethinking the significance of disciplines in higher education*. (International studies in higher education). Routledge.

3. On Being Written

Jon Dron

Why I Write

Almost (but not quite) exactly like Didion (1976), "I write entirely to find out what I'm thinking, what I'm looking at, what I see and what it means. What I want and what I fear." It is certainly true that I do not know what I think or, to a large extent, even what I feel before I write it down. However, my writing is not simply a mirror reflecting some otherwise invisible inner me. My writing is an active participant in my cognition, an extension of my mind rather than an expression of what it contains. Partly, this is simply a result of the act of assembling words. As Richard Powers put it, "I write the way you might arrange flowers. Not every try works, but each one launches another. Every constraint, even dullness, frees up new design" (Kramer, 2006). But it is more than that. As I will later discuss in this chapter, it is the mill, as well as the grist — an active agent in my thinking and a partner — that does some of the thinking for me. It is what connects my mind with yours: a means to create a cognitive space that we may both inhabit together for a little while, separated by time and space. The sense that you are making of what you are reading now is not, however, the same as the sense that I was making when I wrote it. We see the same words from different points of view. You are reading my words from the front; I am writing them from behind. We share the same text much as sailboats share the same ocean, each of us travelling from different starting points to different destinations, blown by the same winds and tides, rocked by the same waves, but experiencing very different journeys. I would love to know about your journey but, first, let me tell you a little about my own.

How I Write

Occasionally, I know my destination before I begin to write. In fact, I sometimes start by writing the conclusion. Often, though, I have no destination in mind at all. I just have an idea for a title, or a phrase that I find appealing (such as "On being written") and I go where its wind blows me. The result of that kind of process is what you are reading now. However I start, whether I know the destination or not, I seldom if ever have more than the slightest idea about how I am going to get there. The course I steer to my destination is very dependent on wind and tide, and I may make long circuitous tacks along the way. There will be obstacles and shallows to avoid, interesting coves to explore, other boats to consider, all of which may make me change course. Now and then, an unintentional gybe thwacks me over the head and my course changes completely before I even notice. I may end up dropping anchor somewhere else. Sometimes, I am completely becalmed, sometimes the waves engulf me. Occasionally I do not even leave the marina.

As the voyage progresses, from the flotsam of words left in my wake I become a *bricoleur*, skimming the froth to salvage pieces that fit together, capturing and keeping harmonious patterns in the chaotic whorls and eddies, occasionally stirring them around to see what new patterns they make. Once a piece of writing begins to take form, it starts to coalesce into a floating island of words alongside which I moor my boat and inhabit for a while, shuffling words around until it feels like a comfortable, coherent place to live. And, sometimes, when it is done, I send it off to drift on the ocean currents in the hope that someone else will find it. For this brief moment, you have stepped onto one of those islands. I hope that you can stay a while. Enough of the sailing metaphors. They can only take me so far.

I am more of an *un*writer than a writer. I usually write a few thousand words each day, in emails, in academic writing, blogs, reviews, feedback that I write for my students, and so on; but I generally unwrite most of them before anyone else ever sees them. To a significant extent, I am the editor, much more than I am the author of my writing, and the editing almost always takes much longer than the production of the words themselves. The words you are reading now are survivors of several massacres: many pages were born and died in the process.

It can be very painful to get rid of words that please me. Some words that I particularly love may enter cold storage in my notes app so that they might one day get another chance to live in the society of others, but most vanish without ceremony. Even the survivors are in peril. There are currently 1,353 unsent emails in the drafts folder of my work account alone, and hundreds in my other accounts. Though I have probably published no more than 150 academic papers, the "papers" folder on my computer right now contains 1122 items, not including many more versions of them that are contained in subfolders. I do not know how many draft blog posts exist on my main blogging site, but it is at least as many as the hundreds you can see. The memory I was born with (or maybe the parts that are left after the ravages I have wrought upon it) is poor, so I am a hoarder of words, even of those that displease me. As regards those that have never left my computer, sometimes I just lost interest. Sometimes I was afraid of offending people. Sometimes I realized I was wrong. Sometimes I found myself in a dead-end, trapped by my own words. Sometimes I discovered that someone else had already said what I had to say, usually much better than I. These were not wasted words, though. Until I wrote them, I did not know what they would say. Every word I wrote contributed to who I am, now, writing this. Every now and then I trawl through them in search of something worthy of further effort. However, only very rarely do I make use of what I find. This is partly because, if the ideas were good, then the chances are that I already used them again in a different work and, if they were bad, there would be no point. Perhaps the biggest reason that I rarely continue to write long-abandoned work is that the writing changed me. It would be a strange partnership between who I was then and who I have become now. It would feel oddly inauthentic to be presenting that person's words as my own (and I would not be able to discuss any disagreements with my co-author).

I do sometimes reread the works that make it out into the open, perhaps years or even decades after I wrote them. When I do, it feels like reading someone else's work. There is much in my old writings that I know that I knew, but I no longer know; some values that I held but no longer hold; and much that I know now that negates what I once knew. Some of it I truly enjoy — it is like rediscovering an old friend — but much of it is truly embarrassing. For instance, I recently re-read my master's dissertation from over thirty years ago on multimedia and education that professed a belief in learning styles, among many other terrible faux pas. But, for all that has changed in my knowledge, understanding and beliefs, it is also sobering, and perhaps a little reassuring, to see how much has stayed the same. Back in 1992 — five years before becoming a full-time educator (and with no intention of ever becoming one), ten years before my PhD defence, fifteen years before my first book — the problems I grappled with remain my preoccupations now and have since formed an unbroken line of themes in all my work. The desire to support learner autonomy, the belief that institutions can be antithetical to learning, my attempts to understand education as a complex system, my search for ways to understand and build technologies so that they can liberate or empower learners, the glimmerings of an abiding interest in motivation, and much, much more are as strongly present in this embarrassingly naïve dissertation as they are in my work today.

Despite my constant regurgitation of half-forgotten ideas and values, when I am writing something new, I usually believe that I am having insights that I am sharing for the very first time. And, in a very important way, I am. Re-use is a feature, I think, not a bug. In all probability, there is not a single word in this book that was written here for the first time. There is without a doubt a significant overlap between the words used by all the authors in each of this book's chapters. Perhaps some of us cited the same sources. But we have all put those words together differently, in combinations that have never once been seen in the whole of human history. What is true for words is as true for ideas that are not only replicated and reassembled but that mutate and evolve in the process. Original thinking, for me, is not an endless succession of novel discoveries or insights; but a constant cycle of renewal, reformulation, reconnection, and reframing in light of what I already know. My writing mines the maddeningly entangled, richly layered web of connected concepts and images in my mind. It pulls strands from the unconscious depths of my memory and sets them before me to become something different every time... the same thread but woven into a different cloth. Each time I write, my writing rewrites me.

Technologies of Writing

Early in my academic career, I observed that full professors (far more than the rest of us) always seemed to carry notebooks with them to events like meetings, seminars, workshops and lectures, in which they constantly scribbled. At first, I assumed that they were recording notes on whatever event they were attending, much as we recommend that our students should do in lectures or when reading, but that was only partially true. In fact, now that I am a full professor myself, I know that they were usually noting down their *responses* to the event, and/or inspirations deriving from it (well, sometimes they were just writing shopping lists: writing serves many purposes). I regret that I have never kept a diary but, for many years, inspired by professors and long before I become one myself, I carried a pocket-sized Moleskine notebook with me at all times. I never wrote more than notes, or sketches, or small *aides-memoires* in them: the constraints of the small format made anything else impractical. They were prosthetic medium-term memories and planning tools, not records that I meant to keep. But I did keep a few, and I am glad of it. I still have some of them stashed away in a box, and they make fascinating reading, snapshots of another me, not a diary, not a finished work, but a work in progress.

For the best part of two decades, though, nearly all my notes have been electronic. Although they lack some of the immediacy and flexibility of expression of their paper brethren, electronic notes (with some provisos and precautions) do not get lost, burned, or stolen. They are dated, searchable, taggable, reorganizable, and reusable. Copying and pasting is seamless. Notes can be any size, from the title of a book I mean to read to the best part of a book I mean to write. Maybe best of all, I can read almost any note I've written for at least the last decade, on many devices, including on one that fits in my pocket that I carry with me most of the time. Too much of what I write is imprisoned on the machine on which I wrote it: not so my notes. Though Moleskine notebooks are small, I would need a suitcase to carry an equivalent number of paper notes, and I would never be able to find anything I was looking for. At first, in the early to mid-2000s, I used note-taking apps like Evernote or OneNote, which were very functional; but their proprietary formats caused endless headaches when I moved to a different kind of device, wanted to move my notes elsewhere, or failed to pay their subscription fees. Some, like Apple Notes, started out openly but morphed into cloud-based apps that rendered them useless to me because they were impermanent, locked into their parent applications. Some simply vanished when their cloud providers abandoned them, moved on, or went bust. I usually had backups, but some notes are, quite unnecessarily, lost forever. For some years I have therefore been using Joplin (https://joplinapp.org/), an open source notes app that allows me to keep my notes on my own server (or any standards-supporting server, as well as some cloud services), to access them from almost any digital device, and to export them to anything else. Behind the WYSIWYG facades, notes are formatted using MarkDown, an open text formatting standard that can be read by countless other apps, and (even in its raw form) without much difficulty by human beings. No one and nothing are ever going to take it or my notes away from me again, unless I do something really stupid, a solar flare destroys all the many devices on which they are stored, or I forget the passwords I used to encrypt their contents. Though Joplin lacks some of the bells and whistles of commercial equivalents, I miss very few of them apart from the means to sketch with a stylus on a tablet or phone, but I can paste in the results of an app that does allow that, so it is not a terrible loss.

Joplin is the epitome of a low-threshold app, a soft, single-purpose, unassuming technology that, precisely because of its simplicity, allows it to become anything I want it to be, and that can be assembled with others to become almost anything. Most writing applications have clear ideas about how the writer will use them: they harden parts of the writing process, from setting margins to structuring a document with headings to inserting citations. In so doing, they take control of some of the writing process. Sometimes that is useful — I have enjoyed using Scrivener, for example, because it is designed for the creation of long manuscripts and provides many tools to assist that process, from outlining tools to virtual corkboards. Such applications harden chores so that we do not have to do them but, in the process, they make us a part of their own orchestration, as much as we make them part of ours. Joplin, on the other hand, has very little innate shape: like all the best soft technologies, it is largely composed of gaps to be filled, in any way I choose to fill them. It serves a great many purposes, from mundane shopping lists and marking to capturing ideas and whole passages that will later appear in a publication of some kind. For instance, one of my favourite folders is labelled "soft-hard stuff," reflecting the fact that it started out as notes and snippets for my long-gestating book, *How Education Works* (Dron, in press), and associated papers (Dron, 2022). However, it has since evolved to be a repository of ideas, pithy sentences that occur to me in the middle of the night or in the shower; things to read, quotations, and so on that are all in some way connected (because they spring from the same source). I can tag the notes so that they can be reorganized in any way that makes sense to me: the folders are just labels, not containers; they are boundaries, not barriers. These ways of organization are my own, not those of the software developers. You could not reconstruct my book or my papers out of this, but you could certainly write a new one. I expect to do so.

My notes in Joplin are an extension of my own mind, not the minds of its creators, and it evolves with me, learning with me as I learn through it. This speaks to the same phenomenon that underpins all the words we write and say. Language is a difficult technology to learn, and writing is possibly even harder but, once mastered, it can express almost anything; it is a very soft technology that contains almost nothing but gaps to fill, with whatever we choose to fill them with, and it can be made a part of almost limitless other assemblies, from promises to poetry. However, it is not all empty space. Each word anchors countless other words and concepts. Metaphors abound, not just reflecting ideas but creating them, fuelling and engendering thoughts, not transcribing them (Hofstadter & Sander, 2013). We think, primarily, in metaphor (Lakoff & Johnson, 1980), and each metaphor opens up new adjacent possibles for us to explore. Often, we make new metaphors from those contained (look, a metaphor!) in the language itself. As Melville (1850) wrote, "The trillionth part has not yet been said; and all that has been said, but multiplies the avenues to what remains to be said." In common with most of our technologies, and perhaps the apogee of them, writing is a partner to cognition, not a slave to it. Although our sentences may be unique, the words we write are, on the whole, not our own. We had to learn them, and so we participate in the collective intelligence of our forebears: their metaphors become the building blocks and active progenitors of our own cognition, and of what we write. They are grist for the mill, but they are also components of the mill itself (Paul, 2021).

Other People

No one writes alone: we weave and re-weave the words and thoughts of others, stretching across countless generations, that provide us with scaffolding on which we create, as well as most of the raw material for our creations. Similarly, the words that we send out into the ether are not transmissions of our thoughts, but threads to be woven into parts of the cloth that makes up the minds of others.

Most of the time, authors see none of the effects of their writing on others, but we get glimpses here and there. The process of publishing an academic paper is, in essence, not far removed from blogging, where replies mostly take the form of peer reviews, and (once published) papers referring back to it. The conversation is, however, usually tediously slow, and far more intermittent than that of any other social medium. Responses from peer reviewers can be very rich and helpful but, as well as being slow, they tend to be anonymous and are only rarely the start of a genuine conversation. The interesting conversations tend to begin when works are cited. I therefore have Google Scholar alerts set up to email me when my work is cited, and I avidly read papers that do so. Rarely, I will return the favour. Once in a while, I come across authors who have done more than just skim my work — those who incorporate my ideas into their own, who argue against them, or who build upon them. These I cherish. Similarly, I appreciate reviews and summaries that tell me how successful or unsuccessful I have been in conveying whatever my writing and I hoped to convey. However, more often than not, my name just appears in a long list of citations, the complex, interconnected ideas in my work reduced to a single concept or label, devoid of nuance, context, or meaning. It does my ego little good to see what becomes of all my hard work, but this is exactly as it should be. I do want my words to matter but, even when they do not, even when they are misunderstood, even when they are reduced to a reference, they have become part of something bigger. Perhaps they are triggers that spawn contrary thoughts, different connections, and dissimilar meanings; perhaps they were the result of a keyword search and the reader got no further than the abstract: no matter. When they leave my computer, they have their own lives to lead, new minds to become entangled with; and that is good. It is personally gratifying to know that, here and there, my writing and I have helped to shape the ideas of another person, but it is just as valuable to be a catalyst, or a barely discernible flavour in a completely different recipe that someone else creates.

For more meaningful and engaging conversations, I prefer to blog and to share my posts through other social media like Twitter or LinkedIn. This is where real academic conversations can begin (often right away, not weeks or months later), where my thoughts can be subject to scrutiny and critique to which I can easily respond, and where I can learn about what I think from others. Blogs can be really useful in more prosaic ways, too. Though I am sure that my published research is a contributory factor, I have often been invited to give keynotes based largely on my blogs alone, and sometimes to submit papers to journals based on their contents. In fact, recently and for the first time ever, I pre-published a finished orphan paper on my blog and, within days, had two offers to publish it in reputable, peer-reviewed, open journals. It is a lot easier to let the journals find you than to try to fit what you think their demands will be. Obviously, this strategy would only work for open content and in open journals, but those are usually the only ones in which I would seek to publish my writing anyway. Predatory journals that prevent others from seeing the work unless they pay a fee, or that charge authors for the privilege of allowing their work to be open, seem to me to be the antithesis of the purpose of academia. The fundamental goal of academia, and thus of academics such as me, is to create more knowledge in the world, whether it is passing on the wisdom of oneself or others, creating something new or, more usefully, engaging with others to create knowledge together.

I am a sporadic but enthusiastic blogger. I started blogging in the late 1990s when I figured that, because I was building and studying the social software, I ought to walk the talk. In keeping with my belief that conversation matters more than broadcasting one's ideas, almost all that I shared back then were commentaries on things that I found on the Web, from papers to electronic and, of course, the blogs of other people. Most were brief but, over the years, the average length has grown, and I have increasingly used them to share my more original ideas. Nowadays, I mostly treat blogs in much the same way as I treat keynotes: they are a less academic way of sharing ideas that are either fully formed and on which I have published extensively; or they are half-formed and to which I want a reaction. Whereas I have seldom given a keynote to more than a few hundred people, and my formal writing (including my books, journal papers, book chapters like this, and conference publications) rarely reaches more than a few thousand readers (usually, not even that), my blogs are sometimes read thousands of times and, occasionally, by tens of thousands of people. A handful have received over 100,000 views. This seems to me to be a good use of my time. I often put as much effort, passion, and time into them as I put into my academic writing. Apart from anything else, it helps me to hone my craft (as any writer will tell you, the only way to become a writer is to keep writing) and, knowing that they will persist for much longer and potentially be read by more people makes me try a little harder. Some are just ephemeral comments that I expect to be forgotten, simply drops in a greater flow. Some that I hope will be noticed are hardly read at all. Some are sleepers, zombie posts that will spark comments a decade or more from when they are written. That's fine: it is all part of the process of being written by my writing and, just perhaps, they may connect with an idea in one of their handfuls of readers, who will in turn pass on their own discoveries, in a cascade that may work its way back to me in months or years ahead.

We are all part of a connected web, a kind of global brain (Bloom, 2000). An individual neuron in a physical brain has no concept of the whole in which it plays a part, but that whole would not exist in quite the same way without it. So, too, with writing. The signals that pass between reader and writer, between you and I, contribute to change in both of us, however small or large it may be. You will read these words and, most likely (unless you have an eidetic memory), forget all, or nearly all of them. That is inevitable. But something within you will be different because we cannot help but learn from everything we do. Words — our own or the words of others — change us.

Shaping our Lives

Words are tools, places to dwell, and active partners in our cognition. This speaks to the most pervasive and underlying theme informing most of my academic work for the past twenty-five years, and where I wish to end this chapter: that we shape our dwellings and afterwards our dwellings shape our lives (Churchill, 1943), and that we shape our tools and afterwards our tools shape us (McLuhan, 1994, p. xxi).[1] This recursive dynamic is the basis of all complex systems in which the parts exist both for and by means of the whole (Kauffman, 2022) — an organism and its cells, a university and its students, or a chapter and its words. The collective intelligence of our cultures and societies is what makes our individual intelligence possible, and it, in turn, is only made possible by our individual intelligence. Writing is a good part of what makes this happen as both an active product and its producer. It is — or should be — a non-rival good that loses nothing and gains much through replication, and its persistence allows us to not only stand on the shoulders of giants but on those of myriad ancestors and contemporaries, whatever their shapes and sizes.

What is written is not just a reflection of a mind but a part of it (Clark, 2008). Through writing (and other technologies), our minds are expanded, becoming extensions of us as well as extending into the minds of others, sometimes including those who will come after us. I hope to still be alive when you read this but, if I am not, a part of me will still exist. The collective mind that results from this intermingling is not a static entity: its very essence is movement and change. We do not become words when we read them, just as we do not become bread when we eat it. In reading these words, you are making what I have written into something I probably never imagined; making it yours, digesting and transforming it to become a small part of you, if only as fuel to sustain you for an instant on your journey. This is not an act of transmission but of re-creation and reinterpretation. In all the things we do, learn, and make, we are participants in a glorious emergent tapestry that transcends while it encompasses us all. Those of us who are lucky enough to write for a living are mostly only spinning strands for others

---

1 Usually attributed to Marshall McLuhan but in fact borrowed from his friend, John Culkin (Culkin, 1967).

to weave, not cloths to admire. Individually, what most of us write rarely has much effect on anything, but it is not nothing. It is part of what makes us — as individuals and as a species — smart (Norman, 1993). This is what makes us more than we are. This is what lets us reach up for the furthest stars and allows us to stare far into the depths our souls.

Writing for me, is both a cognitive and emotional prosthesis, something that helps to form my identity as much as it emerges from it. I am the maker and the made, the writer and the written. Sitting at my desk, writing this now, I cannot know what has become of this little floating island of words that you are reading today. Maybe it has found its way into your home, perhaps it is sitting in a library, or on a computer somewhere in the cloud. Maybe it has become patterns of ink on a piece of paper, maybe you are hearing it read to you by a robot, maybe it is a collection of electromagnetic dots on a screen. However it is reaching you, I hope that you have found something within it that has resonated; that something within you, however small, however contrary to my intent or however trivial, has changed. And I hope that you will go on to share your writing with me, or at least with someone else. All writers pay it forward, giving back what they make out of what they have taken, passing on what they have transformed so that it may in turn be transformed by others. This is how we grow and learn as individuals, as cultures, as societies, and as humankind. It is hard to imagine a more worthwhile purpose than to be a part of that.

References

Bloom, H. (2000). *Global Brain: The Evolution of Mass Mind*. Wiley.

Churchill, W. (1943). HC Deb 28 October 1943 Vol 393 c403. http://hansard.millbanksystems.com/commons/1943/oct/28/house-of-commons-rebuilding

Clark, A. (2008). *Supersizing the Mind: Embodiment, Action, and Cognitive Extension*. Oxford University Press. 10.1093/acprof:oso/9780195333213.001.0001

Culkin, J. M. (1967, March). A schoolman's guide to Marshall McLuhan. *The Saturday Review*, 51–53, 70–72. http://www.unz.org/Pub/SaturdayRev-1967mar18-00051

Didion, J. (1976). Why I write. *The New York Times Book Review 5*, 98–99.

Dron, J. (2022). Educational technology: What it is and how it works. *AI & SOCIETY, 37*(1), 155–66. https://doi.org/10.1007/s00146-021-01195-z

Dron, J. (2023). *How Education Works: Teaching, technology, and technique.* AU Press.

Hofstadter, D., & Sander, E. (2013). *Surfaces and Essences: Analogy as the Fuel and Fire of Thinking.* Basic Books.

Kauffman, S. (2022). Autogen is a Kantian Whole in the Non-Entailed World. *Biosemiotics*, 1–4. https://doi.org/10.1007/s12304-021-09466-4

Kramer, M. J. (2006). *Richard Powers: Each Try Launches Another.* https://www.npr.org/2006/11/20/6515434/richard-powers-each-try-launches-another

Lakoff, G., & Johnson, M. (1980). *Metaphors We Live by* (Kindle ed.). Chicago.

McLuhan, M. (1994). *Understanding Media: The extensions of man.* MIT Press.

Melville, H. (1850). Hawthorne and His Mosses. https://web.archive.org/web/20230529184538/https://web.english.upenn.edu/~cavitch/pdf-library/Melville_Hawthorne.pdf

Norman, D. A. (1993). *Things that Make Us Smart: Defending human attributes in the age of the machine.* Perseus Publishing.

Paul, A. M. (2021). *The Extended Mind: The Power of Thinking Outside the Brain.* HarperCollins.

4. What Lies Beneath

Pamela Ryan

> So I began to have an idea of my life, not as the slow shaping of achievement to fit my preconceived purposes, but as the gradual discovery and growth of a purpose which I did not know… I could not understand at all (at that time) that my real purpose might be to learn to have no purpose.
>
> Marion Milner, A Life of One's Own, p. 12

Let us begin with a little perspective. For a substantive period of my life as a researcher, the phrase "open learning" did not exist. I matured as an academic long before the digital era: I typed up my master's dissertation on an ordinary typewriter, and my PhD on a brand-new electric typewriter. The internet was a dream in someone's head. So, obviously, the field of open and distance learning did not exist. Like several other contributors to this book, I came to open learning tangentially by migrating, in my case, from literary studies to issues about openness in postcolonial theory and thence to open learning. The notion of learning without boundaries had great appeal for me as it aligned not only with my personality (independent, freedom-loving, creative, not very good with rules and regulations) but also with my research interests which always seemed to go against the grain in some way. The poetry of Sylvia Plath was largely unknown and unrecognized when I was writing about it in my master's dissertation. My PhD thesis crossed disciplinary boundaries, blending gender studies, psychoanalysis and literary studies into one research question: "What do women want?" My published research in postcolonial studies focused on border crossings and forced migration. So, openness in education was a natural choice and remains a passionate interest of mine. That sets the scene in one way. The other is more nebulous, more personal, and stems from the quotation by Milner (2011) which opens this chapter.

When I was in my early thirties, I visited a well-known astrologer for a reading of my birth chart. She closed the session with a sentence which has reverberated ever since, and which caused initial consternation and, later, wry acceptance. She said, gravely yet with compassion: "You will not realize your destiny in this lifetime." This worried me deeply. Was I "destined" to be a wanderer, fruitlessly following different paths and achieving nothing? Is one's destiny out of one's control or could I change this "fate"? And what has this got to do with writing and research? Everything, as it turns out. Milner's words are an exact reflection of my predicament and, I have come to believe, my gift.

I write to discover what I do not know.

The title of this chapter is intentionally cryptic, but I hope my brief introduction has given you a clue as to why I chose it. For me, research and writing (the two are not necessarily conflated) are concerned with finding out what lies beneath the surface. I usually begin with a title that excites me without having the faintest idea about how to extrapolate from it. That comes with time, and the process that falls between the conjuring of a title and the writing of a research paper entails a long and slow engagement with ideas and with how best to communicate those ideas.

When Dianne first called for expressions of interest in her new book, I leapt at the chance to write something. The theme was enticing because it entailed a reflexive process on the part of each contributor, and this appealed to my creative bent. The first call was sent out in February 2022 with a deadline set for the end of September. I quickly wrote out a draft outline for my proposed chapter and sent it off. And that was the end of it. Months went by. I occasionally thought, with a fair amount of guilt and annoyance at myself, that I really should get on with the writing, but perhaps because there was no definitive research question or outcome, I found the thinking extremely challenging. Where to begin? Potted biographies are boring most of the time so I did not want to begin there, and if I couldn't begin there, then where? September arrived. I began to panic, simultaneously composing emails to Dianne explaining why I was not going to write the chapter after all. Then a friend told me about a conference he wanted to attend in 2024. The conference is in a field that could not be further from my own: Medieval and Renaissance Studies, and the title is — you guessed it — *What Lies Beneath*. At a time when I should have been thinking about, and writing this chapter, I was immediately smitten with this phrase and began thinking about what I would write if I were a medieval scholar. The title was evocative. I had been reading about mycelia and networks that connect with tree roots that allow trees and other plants to communicate with each other. Beneath us, at any place, is this subterranean network of thread-like fibres that mimic our internet. I would take the idea of the green man, or the search for the holy grail, and link this with my favourite poet, T. S. Eliot. I ran to fetch my very old and heavily annotated copy of Eliot's poems and found the passage from *The Wasteland* which begins:

> What are the roots that clutch, what branches grow
> Out of this stony rubbish? Son of man,
> You cannot say, or guess, for you know only
> A heap of broken images...

I was not sure why these words came into my head as soon as I thought of "what lies beneath" but it makes perfect sense now. I was looking for something, something that was not visible, and all I had to work with was "a heap of broken images." I needed these images to coalesce into a shape. I needed a green tree to grow out of the desert.

Then I stopped. What on earth was I doing? Instead of writing a real chapter for a real book, I was wasting time dreaming up a mythical paper for a conference I had no intention of attending. Talk about procrastination!

And then it struck me. I knew what to do. I would use this moment to write a self-reflexive piece on how I approach and have always approached a research assignment, because the route I take is disappointingly consistent. I sign up eagerly, even greedily; I come up with a title that I really like, then I do nothing. For a long time. But miraculously, every single time, and always at the last minute, I manage to produce something I like, and submit the work on time. Is this a personal vagary? Am I peculiarly lazy? Or is the truth closer when I say that I am scared? Scared of writing. From that fear issues procrastination. The words I quoted earlier, by the astrologer, about my destiny, still reverberate. However, that fear is enormously productive, as is the slow burn between the choice of a title and the writing of the chapter, which allows ideas to percolate. Could this, I wondered, be helpful to other writers? Certainly, I was overjoyed to find Geoff Dyer's book *Out of Sheer Rage* (2012), supposedly his magnum opus on D. H. Lawrence, in which he postpones writing about Lawrence indefinitely:

> ... after years of avoiding Lawrence, I moved into the phase of what might be termed pre-preparation. I visited Eastwood, his birthplace, I read biographies, I amassed a hoard of photographs which I kept in a once-new document wallet, blue, on which I had written 'D. H. L.: Photos' in determined black ink. I even built up an impressive stack of notes with Lawrence vaguely in mind but these notes, it is obvious to me now, actually served not to prepare for and facilitate the writing of a book about Lawrence but to defer and postpone doing so.

I almost wept when I read these words:

> All over the world people are taking notes as a way of postponing, putting off and standing in for. My case was more extreme, for not only was taking notes about Lawrence a way of putting off writing a study of — and homage to — a writer who had made me want to become a writer, but this study I was putting off writing was itself a way of putting off and postponing another book.

So, is procrastination, at least for some people, part of being a writer? Unless you are extraordinarily disciplined by nature, you are likely to put off the moment when you settle down in front of your computer and begin writing. Firstly, there is the desk to tidy. This must be done *now*. The act of sorting and resorting, assigning places for things and reassigning places for things, then carefully cleaning each thing is the first step. Then there is the making of tea or coffee. Then your phone pings, and it might be important. Then there is a knock at the door. Then you are not in the mood to write after all, and besides your brain has the consistency of congealing porridge. Tomorrow then...

Most of us recognize this reluctance to begin a task. Perhaps this reluctance is not merely a natural consequence of fear but a generative precursor to the creative process, allowing different parts of the brain to work on something that is going to be challenging but which needs time to develop, in much the same way as walking or any kind of movement aids the mental or creative mind (see Williams, 2021). So, procrastination per se need not be a liability. But there is a more insidious form of procrastination at which I excel: repression. I pretend that I do not have a deadline. I strenuously avoid thinking about my topic for weeks, even months. Occasionally, I will have a brainwave after reading something in a book or magazine that has no bearing on my topic. I will make a note somewhere, either in the Notes app on my phone or on a piece of paper, or in a notebook that happens to be within reach. Invariably, I can't find that note when I need it.

At this point, the editor of this book should be thinking: what is this woman doing? I wanted my contributors to give sound advice to aspiring researchers, but she is proving to be a terrible role model. I agree. I am not much of a role model. Yet I have published plenty over my long life as an academic, and I have had good responses (usually) to my work, so bear with me.

All research begins with a question — usually "what" or "what if." The more difficult and compelling the research question, the more interesting will be the research journey. If something seems obvious to you, then it will be obvious for your reader. Oftentimes, when we write about that which we are certain, the result is flat. When writing is exploratory, hesitant even, it becomes a kind of "thinking out loud" which enlivens the dialogue between writer and reader. Moreover, as a literary scholar, I have been trained to read texts for their points of difference and for their gaps or silences. I am interested in what is not said, in what is left out of a text because I believe it is important to take nothing for granted but to question received notions so as to reveal their hidden contradictions and tensions. In any discipline, certain beliefs become embedded in their discourse and presented as self-evident, therefore true, and it is the intellectual's task to delve into those tensions and extrapolate the hidden dimensions of a text or an issue.

In line with this thinking, the idea of the palimpsest is rich with possibility. What we think of as self-evident is usually only the top layer of a complex, richly layered architecture. This idea of layering used to fascinate me when I lived in Johannesburg, where, underneath the city, lies a vast network of mine tunnels which cause occasional earth tremors. More poignantly, underneath the surface of many cities in South Africa lie the bones of previous generations. Do you remember the excitement a few years ago when the bones of Richard III were discovered under a car park in Leicester? What lies beneath may be hidden but resonant with history.

This has been a long digression, but it is aimed at emphasizing the central motif of this chapter — that what lies beneath, hidden from view, is fertile ground for research inquiry and research writing.

The word *research* derives from the French word *rechercher* which means "to look again." Research is about looking and looking *for*. It is concerned with digging beneath the surface to find what lies below. Let me explain this by referring to another genre. I have recently joined an art class and am making a study of my local landscapes. I am blessed to be living in a particularly beautiful part of the Western Cape, South Africa, not far from Cape Town. I can see mountains from my kitchen window and can get to the Atlantic Ocean in fifteen minutes. When I started painting mountain scenes, my paintings were very gauche. It took me several weeks to learn how to look — to *really* look. I now notice the subtle shadings when the light falls at an angle, and how to mix paint to best depict light and shade, closeness, and distance. Research involves a similar learning experience. One's first question must be followed up by further and stringent questioning. The initial "what" turns into "what if" and "what then?" Our first gaze is rarely accurate. We have to look behind and to the side of the question, scratching the surface to discover what lies underneath.

In fact, perhaps we can replace the pejorative term procrastination with "slow writing." I cannot imagine the act of writing without a simultaneous act of reading. My best ideas emerge after reading something that makes me stop midstream and think. Somehow those ideas, nudged by what I have just read, get stirred and shaken, put on a slow simmer, then set aside on the back burner. Ideas must go through a slow burn or allowed to rise unhurriedly like a sourdough mix. There is something about this gentle simmer that is immensely productive. Writing cannot be rushed.

If you have survived thus far and are still reading, I have a few tips which have emerged from my own experience as a writer. The first one, as I have hinted, is that writing emerges out of reading. That may seem obvious, but I am not necessarily thinking here about reading that is directly related to the research topic. I read a wide range of material and occasionally my reading will spark an idea which I have to jot down quickly. If I leave my chair to get to my computer, the brilliant idea will vanish along with the choice words I had thought of to elaborate on the idea. But by some miraculous process, the reading moments and the collection of misplaced ideas coalesce at some point and then I am ready to write. A more successful method of note-taking for me is using the old-fashioned notebook to copy notes and quotes by hand. I find this more rewarding as a research tool and have a series of notebooks which I have kept since the eighties (some with characteristically brightly coloured covers) and which I still take pleasure in reading.

It is the circling around the "re" part of the research process that is the ticket to writing success. More often than not, when I am about to write an academic piece, my best ideas come from reading that is completely unrelated to the topic. For example, when I was asked to contribute to a book about open educational resources or openness in academic work, I was reading *The Hidden Life of Trees* in which Wohlleben (2017) shows how trees connect with other trees via a "wood wide web," an intimate network and partnership between fungi and roots. It's a fascinating account of what we do not see — a form of life that is more resilient than anything else on our planet and which has existed for billions of years. The resonances with the internet sparked further thinking about how initially the internet was seen as an open, free form of communication and information sharing but how recently this notion has become tarnished by oversharing and surveillance; and this fed into my chapter on openness and what it means.

Reading a variety of texts from different disciplines has benefited my thinking about open learning in productive ways. In my journey as a researcher and writer, I inclined more and more to taking ideas from other disciplines: psychoanalysis, anthropology, sociolinguistics, and so on. I found being restricted to one discipline confining, whereas ideas from other disciplines lent an extra dimension to my thinking. When I first read Clifford Geertz (2000), the American cultural anthropologist, I was captivated by the idea of *thick descriptions*, a concept Geertz derived from the philosopher, Gilbert Ryle. *Thick descriptions* involve carefully analyzing human actions in terms of their cultural context as well as the influence brought to the analysis by the interpreter (this has intriguing resonances with the thinking in quantum physics which shows how and whether or not the observer influences the movement of neutrons). The example given by Geertz is the difference between a twitch of the eye which is involuntary, and a wink, which is purposeful. Although the two may look identical, there are subtle differences, cued by the context. This is a very simple explanation but it will suffice for now. This idea of the importance of context had huge relevance for my thinking as a literary scholar because I was trained in Leavisite principles whereby the text is all. The scholar of literary texts had no recourse to information outside the text, so bringing to bear on the text information about the author's life or tendencies was taboo. As you can imagine, a study of Sylvia Plath without her biography would be unthinkable these days, but in my master's thesis I stuck rigidly to the poems themselves, sometimes hesitantly mentioning the impact of Plath's father on her work. Now, context is acknowledged to be significant and we are intrigued by facets of a writer's life and loves. We merge these facets into our thinking about the text.

Another helpful borrowing from social anthropology is the topic of "wicked" problems. When I became absorbed by topics outside of literature, such as forced migration, postcolonialism, and identity, I was dealing with wicked problems, those that have no imaginable solution at the time of writing. Think about forced migration, sub-Saharan poverty and unemployment, climate change, and suchlike. These are issues that are so huge, so complex, sometimes so overwhelming, that we would rather not think about them. These are wicked problems. Open and distance learning as a research topic, while it may not be a wicked problem, lends itself to deep thinking about context. For instance, it matters where such learning takes place. Students who study at a distance in sub-Saharan Africa, for example, cannot rely on a steady electricity supply for their online needs while studying. Nor do they always have the financial resources to afford the necessary hardware to access the internet. In a sense then, this becomes a wicked problem as we excavate the reasons underlying poverty and unemployment, poor social benefits, and electricity shutdowns.

My second tip is to remain true to yourself. I am not a conventional researcher. I do not like rules and I do not like to be confined. My most successful articles have occurred when I arrive at ideas sideways. By approaching a topic tangentially, I can examine it more deeply and more creatively. It is similar to reading backwards. Often that simple act can reveal more than was first apparent when reading conventionally. Coming at something from an unusual angle can be fruitful in unexpected ways. This is not to say that research that proceeds logically is less pleasing. My point here is that one method may not suit everyone, which is why the recent trend in South Africa of determining in advance how doctoral dissertations should be set out, via a predetermined set of chapters, fills me with dismay. I like to be creative in whatever I am writing. For example, the final chapter of my doctoral dissertation was set out in two columns. I had reached the end of a very long road without answering my research question. So, after months of internal debate, I decided to "fess up" and present my concluding chapter as a visual display of uncertainty. Two opposing views were presented on the page, so that the reader had to peruse one column, and then the other. One of my examiners nearly gave up on me at that point, but she (fortunately for me) grasped what I was aiming at, and praised me for it, suggesting that of all the chapters, this one should be published.

The lesson here is to be brave enough to stay true to oneself. It has generally worked for me although there have been times when I have suffered for it. I am not suggesting that we become research mavericks. I hope that what will emerge from this confession is an encouragement to follow the path that most aligns to your deepest and truest instincts while finding a way to express those in ways that accord with scholarly norms. To take the best of yourself and align it with the best that scholarship stands for.

My next tip is similarly derived from my own experience. Apart from procrastination, repression, and wayward creativity, I have another "problem" as a researcher, and that is my low boredom threshold. This has given me several challenges along the way because it has meant that I find it impossible to repeat myself. I had a dear friend who was the exact opposite. She discovered Henry James in her English Honours year, went on to write a master's thesis on James, then a PhD, then a book, and so on. She never deviated. As a result, she became a world expert on Henry James and was given an excellent research rating. This was not the case with my research. I discovered Sylvia Plath in my Honours year and went on to write my master's thesis on her poems. This was in the early days of Plath research when there was only one book available on the poet. I therefore relied on close readings of the poems for the bulk of the dissertation. If only I had persevered with Plath, I would now be a world expert. Instead, over the following two decades I read and wrote about, variously, postmodern American poetry, women's studies, feminism, gender studies, postcolonial studies, and, finally, for my PhD, produced an interdisciplinary investigation involving psychoanalysis and women's writing. Not content with that, I entered the field of open educational resources and devoted my research time to investigating how OER could change the face of higher education, particularly in postcolonial territories. In sum, my research interests are varied.

This shifting from one topic to another did not do much to get me a good research rating in South Africa. The feedback suggested that I was "too diverse," that there was not an obvious thread linking my publications, that I needed a clearer focus. Naturally, I was dismayed by this reaction and I wondered if my research career was doomed to mediocrity because I could not be said to be an expert in anything. It was only much later that I found the thread that my reviewers thought was missing. Borders of all kinds and resistance to boundaries, whether these be physical, intellectual, or academic, have been a constant theme in my work. Crossing borders and borderlines has been the connecting thread or *ficelle* that forms the core of my writing career. I have sought out sedimented practices and forms and nudged them aside in favour of an open exploration, a journeying to find out what lies beneath and beyond. I have not found it easy to be contained within a disciplinary border, preferring instead to notice what happens when one discipline is placed alongside or in between another. What new insights are revealed when literary studies finds a neighbour in anthropology, for instance? What stops us from reinventing a discipline, to stretch its seams, and to open it up? This has led to a rethinking of timeworn structural oppositions — indigenous/exotic, inside/outside, home/away — into a more fluid displacement of certainties with questioning and doubt. I prefer to pursue a continuum rather than a fixed line of inquiry. And openness as a field of inquiry is a particularly fertile place to linger awhile, especially if you can find correspondences between openness as a broad concept and open learning as a research topic.

My advice here, therefore, is to do what feels right for you and follow your research passions. No one can write with any verve without being inspired by the topic. At the same time, and to avoid receiving the kind of feedback I received from the National Research Foundation, you need to cultivate self-awareness and anticipate potential misunderstanding in your readership. Make clear the linkages between your lines of inquiry and know that each person's research journey is unique. Far better to keep the momentum in your writing than to hit a brick wall caused by indifference to your topic.

Following on this point, it is important always to be aware of your imagined audience — those who you are writing for and those whom you will address — then adapt your register accordingly. I cannot over-emphasize the importance of audience. The people you are writing for determine your register and approach. I would not be writing in this conversational style if this were a book on a different topic, say, *The Self-Organisation of Students in Distance Learning*. This is another way of saying that you need to pay attention to the norms of the journals you are thinking of submitting your manuscript to if you are writing an article. You have to heed the journal's house style, but it involves more than this. If you are wise, you will read back issues of the journal in question to see what kinds of articles the journal deems publishable. A personal example of not reading an audience correctly follows. When I entered the field of open and distance education as a researcher, I was still very much enmeshed in literary norms and in postmodernist and poststructuralist theory. I attended a conference on distance education in Bergen, Norway, and presented a very abstruse, theoretically inclined paper to a bemused audience. It went down like a damp squib apart from one person who understood my references and applauded with gusto. Learn to pick your conferences. There are those that welcome critical discourse and those that do not. Writing is always intertwined with communication and if you are not communicating with your readers, you are not writing with effect.

In conclusion, writing this chapter has afforded me the opportunity to think freshly and for the first time about the less obvious components of what it means to "do" research in the field of open and distance learning. Looking back over 50 years of research and writing and reliving the precious times I have spent in various libraries across the world has been a joy and an unexpected learning experience. My most treasured memories are of these times in some of the finest libraries in the world and those memories are stored safely away in my notebooks. My last words to you are to be brave, be adventurous, follow your interests, trust your instincts, and follow the rules sensibly. The field of open and distance learning is a vast territory leading to a variety of approaches, and I believe we have not nearly exhausted its fertile possibilities. We are only at the cusp of thinking about what "the commons" really means, and it is an urgent responsibility, in my opinion, that we stand ready to contest all efforts to shut it down.

References

Dyer, G. (2012). *Out of Sheer Rage*. Canon Books.

Eliot, T. S. (1963). *Collected Poems, 1909–1962*. Faber.

Geertz, C. (2000). *The Interpretation of Cultures*. Basic Books.

Milner, M. (2011). *A Life of One's Own*. Routledge. https://doi.org/10.4324/9781315782751

Williams, C. (2021). *Move: The New Science of Body Over Mind*. Profile Books.

Wohlleben, P. (2017). *The Hidden Life of Trees: What They Feel, How They Communicate*. William Collins.

5. Reminiscences and Reflections: No Regrets

Dianne Conrad

Like many of my academic colleagues, I love to write. My writing time feels good, even when I am stuck staring at an unfinished paragraph or — worse — a blank page. Sometimes during this often-gruelling process, my mind wanders off into the nuts and bolts of the enterprise; but it always returns to task once the wheels start turning again.

Here is my chance to further explore this process that fascinates me and gives me such great satisfaction.

I see now in my rear-view mirror that I have always been a writer. In Grade Four, I co-edited the class newspaper with a like-minded classmate. Together, we huddled over a very small typewriter and produced… I cannot recall! But I know we took it very seriously. At the age of twelve, I wrote what I considered a novel but was probably, in truth, more of a novelette. The typewritten, stapled-together pages featured the adventures of a young heroine (twelve-year-old Janet) who lived in Somerset, Bermuda. To this day, I have not been to Bermuda, and I do not know now why it enthralled me; but clearly, I had researched it. Sadly, my younger sister threw my manuscript into the fireplace in a fit of anger one day and thus ended my career as a novelist.

Skip forward many years and I am again enthralled with writing and research.

Getting Started

As a doctoral student, I was reading voraciously, of course, trying to get my hands on everything that seemed relevant to my topic. At the time, I was working as the assistant director of a master's programme and was very involved in curriculum development. Together, these two occasions caused me to often think of articles I was perusing: "I could have written that" or "Why did *I* not write that?" But I had no idea how to start. It seemed a daunting task and I simply did not have the courage. I also did not really have the time, a fact that I will offer as a lesson for prospective writers: it takes time. It's said that writing is lonely, and yes, it can be. We spend a lot of time alone in the room with the computer.

During those years, I was working with Randy Garrison who was the Dean of my faculty at the University of Alberta. Randy was already a noted and prolific writer and, at the time, was just embarking with colleagues on the now-famous research that produced the Community of Inquiry model and the three "presences" of online learning. I bought him coffee one day and point-blank asked how to get started writing. He was very charitable and shared his own writing stories with me. The two that I remember are 1) his advice that by the time you sit down at the computer, your ideas and concepts should be so clear to you that the words should just pour out of you; 2) related to that, he wrote one thousand words in the morning before he tackled his day job at the university.

That was a good start for me. He also said, "just write," which is the advice I often give to others. But I also have to thank Katy Campbell, another colleague at the time, for having a similar discussion with me at another coffee shop; and Margaret Haughey, who was my dissertation supervisor. Both offered advice and support for my desire not just to write but to publish.

And so, in a period of non-writing, when Margaret was reviewing an early version of my dissertation, I began to write. I wrote about what I knew — about the experience of being an online master's programme administrator and working closely with learners. My data were gathered from students in the programme in which I worked and from my own experiences. The article found a good home in the *American Journal of Distance Education* in 2002 and I was launched. Thank you, Michael Moore and Joe Savrock!

Training and Lessons from the Dissertation

My academic background, including a long-ago undergraduate English degree, has shaped me into the learner, teacher, and writer that I have become. I feel advantaged having studied literature and having had the opportunity to write many papers and sharpen myriad writing techniques and skills. As an editor, I observed the difference that basic writing prowess affords an author. As a teacher, I stress this fact to learners and I take the time to do what I can to assist their growth in this area. I have no idea if I am ultimately successful, and in fact, some research shows that students do not pay attention to feedback on their papers. I would hope that this is not the case. Whatever, the virtual "red pen" is inextricably lodged in my hand, forever.

In my more cynical moments, I maintain that the only times I really ever learned anything in my graduate studies were during the writing of theses, specifically the doctoral dissertation. As time goes by, I think I value the dissertation learning even more. Aside from content and research skills, I learned perseverance, fortitude, and a type of tired doggedness that comes with endless late nights, an empty brain, and despair. But I believed in what I was doing and in what I was writing. I believed in the dissertation's potential value as a contribution to the field. Moreover, I *liked* it. I liked the topic and I liked the places to which it took me. I recall waiting with great anticipation for the release of Wenger's 1998 Communities of Practice research; I thought that it would contain the kernels of what I needed to know. It didn't, but the book was still inspiring and relevant. More lessons, all of which I have passed on to learners over the years: There is no "answer," there is no magic bullet, just stay on the trail like a bloodhound. Read, read, read. And the corollary to that: There is a time to stop reading and start writing.

Why and How I Write

I am driven to write because there are things I want to say. There are some things that I always wanted to say but did not have the time to construct the appropriate vehicles. But, over a career, I have found *more* topics that I want to explore. Some of these beckoning interests have accrued from reading others' work, some from my own experience; and, I admit, some from frustration arising from my observations of the workplace and the field. My interests have been varied. Unlike some very strong scholars in our field who have become known for their close attention to certain topics, my parameters have been more eclectic. I attribute this to a short attention span! As a Social Sciences and Humanities Research Council (SSHRC) reviewer, I have noted the dedicated research path of many applicants and SSHRC's emphasis on maintaining the path. This is not my style. "Curiosity" and passion would better describe my approach.

But the curiosity, of course, arises from the surrounding academic environment. At one time in my early career, I was deeply involved in prior learning assessment and recognition (PLAR). As a non-traditional approach in higher education, PLAR required intense championing and marketing of its process. I was keen on both and wrote many articles on its various aspects. I presented at many conferences on PLAR-related topics such as learners' processes, learning, e-portfolios, and infrastructure. The passion I felt for PLAR — and the belief I had in the practice — invested the writing process with energy.

During my first "PLAR period," I was also managing an adult education programme that was delivered at a distance using several modes. I later moved from the adult education programme to a graduate programme in technology and communication; in spite of a different label and a more advanced level of study, my adult education background was never far away. As assistant director of an online programme, I was heavily occupied with curriculum and programme organization and was very involved with the student body. I became intrigued with their learning and with their adaptation to online learning. Many were learning at a distance for the first time. Our programme was rich with potential data and my interest in the online learning process ballooned. It was at this time that the seminal work of colleagues Garrison, Anderson, Archer, and Rourke was creating new energy and theory in the ODL field: I was benefitting from my proximity to these scholars and the exciting environment that they created. Again, the energy generated by my commitment, interest, and *belief* in what we were doing was more than enough to keep me writing and conferencing.

I was learning at this time about the value of networking and conferencing, although neither came naturally to me. I am at my core reserved and shy; teaching rooms full of adult learners had given me coping skills, however, somewhat akin to being on stage for a certain amount of time. I could manage that! I also endured, for my entire career, a sense of "come from behind."[1] That is, I was always "catching up," and was in awe of those who were already more established and more published than I was. That perception continued to cause me some insecurity and stage-fright in large gatherings.

Writing, on the other hand, was safe and secure; and I had confidence in my skill at the keyboard. If I had been a fiction writer, my agent would have been hard-pressed to get me out to market the product! But sitting in the quiet of my home was a comfortable and even enjoyable way to express myself.

How one learns or writes is an important part of this book's theme; creative processes have always interested me. For my doctoral dissertation, I considered where learners did their learning and, because of that, I travelled to interview my participants in their "natural" learning habitats, be they homes or offices. I based my judgement of the environmental importance to the creative process on my own senses: I noticed over the year that I attended to business matters more efficiently and professionally if I was sitting at the computer rather than on the sofa in front of the television. I graded papers more effectively and with greater confidence in certain places. And so forth.

My Writing Process

It is an understatement to write that substantial differences exist between the fields of hard science and those of social science and humanities. As an education scholar and a "soft science" researcher, I have little knowledge of hard science research, other than that novice scientists aspire to be accepted onto an established research team, led

---

1 In a nutshell: I began my graduate studies at age forty during a divorce and I single-parented my children in poverty conditions in a city where I had no relatives or support. Hence, when I finally joined the "PhD" club at age fifty-four, I assumed I was about twenty years behind everyone else who had had a more direct route to that goal. Fortunately for me, I was youthful-looking and I do not think my colleagues realized that I was older than most of them. I certainly did not realize that so many of the scholars that I idolized were actually younger than I was. In a way, my desire to "catch up" is what has kept me motivated and inspired to continue to teach, research, and publish beyond retirement.

by a productive senior researcher who is usually funded for their work. Such teams publish papers that feature many authors as compared to papers emerging from the social sciences and humanities sector, where single authorship is as common as papers with multiple authors, but usually not more than six.[2] From personal experience, however, I know that "hard" scientists do not consider social science and humanities research as valid research, especially when qualitative in nature.[3]

My own tendency in research endeavours, mentioned above, was to investigate those aspects of my field and practice that interested me or caused me to question. I have been fortunate always to have access to study participants. In my role as dissertation supervisor, I have seen learners whose intended research interests are thwarted by the impossibility or difficulty in obtaining participants for the study. As a supervisor, I caution against entering research situations that for many reasons — logistical, social, political — are not going to yield results.

Researchers must also consider the participants from another angle. I learned this lesson (I thought the "hard way") years ago when conducting research for my master's degree. As I was studying learners who were engaged in distance education at a time when such learners were in short supply in Canada, I chose Athabasca University as my locale and requested permission from that institution to contact their students. After much delay and fuss, I was asked to appear on-site at Athabasca University (AU) to be interviewed by their distance education faculty. It was a cold February day when I drove from Edmonton across the bleak and snowy prairie to meet these people, all of whom I knew by name but not personally at this time. I was terrified. (Remember, I considered myself "young" at the time, and therefore naïve; and my inquisitors older and experienced in the ways of everything-research.) In the long run, it emerged that Athabasca faculty were simply tiring of the larger, traditional university to the south of them continually using AU students as research subjects. They wanted to see "boots on the

---

2   An exception to this commonality, for example, is a recent set of papers written by the COER (Centre for Open Education Research) group from Germany, a cooperative assembled by Olaf Zawacki-Richter and populated by graduate students and global scholars. Working collaboratively on a multi-year project, COER's published papers display a very long list of contributors.

3   I was once told so in no uncertain, in fact, belligerent terms, by a well-established university chemistry scholar.

ground." They wanted to hear me discuss my rationale and purpose. It all worked out well; and that initial visit to a lovely small town on the banks of a grand river presaged my move there to take up a position at AU fifteen years later.

If the master's thesis served as an introduction to some of the foibles of conducting research, the doctoral dissertation amplified the presence of hiccups and foibles. One encounters inspiration and de-motivation from unexpected sources. One grabs the inspiration from wherever it presents itself — literature, friends, happenstance — and accepts and strategizes the hurdles. In my case, my supervisor did not share my vision of what I wanted to do; I understand now that I would have drifted too far into the psychology realm and was not sufficiently trained in psychology to take that approach. And perhaps, neither was she. We compromised on the topic, leaning more heavily into the pedagogical side of learning. Negotiation is always the way forward.

The dissertation process can be very lonely. After progressing through the programme with peers and/or in a cohort setting, as I did, one is suddenly alone, left to manage a path through endless literature, the collection of empirical data (usually), and the massive task of organizing all those pieces into a readable and coherent work that must follow, to the letter (usually), institutional guidelines. The writing of the work is bookended by two oral exams, the first allowing you permission to proceed, having exhibited your competence to do so; and the second to "defend" your work to a committee of experts in the field. It is daunting, to say the least, and successful completion requires dedication, flexibility, and a thick skin.

"Situated" Writing

We all face and contend with situational issues as we write, as mentioned above in my description of my doctoral research. Nobody lives or writes in a vacuum — or without circumstantial effect. My own writing was relegated to evenings and weekends because of my personal situation (see footnote 1). I have always held an administrative position in post-secondary settings: I began that career journey when I accepted a position as Programme Manager for an adult education programme, having cut my teeth in that university faculty by serving as a Research

Assistant to my mentor, Walter Archer. Very generously, he hired me for the position when it became available, conveniently for me, just as I was completed my master's degree. From that time on, I taught as well but always on a part-time basis, to supplement my income. But I realized that I really enjoyed the administrative work of organizing and "running things," and so, even though I was invited to apply for actual tenure-track academic positions, I chose to remain in administration, wearing two hats, teaching steadily on contract here and there, both face-to-face and by distance. (See also Nichol's chapter, where another administrator tells his story.)

The writing, therefore, was also part-time, but I was so energized by the process that I never tired of sitting down at night after the kids were in bed to plug away at it. Weekends, holidays... I just kept at it. Success came early and that affirmation encouraged me even more. I relate this history for those readers who might be experiencing the same hardships that I was at the time, notably, poverty and never-ending stress.

It was wonderful to be asked to contribute to an edited volume or to have a journal piece accepted. Although I never held a tenure-track position, my publication record left many colleagues not realizing that fact. And I tell *this* story to encourage those readers who *want* to write and publish, regardless of which hierarchy you fit or do not fit into.

Perhaps my position as an administrator rather than a tenure-track academic contributed to my "lone wolf" stance as a writer — or perhaps not. Whatever the reason, I tend to work best alone. Many other notable authors in our field have worked successfully in teams or at least with a colleague (see, for example, Garrison's chapter, which outlines the benefits of collaboration).

Perhaps my eclectic choices of topic were best addressed alone, thus allowing me to do what I wanted. If I had been tenure-track and searching for funding in order to grow my CV, it may have been more strategic to buddy up with colleagues, especially those with sturdy reputations! But I did not need to do that, and that allowed me more freedom. That said, my topic choices were not pie-in-the-sky; they were solidly fixed within the field and, as such, were well-received and cited.

I must also admit that I preferred my own writing to the styles of some colleagues. As mentioned earlier, I am fussy about the mechanics of writing, more so than many, and this fact has worked well for me. In truth, I think I have been invited aboard some collegial writing projects because of my ability to punctuate and edit. And I have accepted some of these invitations because I understand that that is my intended role, and it has not bothered me that, as such, I am not the first author. (However, in several cases, my attention to the work has served to "move me up" the authorial hierarchy! And so it goes.)

The Logistics of Writing

Writing requires discipline. I have known some very fine writers whose disciplined approaches define certain hours of the day for sitting at the computer. My own process is not so regularized. *If* I am pressed for time or working to deadline, I will commit myself to sitting down and creating some number of words every day. If the pace can be more relaxed, I wait until the moment is right, until I can feel the creative juices flowing. Those are precious and enjoyable times: the words flow, the keyboard crackles, and pages fill up. In between those high-productivity spurts, however, the mind does not stop formulating and playing with ideas. The research continues, usually via Google as a starting point, then progressing to university library collections and search engines. I find Google remarkably useful and easy to navigate. When I am actively writing, I also keep a close eye on newspapers and other news sources for new or current developments that may relate to my topic.

One of the most frustrating things for a writer is to have to track down a reference source after the fact. In spite of great diligence, this annoying necessity usually occurs at least once in any writing project. I cannot emphasize strongly enough the importance of keeping a close eye on the compilation of references.

I must admit to being very old-fashioned in my use of technology. I do not use a programme for footnotes or any other sort of formatting; I do it all manually. I enjoy the "tiddly" aspect of creating my formats; the repetition and detail sharpens my attention span, which is normally short. As I write, I gather the footnoted material and assemble it in a separate file, updating and saving constantly. Similarly, each draft is saved with the daily date. And weirdly, toward the end of the project, when I am terrified of a computer crash or glitch that renders me helpless, I send penultimate drafts to trusted members of my family for safe keeping, usually with instructions that say, "Do not open or read! Please just store in a safe place."

I have had a very satisfying writing career. My first publication won a prestigious award. My dissertation won a prize. My curiosity-driven approach has allowed me to "follow my nose" and exercise my imagination. I think I have been a useful mentor to those who have asked me for advice and to my students, with whom I always share ample writing tips and even conduct mini-workshops. I am detailed and old-school; I believe in punctuation, apostrophes, and hyphens!

My regrets in my writing career are few. I do recall being asked to contribute a chapter to a colleague's book many years ago; shockingly (to me), it was rejected. That was hurtful and I did not understand the rationale that was presented to me. But I was young and just skulked away, storing the unwanted piece in the depths of the computer. Years later I retrieved it, read it over, and was still stymied by its rejection. Another time, I was unable to finish a piece and shelved it. Again, years later, I took it out, re-read it, and marvelled to myself at how good it was! Sadly, that particular era in our field's rapid evolution had passed by then and my topic was no longer cutting-edge or relevant. A lost opportunity.

When serving as editor of a large journal for several years, I have seen scholars "dust off" and resurrect what was certainly an older work, sometimes in pursuit of tenure or some other imminent goal. Authors have even admitted this motivation in a note to the editor. Clearly, this tactic is not a good idea. Honour and integrity should always shine brightly on the academic writer's radar.

Advice to the Novice or Hesitant Writer Who Seeks Publication

The best advice I can offer is *get started*. And, after that:
1. Seek out advice and ask questions of deserving colleagues.
2. Be very interested in your topic.
3. Keep a file of potential sources/ideas/quotes... whatever.
4. Acquaint yourself with the nature and scope of your intended audience/place of publication.

5. Ask questions of the editor if relevant.
6. Re-read, re-visit, revise. Edit, edit, edit.
7. Do not fall in love with your own words. Be ruthless with yourself.
8. Comply with guidelines, word length, format, etc. *Pay attention*!
9. Be prepared for revisions and do not be discouraged.
10. Respond to your reviewers with courtesy and the relevant/requested information.

Concluding Remarks

I have read in some of the other chapters in this book of colleagues' research writing hardships and barriers; and I have certainly experienced — and detailed here — those of my own. But, as has been offered by others, my takeaway advice is *just write*. Start something. Obviously, it is best to tackle something that you know and are passionate about. The process of researching and writing can be lonely, long, and arduous. But it can also be extremely satisfying, even comforting. And it has been mentioned that it is nice to see your name in print. After my first book was published, one of my kids personalized a coffee mug for me. With a picture of the book's cover were these words; "I wrote a book!" Very nice indeed.

6. Intrinsic Motivation, Agency, and Self-Efficacy: Journeying From "Quasi-University" Student to Steward of the ODE Community

Junhong Xiao

This chapter aims to portray my professional career as a researcher and steward of academic publications. It starts with a brief account of my very humble background in education, before going on to explain the motivation behind my lifelong interest in research and writing. It then describes how mentorship helped me to turn into a full-fledged researcher as well as why and how I left my familiar fields of study in my prime and joined the open and distance education (ODE) research community as a 'green hand', eventually becoming an international steward after overcoming sustained adversities. The chapter interprets my journey through the theoretical lens of intrinsic motivation, agency, and self-efficacy and concludes with tips for early-career researchers.

From a "Quasi-university" Student to a Professor: A Brief Self-portrait

China's national higher education matriculation examination was suspended during the devastating Great Proletarian Cultural Revolution (1966–1976). The examination, called 高考 and pronounced as *gaokao* in Chinese pinyin, was resumed in the winter of 1977, and has since then been held in summer once a year. This is the only way to be enrolled in a full-time residential programme at a campus-based higher education institution in China except during the Cultural Revolution. I sat the 1980 examination and was enrolled as a student at a "quasi-university" (专科学校, pronounced as *zhuanke xuexiao* in Chinese pinyin), a pre-service teachers' college which offered three-year programmes leading to the award of a junior college (专科, pronounced as *zhuanke* in Chinese pinyin) diploma, instead of an undergraduate degree awarded to graduates of a four-year university programme. I majored in English, learning the basics of the language. There was no writing course or training in research methodology. We did not have a native English teacher; the only authentic English we heard was when listening to the news programmes of the British Broadcasting Corporation (BBC) and the Voice of America (VOA) every evening. The only chance we had to meet a native English speaker was a visit by an American writer whose father was a priest in China before 1949.

Unlike many classmates from politically privileged family backgrounds, I cherished each and every day at college because higher education was nothing but a rosy dream for young people such as me during the Cultural Revolution, a topic I will pick up in the next section. I was soon a "celebrity" for my diligence, becoming the best student and the teachers' favourite. I did not have to spend much time doing the courses, so I stayed in the library after class, reading whatever English materials I could lay my hands on, from English novels to barely intelligible academic books, for example, Noam Chomsky's (1957) *Syntactic Structures*. My efforts paid off. It was because of my excellent school record that I was given a teaching position at my alma mater as an exception. I do not have a bachelor's degree, master's degree, or doctoral degree. My highest qualification is a Postgraduate Diploma in Professional Studies in Education (Applied Linguistics) from the Open University in the United Kingdom (OUUK). This was the humble origin from which I strove to be a respectable professor and journal/book/conference steward.

Research and Writing Gives Meaning to My Life

My motivation for research and writing can be traced back to my childhood. My grandfather owned vast tracts of farmland and a large fishing-net-manufacturing company in old China, that is, before 1949. When New China was founded, we were categorized as members of the exploitative ruling class of the "old" society, hence our transformation from the "ruling" to the "ruled" class in the "new" society. In that historical period, it was not unusual for offspring of the "ruled" class to be discriminated against unfairly, and even brutally in some cases; and to be the target of bullying, among other things, at school. Knowledge became an effective weapon to protect myself and regain my dignity. If I could help my classmates do their daily homework or cheat on examinations by passing answers to them, school life would be less threatening and humiliating for me although the right to higher education was unthinkable due to my family background. Gradually, I found peace, safety, and dignity in the world of knowledge and pure joy in pursuing it, hence becoming more and more curious and even dreaming of sharing new discoveries with other people. This curiosity continues to be a source of motivation and inspiration today, echoing Vygotsky's (1994) concept of *perezhivanie* (emotional lived experience), which refers to the way one "becomes aware of, interprets, [and] emotionally relates to a certain event" (Vygotsky, 1994, p. 341).

Knowledge was the only spiritual home where I could forget everything unpleasant. Ryan and Deci (2000a) state that there are intrinsic and extrinsic motivations. Interest in research and writing has always come from the bottom of my heart; intrinsic motivation far outweighs extrinsic motivation in my case. My first paper (Xiao, 1983) was written in the third/final year of college and published in one of the four major Chinese journals of foreign language teaching and research (FLTR) in July of 1983, the same month I graduated. I still feel as excited and thrilled as I was then because this was the first time I researched and wrote to share my new discoveries, thus realizing my childhood dream. In the following four decades, I have published papers every year.

My perseverance in research and writing was further strengthened by two early-career events. In 1986, I happened to learn about an exchange programme between Simmons University (previously Simmons College) in the United States and China. Unlike similar programmes, interested scholars submitted applications directly to the representative of the university, David Perry, who was sent to teach at Wuhan University at that time. I did not have a bachelor's degree essential to the application, so I wrote a long letter to him, explaining my situation and sending him several papers that I had published in major journals.

He gave me an opportunity. After an interview of about one hour (it was supposed to be twenty minutes), Professor Perry gave me Ernest Hemingway's short story "The Snows of Kilimanjaro" and asked me to write an English review of one thousand words within two hours. I analyzed the use of stream of consciousness from a linguistic perspective, which, together with the interview, clearly left a good impression on him. With his recommendation, I was awarded a full scholarship to study for MA degree. However, I was not permitted to obtain my passport because my employer did not want to take political risks for this "private" exchange.

The following year, I planned to sit the national postgraduate matriculation examination and enrol at a full-time MA programme with the encouragement of several professors from the Guangzhou Institute of Foreign Languages who knew me through my publications. To my despair again, my application for approval to register for the examination was denied, this time "due to shortage of teaching staff." Honestly speaking, I could not have recovered from these heartbreaking blows if I had not seen their positive side. I came up with the theory that such opportunities would have been unthinkable but for my dedication to research, a belief which greatly promoted my agency and enhanced my perceived self-efficacy.

My zeal for research and writing has remained unabated today, even after I was promoted to professorship in 2009. In my case, even if I do not conduct any new research or publish any new paper, I will be entitled to my professorship until my retirement. But I continue to research and to write as an active member of the international community of open and distance education (ODE) because this is part of me, giving meaning to my life. For me, teaching, researching, and writing are the three most meaningful activities in my professional career through which I can realize the value of my life. Believe it or not, what sustains my lifelong academic pursuit is more intrinsic than extrinsic. I research; I write; I contribute; I share; and I rejoice. This is who I have always wanted to be and who I really am.

Meeting a Mentor Who Re-defined My Identity

I did not receive any training in research methodology and academic writing at college. As mentioned above, I researched and wrote purely out of curiosity in the first place. Without systematic training, I had to grope my way to be observant, analytic, deductive, and inductive in order to grasp the required skill. My early research interests were linguistics as well as applied linguistics and my readings were mostly related to these disciplines. With what I learned from linguistics, I was able to identify features of a good paper and imitate them in my own writings. Nevertheless, I soon found myself stuck on a learning plateau, feeling at my wit's end, and desperately wanting to break through it. I was experiencing frustration and pains, getting lost and doubting myself. It was around this time that I met my first and life-changing mentor, Guowen Huang, a linguist.

I first met Huang at a summer workshop on applied linguistics run by a group of professors, including him, in 1986. He was an editor of a major Chinese FLTR journal. I was a contributor to this journal and we had known each other through letters. But this was the first time that we had met in person. A pleasant surprise from this meeting was the discovery that we were from the same area of China, speaking the same dialect and feeling an immediate sense of kinship. He was, and remains, my model and mentor. In 1988, when he won a scholarship to the University of Edinburgh to do a PhD, we were just beginning a collaborative study on the grammar of the English complex sentence. Not long after he started his PhD studies in the UK, we resumed our research and began to publish research findings in Chinese journals. This collaboration lasted eight years until 1996 when our research culminated in a monograph entitled *Aspects of English Complex Sentences: From Sentence to Text* (Huang & Xiao, 1996) in addition to a dozen Chinese journal publications. It was throughout this collaboration that I received systematic "training" in research and writing.

In terms of research methodology, whenever we moved on to a new topic, my mentor would tutor me, for example, on how to identify an issue worthy of exploration, search for and review relevant literature, collect data, analyze the data collected, interpret findings, and avoid pitfalls. Whenever I was confused, I would write to him for advice. Bit by bit, I learned how to do research in accordance with the established practice of the academic community. Many friends found it hard to believe that I learned research methodology not from formal education, but from my mentor. It was the same with learning to write. If he wrote the first draft of a paper or chapter, I would use it as an exemplar and conduct a thorough analysis of its generic structure, coherence, language, citation/reference format, and so on. If I wrote the first draft, I would always stick to the citation/reference format he taught me but try something slightly different in other aspects. My mentor gave me feedback each time, so I wanted to take advantage of such opportunities to test my creativity and originality. I found that many authors evolved their idiosyncratic style and I longed to develop mine, an ambition which might have been unrealistic then but was definitely a sign of perceived self-efficacy.

I learned techniques and skills of research and writing from this hands-on experience. I noticed the transformation happening to me: I had more confidence in my research and a clearer mind when writing up a paper. But it was an ensuing mentorship programme that catalyzed my growth into a more rigorous researcher. After staying for eight years in the UK and gaining a second PhD degree from the University of Wales, Cardiff, my mentor accepted an invitation to be a full professor at Sun Yat-sen University and returned to China in 1996. With his assistance, I went to this university as an academic visitor, studying functional linguistics under his supervision for a semester. He would give me a batch of books to read every week, asking me to write down my interpretations, puzzles, and queries. Every Saturday evening, he would be waiting for me in his study and listening to my report on the week's reading, explaining to me what had been misinterpreted, solving my puzzles, clarifying my queries, and discussing controversial issues. Soon I was able to read and argue through a logical and critical lens, an essential attribute and highly desirable mindset for a rigorous researcher. What I learned from my mentor has become part of me as a researcher/writer and has accompanied me to the evolving field of ODE.

Moving into a New Field of Study

After being denied the requests for permission to obtain my passport and to register for the national postgraduate matriculation examination, two events that still hurt sometimes, I left my teaching job at my alma mater in August 1988, and joined the Open University of Shantou, a local branch of the Open University of China (formerly known as China Central Radio & Television University). However, I continued to research and write as an (applied) linguist until 2000 when I decided to shift my research interest to ODE. Again, it was curiosity that aroused my enthusiasm in this new area. I found that papers in Chinese ODE journals seldom cited English-language literature and that if they did, the studies cited were mostly Chinese translations some twenty years ago and might be out of date. I wanted to make a difference because I believed I could. So, despite the fact that I had published over thirty journal papers and several monographs and edited books on linguistics and applied linguistics, I decided to move into this new field, to the bafflement of colleagues and friends, including my mentor.

An opportunity came in 2000 when the China Scholarship Council (CSC), a non-profit organization funded by the Chinese Central Government, accepted individual applications for scholarship to academic visits outside China (government-funded opportunities of this kind used to be allocated to designated institutions which then recommended their candidates). I submitted my application with a research proposal on ODE in the UK; to be honest, I did not have much confidence because of the intense competition. It took me quite a while to believe that I was among the lucky few winners when I saw my name on the list released at the CSC website in July 2000. Needless to say, the OUUK was the destination of my choice. Learning from my experience as a researcher of linguistics and applied linguistics, I knew the first thing to do when stepping into a new field was a systematic mastery of its foundational theories and seminal works. So, during my stay at the OUUK from 2001 to 2002 as a Visiting Research Fellow, I read those foundational theories, including its Master of Arts in Open and Distance Education modules, taking copious notes, meeting many ODE researchers and writers of the modules for further advice, and reflecting on directions of my future research.

However, when I returned to China one year later, I was less confident and optimistic. There was no way for me to access new book and journal publications in the international community via the university library. As a matter of fact, the local branch where I worked did not even subscribe to any Chinese academic databases. I bought Chinese books and subscribed to Chinese journals with my own money. But it was extremely difficult, if not impossible, to personally purchase or subscribe to publications outside China, not to mention the likelihood of losing the package in the process of delivery because not all postal workers know English. Luckily, open-access publications were increasingly available. I also tried whatever I could to acquire these resources. For example, I signed up for Academia.edu, ResearchGate, and LinkedIn and stayed connected with colleagues around the world, the majority of whom were always happy to share. Later, as I became a board member of journals in the field and a contributor to and editor of books, I had more and more access to new publications. When I was adequately resourced, I started to write for an international readership.

This transition to a new area of study was an agentic endeavour underpinned by intrinsic motivation and perceived self-efficacy.

Becoming a Steward

I published my first paper written in English in 2005 (Niu et al., 2005). Since then, my writings have mostly been published in international journals. Meanwhile, I acted as a reviewer for journals and conferences. My thorough and rigorous attitude to reviewing also contributed to my reputation as an ODE researcher. In 2013, I was invited to be on the editorial board of *Distance Education*, and the following year on the editorial board of *System: An International Journal of Educational Technology and Applied Linguistics*, two high-impact journals listed in Social Sciences Citation Index (SSCI). From 2014 to 2022, I was the associate editor of *Distance Education*, and on the editorial boards of several other international journals. In January 2021, I joined Insung Jung and Olaf Zawacki-Richter as Co-Editors of the *SpringerBriefs in Open and Distance Education* series.

My involvement with *Distance Education in China* (DEC), a peer-reviewed Chinese journal, deserves an additional note. In March 2013, I was commissioned to launch and chair its International Forum where invited papers from international researchers were translated into Chinese and published in each issue of the journal. From the March 2013 issue to the July 2022 issue, 121 papers contributed by 155 researchers from twenty-eight countries were published by the journal, an unprecedented "marathon" undertaking in the history of Chinese journal publication. I had sole responsibility for everything, from inviting colleagues to contribute, reviewing and giving feedback, to translating and writing a scholarly commentary for each paper. I experienced frustration, anxiety, and even despair working in this time-consuming capacity. However, all my sacrifices were worthwhile because these papers were well received by Chinese readers and I myself have matured into a better researcher by learning from an expanding network of international colleagues.

Being a steward is an altruistic commitment to maintain the quality of publications and assist contributing colleagues in honing their skills. Therefore, it requires not only unselfish devotion but also adequate research literacy. Meanwhile, being a steward is more than a gesture of "giving/paying back" what you had taken from other stewards or knowledgeable others before; it is also a valuable opportunity to learn from other researchers and keep improving yourself as a researcher/writer. Therefore, I have always taken this job very seriously, an experience from which I have learned a great deal and which has greatly enhanced my perceived self-efficacy.

Resolving Identity Conflict

China is a collectivist culture favouring group interests over individual goals or desires. In such a culture, one is not defined by personal uniqueness but rather in terms of those common qualities of the group one belongs to. Hence, uniformity and conformity are the expected norms while expression of personal ideas and disagreement should be cautiously handled, if unavoidable. Authorities are to be respected and not to be challenged. However, constant exposure to and immersion in more individualist-oriented cultures has fostered my aspiration to make a difference in the world, including research and writing, in my own way. I have always felt more comfortable getting along with international counterparts than with domestic colleagues. Therefore, it was a hard decision to make whether to align my identity with my ought-to self, i.e., what other people in my local community expect me to be; or my ideal self, i.e., what I would like myself to be (Higgins, 1987). This dilemma was far more challenging to resolve than lack of skills, resources, and opportunities because I had to face it every day. After balancing the pros and cons of either choice, I decided to follow my ideal self which was obviously in conflict with a collectivist culture. On the one hand, I continued my engagement with the international ODE community, gradually gaining my acceptance as a full-fledged researcher in this circle and later even becoming a steward, or academic caretaker. On the other hand, I did not give up the domestic stage. Especially after I was put in charge of the DEC International Forum, I constantly had my voice heard, a voice which is often not in harmony with the "mainstream" discourse of China's ODE community. I wrote a scholarly commentary for each invited paper to highlight its relevance to the Chinese context, emphasizing the importance of listening to different voices and embracing a diversity of perspectives. Gradually, my voice could no longer be ignored by other Chinese ODE researchers, most of whom I believe are impressed by the uniqueness of my perspectives on many ODE issues in the Chinese context.

Intrinsic Motivation, Agency, and Self-efficacy: My Secrets to Success

Looking back on my forty-year career trajectory, intrinsic motivation, agency, and self-efficacy have played a key role at each stage, especially in decision-making and decision-implementation.

Dörnyei's (2005) theory about teacher motivation is equally applicable to my motivation as a researcher when he argues that the intrinsic component is a main constituent of motivation and "related to the inherent joy of pursing a meaningful activity related to one's subject area of interest, in an autonomous manner, within a vivacious collegial community... " (p. 160). From the perspective of self-determination theory, intrinsic motivation is also "an inherent tendency to seek out novelty and challenges, to extend and exercise one's capacities, to explore, and to learn" (Ryan & Deci, 2000b, p. 70). Although my pursuit of new knowledge originated from an extrinsic motivation "in order to attain a separable outcome" (Ryan & Deci, 2000b, p. 71), for example, for self-protection and dignity; it gradually developed into something that gives me inherent joy and curiosity, both of which have been motivating and inspiring to me throughout my entire professional life. Moreover, because of my strong and persistent intrinsic motivation, I do research and writing out of my own free will and take advantage of every possible opportunity to establish a "vivacious collegial community"; that is, my personal network of researchers around the world. I never retreat from whatever obstacles come my way and never stop exploring and learning. This is because intrinsic motivation stays when one can be in control, overcome challenge, and believe what one does is of social value and significance (Ryan & Deci, 2017). For me, research and writing are genuinely satisfying experiences which result in what Csikszentmihalyi (2008) refers to as a state of flow.

The interplay between motivation and agency — "the power to originate actions for given purposes" (Bandura, 1997, p. 3) — is self-evident from the accounts above. There is an obvious element of motivation, especially intrinsic motivation in any agentic engagement. According to Bandura (2006), human agency has four core properties: (1) intentionality, (2) forethought, (3) self-reactiveness, which "involves not only the deliberative ability to make choices and action plans, but also the ability to construct appropriate courses of action and to motivate and regulate their execution"; and (4) self-reflectiveness, wherein "people are not only agents of action. They are also self-examiners of their own functioning" (p. 165). Each of these properties is motivation-related.

I received my higher education at a "quasi-university." International colleagues might not be able to imagine the scarcity of learning resources and qualified staff at the lowest-level higher education institutions in China over forty years ago. Looking back, I myself can hardly believe how I have managed to master English even without a native English teacher, not to mention becoming an active researcher and member of the international ODE community. I can hardly imagine how much I have overcome, and how much I have sacrificed, to be what I am today.

But beyond any doubt is my point that my agentic engagements are not so much externally driven as inherently motivated. When an extrinsic motivation is satisfied or if it remains unsatisfied for too long, agency may wane and die out. However, an intrinsic motivation may last as long as one's life and remain an endless source of agency while successful agentic engagements reinforce intrinsic motivation in turn, so that you aim higher and higher. This is a lesson learned from my personal experience, echoing the argument that motivation is a mediator of personal and contextual characteristics and actual performance (Trigwell et al., 2004). The importance of agency is also demonstrated in the mentorship with which I was blessed.

Perceived self-efficacy — "people's beliefs about their capabilities to produce designated levels of performance that exercise influence over events that affect their lives" (Bandura, 1994, p. 71) — has a direct impact on one's motivation, affect, and agency. I was vaguely aware of my self-efficacy when I "helped" my classmates do their homework and cheat on examinations in my childhood. However, it was not until I published my first paper in a major journal as a student at a "quasi-university" that I had a keen awareness of self-efficacy. And my perceived self-efficacy has become an important asset when making my decision at each turning point of my career. For example, it was because I had full confidence in my capabilities to make a difference in the field of ODE that was new to me that I resolutely gave up my research interest in the familiar disciplines of linguistics and applied linguistics, a choice which was favoured by none. It was also because of my perceived self-efficacy that I decided to follow a path which led to what I *wanted to be* rather than what I was *expected to be*, a choice which was paved with adversities and therefore required stronger motivation and higher agency. My experience echoes Bandura's (1989) theory that people "readily undertake challenging activities and select social environments they judge themselves capable of handling" and that "efficacy-activated processes... enable people to create beneficial environments and to exercise control over them" (p. 1178).

Advice to Early-career Colleagues

- Identify your intrinsic motivation for research and writing. It is alright to conduct research out of external motives from time to time. However, intrinsic motivation is critical if you want to sustain your interest and become a researcher in a strict sense.

- Find a good mentor and exercise your agency to foster a productive mentorship. Mentors will not take you seriously unless you yourself are serious about your pursuit.

- Have faith in yourself. Needless to say, this faith should come from your past and/or current actual performance, rather than the result of pure imagination or assumption.

- Learn to think critically. Always challenge what you read instead of blindly accepting what is presented to you. To challenge what other people say is to better understand them, not to disbelieve them. A critical mindset is the source of creativity, innovation, and originality.

- Be well versed in key theories and seminal works in your chosen field of study and keep updated on new research outputs regularly. Making a last-minute effort to catch up on the knowledge base of your study is not an effective strategy.

- Show your respect for stewards by following to the letter the author guidelines set by your target publication outlet. As is the case with mentorship, unless you present yourself seriously, including as a stickler for formalities, others may, subconsciously, take your work less seriously.

- Be happy to give back when you are ready. Giving back is a win-win transaction. You are improving yourself as a researcher when you are helping other people to improve their research.

Concluding Words

In summary, intrinsic motivation, agency, and self-efficacy interact with each other in turning someone such as me from a very humble background to a steward, a caretaker, within the international ODE community. Intrinsic motivation may be the source of agency at the beginning, both of which interact to lead to self-efficacy. Nevertheless, as one stays on track, all three are so intertwined that it is impossible to tell which one is the result of the other or other two. Their interplay results in a synergy conducive to sustaining motivation, boosting agency, and enhancing self-efficacy. These are the three proven keys to success, at least in my case.

References

Bandura, A. (1989). Human agency in social cognitive theory. *American Psychologist, 44*(9), 1175–84. https://doi.org/10.1037/0003-066X.44.9.1175

Bandura, A. (1994). Self-efficacy. In V. S. Ramachaudran (Ed.), *Encyclopedia of Human Behavior* (Vol. 4, pp. 71–81). Academic Press.

Bandura, A. (1997). *Self-efficacy: The Exercise of Control*. W. H. Freeman.

Bandura, A. (2006). Toward a psychology of human agency. *Perspectives on Psychological Science, 1*(2), 164–80. https://doi.org/10.1111/j.1745-6916.2006.00011.x

Chomsky, N. (1957). *Syntactic Structures*. Mouton.

Csikszentmihalyi, M. (2008). *Flow: The Psychology of Optimal Experience*. HarperCollins.

Dörnyei, Z. (2005). *Teaching and Researching Motivation*. Foreign Language Teaching and Research Press.

Higgins, E. T. (1987). Self-discrepancy: A theory relating self and affect. *Psychological Review, 94*(3), 319–40. https://doi.org/10.1037/0033-295X.94.3.319

Huang, G., & Xiao, J. (1996). 英语复合句——从句子到语篇 (*Aspects of English complex sentences: From sentence to text*). 厦门大学出版社 (Xiamen University Press).

Niu, J., Xiao, J., Wang, Z., & He, L. (2005). Exploring an integrated approach to web-based course assessment. *Asian Association of Open Universities Journal, 1*(1), 38–44. https://doi.org/10.1108/AAOUJ-01-01-2005-B004

Ryan, R. M., & Deci, E. L. (2000a). Intrinsic and extrinsic motivations: Classic definitions and new directions. *Contemporary Educational Psychology, 25*(1), 54–67. https://doi.org/10.1006/ceps.1999.1020

Ryan, R. M., & Deci, E. L. (2000b). Self-determination theory and the facilitation of intrinsic motivation, social development, and well-being. *American Psychologist, 55*(1), 68–78. https://doi.org/10.1037/0003-066X.55.1.68

Ryan, R. M., & Deci, E. L. (2017). *Self-determination Theory: Basic Psychological Needs in Motivation, Development, and Wellness.* Guilford Publications.

Trigwell, K., Ashwin, P., Lindblom-Ylänne, S., & Nevgi, A. (2004, June 18–21). *Variation in Approaches to University Teaching: The Role of Regulation and Motivation* [Paper presentation]. The European Association for Research on Learning and Instruction (EARLI) Higher Education Special Interest Group conference, 2004, Stockholm, Sweden.

Vygotsky, L. S. (1994). The problem of the environment. In R. Van Der Veer and J. Valsiner (Eds), *The Vygotsky Reader* (pp. 338–54). Plenum Press.

Xiao, J. (1983). Unattached Participle 浅说 (On unattached participle). 《外语学刊》 (*Foreign Language Research*), 3, 19–22. https://doi.org/10.16263/j.cnki.23-1071/h.1983.03.003

7. 1001 Nights of Research: The Good, Bad, and the Ugly Magic Carpet Ride

Jennifer Roberts

According to Webster and Mertova (2007), narrative inquiry is a methodology that researchers can employ that provides a "rich framework through which they can investigate the way human beings experience the world, as told through their own individual stories" (p. 3). In the same light, Connelly and Clandinin (1990) say that what we know about education comes from sharing stories of our own educational experience with other people.

As an academic researcher, I cannot help myself: I need to find a theoretical framework to guide my story and journey. This chapter provides a rare opportunity for me to cast aside the formalities and rigour of academic writing for a short while. So, faced with this exciting challenge, I will weave my academic stories together to form a narrative — my journey through academia and the world of academic publishing. As a unapologetic teacher, my hope and wish is that I can impart some insight and wisdom to a new generation of distance education researchers.

There are underlying themes running through my academic story and I will touch on each of these as I write, and then try and interlace them into a comprehensive whole. As I sit and write now, at the beginning of this process, the first theme that comes to mind is that I am a late arrival to the world of academia, and I found myself drawn into distance education by being in the right place at the right time. My story will be told as one who entered academia later in life, navigating a world that was alien to the business field where I had previously worked.

I will also touch on some personal aspects of the reasons for doing a PhD (mid-life crisis, acrimonious divorce, development of self-efficacy) and my journey through the field of distance education, both as a student and then later as a researcher/professor (This will also include the very real condition called Imposter Syndrome and my views on the prevalence of narcissistic traits prevalent in some academic spaces).

In addition, if space permits, I would like to include publishing aspects relevant to authors from developing countries such as cognitive or confirmation biases of editors towards researchers from "other" countries. As a research professor residing in a developing country (South Africa), I find this to be a very real issue and so I will relate a few stories that have led me to explore this phenomenon and present this evidence.

Distance Education: An Interdisciplinarity Field

It is only in recent years that distance education has been acknowledged as an academic field. An academic field is often defined by the research that has been published in that field. Distance education is relatively new and initially attracted a fair amount of criticism for its lack of theoretical frameworks, for being descriptive, and for the use of poor research methodologies (Bernard, Abrami, Lou & Borokhovski, 2004; Perraton, 2000). Part of the scepticism of distance education as an academic field of study stems from its interdisciplinary nature.

I am inquisitive and detail-oriented by nature. It is a standing joke in my family that I can recall insignificant details of events that occurred many years ago (the colour of a dress that someone was wearing at a party over forty years ago — you get the gist!). This remembrance of minute details led me to pursue undergraduate studies in statistics and sociology, a masters in socioeconomics and finally a PhD concentrating on curriculum design in distance education. As such, I consider myself to be a truly interdisciplinary scholar and it is this interdisciplinarity that cascaded me into the academic field of distance education. Distance education is by its very nature an interdisciplinary field and draws on the nexus of other academic fields which may include education, technology, sociology, psychology, communication, and philosophy, amongst many others.

My Own Stories

My first story concerns my own PhD study, which, as mentioned earlier, was an interdisciplinary one, where I stated a research problem and addressed it through various sub-studies, each with its own paradigm and methodology. My concluding chapter brought together the assorted studies that I had conducted to answer the research question from a holistic point of view. As is customary, my final thesis was sent to three different examiners. It is often challenging to appoint examiners (and reviewers for journal articles and book chapters) when they include different fields of study in the research work. In my case, two of the examiners understood the concept of interdisciplinarity and provided interesting and sound reviews, which I willingly incorporated into my final thesis submission. The third examiner however, stubbornly refused to acknowledge that a PhD could be extensive rather than intensive. He dug his heels in to insist that I should take one of the individual studies and extend the scope and depth of it — and ignore the other data that I had collected. I am happy to report that a fourth examiner was appointed who overwhelmingly saw the importance of my comprehensive approach to answering the research question and integrating all the findings. The moral of this story is that the field of academia is dynamic and evolving rapidly, and in some instances, scholars are resistant to changing their epistemological viewpoints.

Before my academic life, I worked in the retail industry, using my statistical knowledge to forecast buying trends, patterns, and sales. Retail management is not for the fainthearted as it is driven by accurate forecasts and profits. It is a "just in time" environment where each small error could convert into the loss of large sums of money. Another interesting aspect to the retail business is that it employs people who are creative, vibrant, and sometimes viewed as "slightly eccentric." This is the nature of the business. Drama, histrionics, and a sense of urgency dominate this landscape. There are big personalities and egos at play, and one would be unwise to think that this is the opposite to the confines and rigour of the field of academia. I will discuss this further in the chapter when I reflect on my experiences of academic vanity.

At the age of forty, I underwent my first midlife crisis, and instead of joining the bridge club, engaging in risqué adventures, or travelling the world to "find "myself, I decided to continue my academic studies and enrolled in a master's programme, which was presented in a hybrid format through a university in the United Kingdom. The lecturers travelled to South Africa every six weeks, and we would convene for an intensive weekend session with them. During the time that they were not available, the studies continued in correspondence mode. This is where the concept of self-directed learning became apparent as we were totally on our own for the six weeks between visits and this was in the very early days of email and internet. Communication was thus limited or barely existent, as those were the days before the advent of technology-enhanced education through social media.

At this time, I felt myself drawn to the library at one of the South African universities where there was a reciprocal arrangement with the UK university. I spent days, and even weeks, immersing myself in the library, and opening a world of knowledge that I could not even had imagined existed. I was a rookie researcher and knew that I had to find all the information for myself as there was no one to hold my hand. I am grateful for this opportunity because it was the perfect training ground for my future career as an academic researcher. If there is one piece of advice that I would like to pass on to new and emerging scholars, this is it: You are the master of your own development. Read deeply and find the right people to answer your questions.

The next story relates to my later-life PhD studies and the importance of aligning yourself with a substantive mentor. The value of mentoring in the academic journey is often bypassed and its positioning is not fully understood. I was undergoing my second midlife crisis, as well as recovering from an acrimonious divorce. I needed a new focus, and I will admit that I used the PhD study as a crutch to see me through this trying time of my life. Around that time, I met a fellow parent at a school committee project meeting — an esteemed academic professor. He saw something in me and provided encouragement to immerse myself in and complete my PhD study. We spent a great length of time debating, questioning, and arguing; and in his sage and gentle manner, he guided me on my PhD journey. He must have had the patience of Job, but most of all, he believed in me and encouraged my journey to its conclusion. One of the most special times in my life was at my PhD graduation when he was the guest speaker. He quoted from that classic movie "The King and I" when Anna sang to her pupils, "It is a very ancient saying, but a true and honest thought, that when you become a teacher, by your pupils you'll be taught." This is true mentorship: When it becomes reciprocal — as much as he taught me, he also learned from me.

I fell into the field of distance education. I had completed my PhD at the University of South Africa (Unisa), which is the oldest distance education university in the world, and my research topic for my thesis had centred on curriculum design at a distance education university. I was clearly ahead of my time as I incorporated virtual reality, new learning pedagogies into my research and used mixed methods which were novel then. The Institute for Open and Distance Learning (IODL) at Unisa had advertised for research staff for their research institution, and after a series of interviews, I was offered a senior researcher position. I thought that I knew all about distance education; little did I realize that the field was rich with theoretical frameworks, pedagogies, research methodologies, and philosophical stances.

I was thrown into the deep end and expected to create my own research identity and forge niche areas.

There was no training, orientation, or guidance — just an expectation of research outputs and postgraduate supervision success. This is where I had to draw on the lessons I had learned in self-directedness. To me, self-directedness is when you take responsibility for your own learning and career advancement. You understand that you cannot rely on anyone else to guide you and that you are accountable for your success. In my case, this involved extensive reading (once again back in the academic library), arranging meetings with senior academics to "pick" their brains, attending as many seminars, conferences and talks as possible, and most importantly, being the catalyst for arranging regular debates, presentations, and discussions with colleagues.

The Nature of the Academy

I was intrigued to find that, while I met up with Unisa colleagues at international conferences where they presented interesting research papers, the audience included very few academics from my own organization. Somehow this felt wrong to me — that our own university faculty did not get the opportunity to listen to these presentations. I then created a "Research Café" back at Unisa, where these colleagues were invited to present and share their work in a collaborative environment, understanding that, as academics, we are keen to create an international audience for our research, but we need also to be mindful that our own contextual environment is just as important. Through these Research Cafés, I was also able to disseminate my research within my own university, which led to collaborations with other departments. An example is my work on the future and changing roles of distance education staff. This research had been presented in Australia and India, but when I shared it at my own university, members of the Human Resources (HR) department invited me to assist with their Talent Management programme. In addition, I entered an interdisciplinarity collaborative project with the director of the Continuous Professional Development (CPD) department to continue this research as a longitudinal study.

Academia was like no other job that I had done before, and I could see how easy it is to lose yourself in its bewildering maze. I wished that someone had told me that this was going to be the scenario. I also found out how judgemental this field is: you are often engulfed in the pejorative frame of mind that is possessed by many academics, and my fear was that this mindset would become inculcated into me as well. My experience is that there is no handholding or encouragement — that is the nature of academia. I have often said that this field forces your skin to grow thicker and teaches lessons about overcoming sensitivities and insecurities.

I have seen many new academics faltering in this environment, and I believe that this is not unique to Unisa or developing countries such as South Africa. Many colleagues from various countries have echoed these sentiments and thoughts; my perception is that this is a universal reality as many other colleagues have expressed the same views about their countries. However, I do not wish to sound victimised nor negative. It is difficult to express the sense of achievement when you have been pushed far out of your comfort zone and dug deeper than you thought possible, but, at the end, achieved success.

Publish or Perish

My very first published research article is an example. This article was based on aspects of my PhD thesis so I thought it would be a straightforward process, not realizing the complexities of academic publishing. I was therefore distraught when the article was returned from the reviewers and minor corrections were necessary. Little did I realize that this was the easiest article that I would ever publish, and the voyage would get far more competitive and difficult as I forged ahead into my article publishing journey. I refused consolation from my mentor and did not really believe him when he told me that this was one of the best reviews that he had seen, and that I should be elated.

I have recently read the review reports for an article submitted for publication by esteemed colleagues who are highly rated researchers; they were harsh. Their article has subsequently been published in a high impact journal where the readers would not imagine that the article had been brutishly reviewed. This, however, is the name of the game and it is why I mentioned the need to overcome personal fragility and self-doubt.

My advice is to find a niche research area and prepare yourself to be competent in your knowledge and expertise, so that you can present critical arguments from a point of self-confidence. I became an "expert" in staff development in distance education as well as the development of research capacity and training in developing countries. Too often we try to be all things to all people and find ourselves lost in the pool of researchers. My most cited single-authored article centred on a study into the future roles and competencies of distance educators, in light of the move to online teaching and learning. Currently, I am participating in a project to design an ODL research framework for developing countries and have already published a few articles on this topic.

The Value of Networking and Conferencing

Networking is paramount and, in my experience, the optimal way to do this is through attendance at local and international conferences. This is not straightforward, though, as it involves bureaucratic and challenging administrative issues to obtain funding for such travel. I was fortunate to be awarded with a research grant that enabled me to travel extensively. I have attended and presented my research at many ICDE and EDEN conferences and as a result received invitations to present keynote lectures at other conferences. I cannot overemphasize the importance of putting yourself out there, even if this is not in your nature. As a result of the networks that I created by attending some of these conferences, I am now a "permanent" conference organiser for a digital learning conference in Eastern Europe, have presented seminars in India and was a founding member of the international organization, the Centre for Open Education Research (COER) which is funded by the German government.

Serving on the Australian ODLAA executive committee provided me with exposure to the Australian distance education environment and certainly broadened my narrow landscape. A highlight was when I was appointed programme director for their international conference in 2017. Presenters represented many countries and afforded me the opportunity to meet and discuss differing perspectives of distance education globally. The community of distance education academics in the world is not large and therefore the opportunity to meet and interact with some of the top players in this field was priceless. The networking opportunities are the groundwork for future collaborations, international project teams and invitations for speaking at international conferences. It is the gateway to your academic future. A bonus is that I have managed to form friendships that go beyond that of being just colleagues. I have fond recollections of sailing up and down the Bosphorus in Istanbul with a colleague from China, late night dining (rather raucously) in Oldenburg in Germany, walking along the Yarra river at night in Melbourne, watching the Kremlin Ballet company production of Swan Lake in Moscow and singing loudly in the Irish pubs in Dublin.

Perceptions of the Professoriate

I mentioned earlier the perception of academics as wise, grey-haired, elderly teachers who desire to impart their knowledge to the next generation. One conjures up the image of a gentle, humble person who is enthusiastic about his or her subject, as well as engaging in teaching and learning. I typed in the word "professor" into Google Images and most of these images confirm this stereotype. I am certain that many of these professors do exist, but in my experience, they are rare. Rather, I have encountered many people in academia who think very highly of themselves, need admiration, believe others are inferior, and lack empathy for others. I do not profess to be an expert on personality traits, but my experience, research, and reading have led me to gain a richer understanding of the motivational drives present in many academics.

I have been to international conferences where a certain sector of the audience would delight in asking difficult and unnecessary questions, particularly to novice researchers; and then seemed to derive satisfaction from embarrassing them. I have often felt that this profession lacks empathy and nurturing which are two qualities necessary for effective teaching. In some cases, chasing the limelight seems to be the perceived goal in academia, whereas my feeling is that we should be working co-operatively to enhance education. However, I remind myself that for each of these people who need a sense of entitlement and require constant, excessive admiration, there are many others who have made my career so fulfilling.

I have a close friend who occupies a senior position in a financial institution. Her career success can be seen by her material acquisitions — annual dividends and bonuses allow for the purchase of a new vehicle at regular intervals, a holiday house by the sea and high-end fashion garments. Career success in academia is judged differently, through publications, presentations, awards, and self-acknowledgement. Opportunities for publication in high impact journals are limited and the supply far outstrips the demand. Many universities operate in a managerial style and are policy-driven. Success is determined through a system of metrics and can become extremely competitive. Journal article reviews are often conducted by peers who are competing for the same space as you in the narrow pool of academic journals. It is therefore understandable that the hypercritical stance taken by some reviewers certainly exists. How often have you heard of an article that received a scathing review from some reviewers and editors, only to be accepted by a similar journal with minor changes needed?

In my own experience, I have found that sometimes the new researcher "treads lightly" on the toes of more experienced ones, resulting in the wiser ones feeling the need to protect their knowledge. Be aware that the open education movement, which incorporates Open Education Practice (OEP) and Open Educational Resources (OER), relies on transparency and the free sharing of ideas, knowledge, and concepts. Academia is still, in my opinion, very hierarchical and competitive.

I gave a presentation to a group of senior academics at an international seminar a few years ago. I was asked to present an explanation and analysis of the role of colonization on higher education from a South African perspective. The presentation was well received by most of the delegates, and I was thrilled to hear from a highly esteemed academic that this was one of the best explanations and analyses that she had heard on the topic. A short while later, I heard through another delegate, that someone else had told her that my work was sub-standard and superficial. So, whom do you believe and how do you respond? You must believe in yourself.

Most research emanating from developing countries is context-specific and centres on the unique challenges of these countries. Many developing countries face challenges with regard to broadband connectivity, access to wi-fi, lack of funding for hardware, an inconsistent electricity supply as well as insufficient levels of digital literacy skills (Daya, 2020). There is a perception that the quality of research originating from developing countries is below the accepted standard for international publication (Harris, 2022; Salager-Meyer, 2008). My experience is that editorial bias exists and that some journal editors have an inherent cognitive bias towards researchers from "other" countries. This is called the *availability heuristic* and it is the tendency for someone to estimate the probability of something happening based on past examples (Giblin & Stefaniak, 2021; Yamashiro & Roediger, 2021). It could also fall under the guise of confirmation bias where the editor possesses an existing or previous belief that research from developing countries is inferior (Schuum, 2021).

Believe in Yourself: Self-confidence and The Imposter Syndrome

The judgemental nature of academia can also lead to the prevalence of the Imposter Syndrome (IP) that occurs when persistent doubt concerning one's abilities or accomplishments are accompanied by the fear of being exposed as a fraud despite evidence of one's ongoing success. Many of us accept the negative remarks that are thrown at us and dwell on them, rather than celebrate the positives. According to Brookfield (2002), critical reflection can be a worthwhile intervention. In particular, he describes group reflection as providing an environment that can alleviate the isolation a teacher/academic feels due to fear of exposure. Recognizing that colleagues also experience similar feelings can go a long way to providing relief from the anxiety caused by IP.

A colleague is currently finalizing his PhD which focuses on IP at my own university. I was selected as a participant in his research, which involved an in-depth interview. I found the process to be cathartic as it was the first time that I understood the extent of this syndrome and this interview provided the impetus for me to critically reflect on the reasons for this fear that I had developed. I began to understand that in my previous jobs, I had never felt like a fraud and imposter; and that this syndrome, in my case, was specific to my academic persona. Self-reflection forms a necessary part of self-directedness and the joy here is to find the nexus between understanding the cause of our heightened anxiety and fear of exposure and curtailing the possibility of developing self-aggrandizing traits.

As a new researcher, you must understand that negativity can indeed breed self-doubt. Reflect on the disapproval, understand where it is coming from (and, in many cases, it is our own uncertainty and insecurities); dust off your tiara, straighten your crown, and move on.

In Conclusion

In summary then, I would offer the following advice to new academic researchers:

- Embrace distance education as an interdisciplinary academic field where you can integrate academic disciplines by bringing together different perspectives.
- Find a mentor who believes in you and encourages your development.
- Understand and fully incorporate self-directedness into your academic development. You are your own north star.
- Believe in yourself without becoming arrogant or egotistical.
- Accept criticism without becoming oversensitive. Understand that you are not being critiqued as a person.
- Do not fall into the trap of feeling like an imposter. Remember to practice regular self-reflection and maintain frequent conversations with other colleagues.

As my own academic career moves into its latter years, I am excited to see that a new generation of enthusiastic researchers is entering the exciting field of technology-enabled open, online distance education. I would like to see interdisciplinarity, openness, and a culture of care and mentorship dominate the future landscape of this exciting and rewarding field of research.

References

Bernard, R., Abrami, P., Lou, Y., & Borokhovski, E. (2004). A methodological morass? How we can improve quantitative research in distance education. *Distance Education, 25*(2), 175–98.

Brookfield, S. D. (2002). Using the lenses of critically reflective teaching in the community college classroom. *New Directions for Community Colleges, 118, Summer*, 31–38.

Connelly, F. M., and Clandinin, D. J. (1990). Stories of experience and narrative inquiry. *Educational Researcher, 19*(5), 2–14.

Daya, R. (2020). Digital literacy: An investigation into perceived competencies of Open Distance Learning students in the Eastern Cape province in South Africa. *UnisaRxiv*. https://doi.10.25159/UnisaRxiv/000031.v1.

Giblin, J., and Stefaniak, J. (2021). Examining decision-making processes and heuristics in academic help-seeking and instructional environments. *TechTrends, 65*(1), 101–10.

Harris, J. (2022). Mixed methods research in developing country contexts: Lessons from field research in six countries across Africa and the Caribbean. *Journal of Mixed Methods Research, 16*(2), 165–82.

Perraton, H. (2000). Rethinking the research agenda. *International Review of Research in Open and Distributed Learning, 1*(1), 1–11.

Salager-Meyer, F. (2008). Scientific publishing in developing countries: Challenges for the future. *Journal of English for Academic Purposes, 7*(2), 121–32.

Schumm, W. R. (2021). Confirmation bias and methodology in social science: An editorial. *Marriage & Family Review, 57*(4), 285–93.

Webster, L., & Mertova, P. (2007). *Using Narrative Inquiry as a Research Method: An Introduction to Using Critical Event Narrative Analysis in Research on Learning and Teaching*. Routledge.

Yamashiro, J. K., & Roediger, H. L. (2021). Biased collective memories and historical overclaiming: An availability heuristic account. *Memory & Cognition, 49*(2), 311–22.

8. Creative Academic Writing and Anatomy of a Scholarly Paper

Aras Bozkurt

Academia is full of people who have a lot to say but write very little, and people who have little to say but write a lot; the best amongst us are those who achieve the most appropriate balance between the two.

Petar Jandrić

Creative academic writing is a process and every final product is a scholarly art. This chapter consists of two sections. The first section introduces several creative approaches to better shape a scholarly paper and explains how authors can adopt innovative strategies. Assuming that expertise comes from mastering the structure of a scholarly paper, the second section explores the anatomy of a scholarly paper and provides some practical tips that can aid in writing well-structured papers.

The purpose of research is to solve a mystery, find an answer, and share this knowledge with other individuals all over the world. Sharing has many forms, and the most essential one in the scholarly landscape is writing about the research in question. In addition to writing for the purpose of sharing, writing is an act of documenting research and making it accessible and tangible.

Why I Research and Write: Curiosity and the Need to Learn

The palest ink is stronger than the sharpest memory.

Anonymous

Why do I write scholarly pieces? That question seems very basic but my answer to that question is deeper and more sophisticated. In addition to reporting and documenting my research, I write to document my exploration and learning journey. In this process, everything starts with curiosity — my curiosity drives my inquiry, my inquiry meets my learning needs and expands my worldview. It is certain that scholarly writing (e.g., articles, conference papers, books, book chapters) has many purposes such as advancing the field, exploring a phenomenon, getting a broader understanding of the research in question, reporting empirical findings, or, perhaps, meeting the expectations of the scholarly community. I, as an editor, author, and researcher, pursue similar goals, but one of the reasons that I write is to nurture my curiosity and meet my learning needs.

Verba volant, scripta manent [spoken words fly away, written words remain].

Anonymous

Before I begin to write, I sharpen my thoughts, develop a clearer vision of the topic, and build a cognitive map as I force myself to read more deeply on the topic. I, therefore, sometimes write about the topics that I want to explore and become a nomad traversing bits of information, cross-pollinating between diverse views, ideas, and discussions. In the end, above all, I write to nurture my thoughts and enhance and enrich my cognitive inner world. When I write, I know that the output is more than a scholarly paper and a contribution to the related literature; it is part of my identity, the way I express and reflect my ideas. My writing, therefore, is important to me; and I must be sure about the final product because these scholarly writings are my intellectual fingerprints that are unique to me. Finally, writing is a form of sharing, and sharing what you know or think about is a form of caring for the world we live in, the societies we interact with, and the individuals we communicate with.

In this chapter, I am going to share some of my discoveries and insights regarding academic writing. These insights — and the advice that accompany them — have developed over many years and have served me, personally, well.

Each section below attends as fully as permitted by chapter length to the various aspects of academic writing. Each section is prefaced by a quote that I think cogently captures its essence.

Reading Before Writing

Reading is to the mind what exercise is to the body.

Joseph Addison

One of the most critical steps in writing a scholarly paper is reading. Writing articles requires prior research, which necessitates further reading even if you have expertise on the topic. Thus, you should read, read, and then read again before you start writing. We have to read what others have written to learn and gain deeper insight into how they approached the topic, what are the limitations and strengths; and most importantly, if they exist, what are the gaps in related literature. Besides, meaningful deep reading will also allow you to gain more expertise on the topic, and your expertise will increase even more when you write on the same topic.

Reading, in some cases, can be painful. You will most likely download hundreds of articles and store them in a folder. In some cases, authors blindly download everything, but you should be selective as the pile can become a heavy weight and reading a heavy weight of material can be quite boring. Organize your downloads (i.e., by publication year and author surname) and create a blank page where you can take notes as you read. At this point, remember that you do not need to read every single detail; you can skim through the articles so that you can do a more detailed reading after identifying key resources. If you create a bibliography using this process, you will ease your pain when you must give a report of your reading.

Before starting writing, you should also consider your audience and remember that writing is a way of communicating with them. Therefore, you must digest what you read, organize your ideas, outline a structure that ensures a seamless, smooth flow and a rich reading experience, and most importantly, make sure that your audience will be able to connect the dots when they read your entire paper.

Writing Through and Editing

> The process of editing is what I enjoy most — putting the pieces together and making sense out of them.
>
> Christian Marclay

Do not strive for perfection. Just write as the inspiration comes and when you come up with an innovative idea, just write it down. These ideas come all of a sudden and likewise fly away all of a sudden. Personally, I do not worry about grammar and right word choices. I believe that function — delivering a message — comes first; and then form, following structural and stylistic issues, comes second. So, it is of utmost importance to sketch what you are thinking and then you can polish it later.

> We are the products of editing, rather than of authorship.
>
> George Wald

When you have a draft paper with the main arguments, you can start editing your paper. At this point, remember that as we dive in deeper while reading and exploring, we can experience *scholarly blindness*, which means that dots are connected in our cognitive world but we might have failed to connect them on paper. As we work on a paper, our brains can trick us into connecting these dots automatically. Therefore, it is a good strategy to leave the paper for a while and reset our short-term memory so that our brains have a fresh beginning and we can identify unconnected dots on our paper. That is, if you put your work on hold and allow it to lie fallow, the resulting product will be an improvement.

> The first draft reveals the art; revision reveals the artist.
>
> Michael Lee

Editing can address grammar, word choice, and structural and organizational issues. Printing and reading your paper, reading it aloud, and having someone who is not familiar with the topic read it are other effective strategies. After editing your paper, ask an academic buddy to read your paper and give feedback and constructive criticism from an external perspective. Allowing someone else to critically review your paper is a good strategy to make it better. However, do not forget that there is no perfect final paper, but you can demonstrate perfect effort.

Planting Intellectual Seeds

> We connect the dots in the drawing with our mind. We give them a meaning, a figurative sense, which is self-reflexive in that it creates us, because we are the experiencer of the moment.
>
> Frederick Lenz

Writing a scholarly piece is not a simple act, but rather, it is a form of planting intellectual seeds that will eventually grow and blossom in someone else's inner cognitive world. This notion implies that you should be careful about what you write and how you approach the way in which you report your thoughts or your findings. In this regard, we can assume that your paper will report many dots and that you aspire to the level of understanding may vary according to your purpose. You can write to inform people, give them a critical understanding, help them to explore a phenomenon, and help them to gain deeper insight or wisdom. It is, therefore, important to decide how your intellectual seeds will grow and when they turn into something green, how they will contribute to someone else's worldview.

Scholarly Papers Form an Intellectual Network

> We can only connect the dots we collect, which makes everything you write about you. Your connections are the thread that you weave into the cloth that becomes the story that only you can tell.
>
> Amanda Palmer

In many cases, people assume that academic papers are documents reporting research or arguing a new idea. Beyond their textual nature, they form an invisible intellectual work as they connect different ideas or papers in the scholarly landscape. In addition to creating a form of art by selecting words and expressions purposefully, citations and references create a network that is identifiable through some visualization techniques.

> You can't connect the dots looking forward; you can only connect them looking backwards. So, you have to trust that the dots will somehow connect in your future.
>
> Steve Jobs

Words, terms, or expressions, for instance, can create a discourse network based on their co-occurrences. Aras Bozkurt and Olaf Zawacki-Richter's (2021) study proposes a visual synthesis of scholarly publications in the intellectual landscape (Figure 1). The authors analyzed the titles and abstracts of 1,362 articles published between 2014 and 2019 and visualized them through text mining. Their analyses proposed a network-based concept map in the field of distance education.

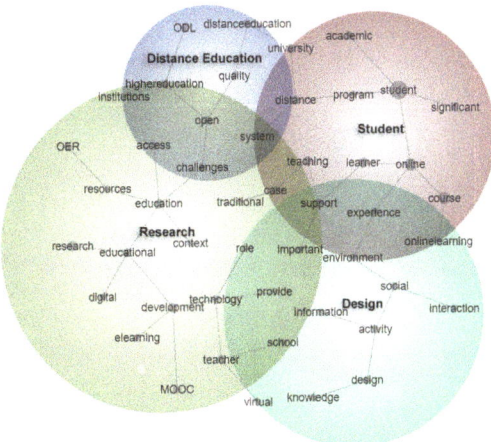

Fig. 1. A concept map showing the research patterns in distance education studies (Bozkurt & Zawacki-Richter, 2021).

A current and relevant example of connectivity within the field is Bozkurt, Kadir Karakaya, Murat Turk, Özlem Karakaya and Daniela Castellanos-Reyes' (2022) study on the impact of the COVID-19 pandemic. In their study, the authors created a network graph depicting the citing and being-cited patterns in COVID-19 and education-related peer-reviewed publications (Figure 2).

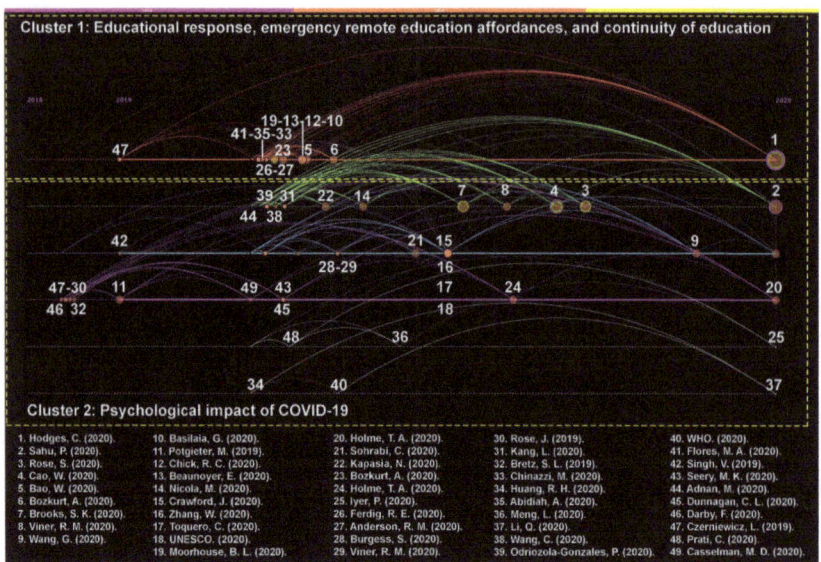

Fig. 2. A network graph showing citing and being cited patterns in COVID-19 and education papers (Bozkurt et al., 2022).

> Everything's intentional. It's just filling in the dots.
>
> David Byrne

The above examples and figures are good proof that every word, expression, citation, and reference should be selected purposefully since they form an intellectual network. This view also gives more responsibility to authors because writing a scholarly paper is a form of reporting a research process or documenting innovative ideas systematically and more critically and purposefully. The above visual proofs from selected articles imply that writing a scholarly paper is not a random act, yet a purposeful one that forms, shapes, and informs an intellectual work.

Mystery Unlocked: Metaphors, Easter Eggs, and Hidden Messages

The metaphor is probably the most fertile power possessed by man.

José Ortega y Gasset

We can forge our arguments in different ways such as using metaphors, placing Easter eggs, or leaving hidden messages. In some cases, such an approach can be confusing and risky for writing a scholarly paper, but it is still a creative way to make your papers more engaging and mysterious to arouse some curiosity. To make this point, two editorial papers will be given as examples. The first one, entitled "In pursuit of the right mix: Blended learning for augmenting, enhancing, and enriching flexibility" by Bozkurt and Sharma (2021), is about combining on-site and online learning by blending the strengths of one modality and neutralizing the weaknesses of the other to provide flexibility. In this editorial, the section entitled "Blending to Achieve the Right Mix!" has metaphors from the movie *The Matrix* that imply the importance of choosing the right modality using the red and blue pills; and another metaphor from the book *Alice in Wonderland* to imply the importance of deciding "on the use of sequential or parallel designs, as well as consider[ing] the factors of time, space, path, and pace to adopt an ideal blended learning model" (Bozkurt & Sharma, 2021, p. 2).

> Onsite and online learning is not a choice of red or blue pills (The Wachowskis, 1999), nor is the purpose of blending to create an ecstasy for synthetic stimulant and hallucinogenic effects. In fact, the goal is to chase the white rabbit (Carroll, 1865) to blend and get the right mix.

Developing these metaphors, the authors placed a white rabbit on the left corner of the first page and two pills in red and blue at the end of the paper. In the acknowledgement section, there is another reference to Grace Slick, who wrote the song "White Rabbit." The acknowledgement section also thanks Lewis Carroll and his character Alice for inspiring many of us and introducing Wonderland and the White Rabbit. Yet, only very careful and curious eyes can see the second part of the acknowledgement as it is written in white and not visible in regular reading.

Another example is also from Bozkurt and Sharma (2022) who wrote the editorial "Digital Transformation and the Way We (Mis)Interpret Technology." In this article, the authors pay tribute to the father of science fiction, Jules Verne, in visible form, and also give thanks to the fictional character Optimus Prime from the movie *Transformers*, which is written in white letters and not seen if you do not read the paper to discover such hidden messages. Because the editorial is about the digital transformation process, there is a pale image at the end of the paper depicting the transformation process of a caterpillar into a butterfly.

These examples are given not to imply that all papers should include metaphors, Easter eggs, or hidden messages, but these examples show that the authors perceive their editorials as pieces of art and use such tricks and design elements to convey their messages in different forms, and perhaps, in more powerful ways. However, it should also be noted that before crafting scholarly papers as in the above examples, those who are in their early academic career or who are MA or PhD students should master the anatomy of a scholarly paper first. The next section will address this issue.

Anatomy of a Scholarly Paper

In essence, most nonfiction papers fall into two categories: research papers and topic papers (Straus, 2012). While research papers are more organized and follow a certain structure as they adopt a methodology, topic papers can reflect a free, but coherent, concise, and scholarly tone. In any categories, authors are expected to provide a clear message, create a logical framework, demonstrate confidence by backing up the arguments by citing the related literature, engage readers' emotions, and avoid formal, impersonal language (Gevin, 2018). Addressing a wider audience and being clear in the way we report our findings so that readers can understand our arguments is important for scientific communication (Fozdar, 2022; Warren et al., 2021) and even for being cited more frequently. In its essence, a good paper is written for a purpose (Perneger & Hudelson, 2004) and shaped around research in question.

Publishing scholarly papers can be a challenge for many authors, even for experienced ones (Hartshorne et al., 2021). Therefore, paying attention to details before submitting your paper (see Dennen & Lim, 2021; Hodges & Curry, 2021; Johnson et al., 2021; Moore & Dickson-Deane, 2021) will also seal the fate of your paper (Naidu, 2021). In this sense, the following section explores the anatomy of a paper and explains the points to pay attention to while writing a scholarly paper.

Title, Abstract, and Keywords

This section is a micro-representation of the paper and can be considered independently since most databases will present these sections firsthand. Please also note that if 1,000 people access your paper, 1,000 people will read your title, 500 will read the abstract, 250 will read the keywords, and approximately 100 of them will read the entire paper. Thus, it is of utmost importance to forge these sections carefully.

Title

Make sure that your title reflects the scope and nature of your study. It should be relevant, informative, and able to arouse curiosity. Refrain from using clichés in the title because clichéd titles might shadow the true potential of your paper. Use a maximum of twelve to sixteen words in the title; considering that most of the publications will appear online, please also consider the perspective of search engine optimization and use a title that is easy to find and visible in online spaces. The title should not include technical jargon so that it will reach a broader audience. In many cases, the title, along with the abstract and keywords, is the showcase of your paper. Therefore, select words or phrases that help the reader to understand the purpose and scope of the study. Note that the title is the very essence of your study and serves as the signature of the author. The title gives the first impression, and most readers will decide whether they should read the paper after reading the title.

Abstract

The abstract gives readers a preview and informs them what comes next. The abstract should be one single paragraph and have a structured format. It should include an introductory sentence and should also address the aim, method and significant findings and takeaways, and conclusion of the study. Remember that, in addition to the title, some readers engage with the abstract and then decide whether to read the whole study. Do not use in-text citations in the abstract since the abstract appears as a separate section in many academic databases. An abstract should be approximately 250 words, which means that you must craft it carefully so that it properly informs the readers and gives your work the value it deserves.

Keywords

Your keywords identify how, where, and when your study is seen in online spaces. Your keywords should be representative and distinctive. To identify the appropriate keywords, ask yourself the following: "Which keywords should I use to find such a paper on the internet?" Keywords are also used by editors to assign reviewers, which implies that you should pay careful attention to the choice of keywords. By default, many publications require a total of five keywords which limit their number and further necessitates selecting them meticulously. You should refrain from using keywords that are too generic or non-specific.

Introduction, Literature Review, and Theoretical or Conceptual Framework

The purpose of the introduction is to provide a background, to offer a description of what the paper is about, and to warm up readers. Metaphorically, the introduction serves like a trailer for a movie. In this section, you can introduce the scope, context, background, core studies, basic terms, and definitions. After providing the background and informing readers of the structure of the study, you can also write about the main purpose of the study. An introduction is also vital in terms of hooking the reader. Therefore, the introduction should be concise and engaging. Strategically, after providing the background, authors are expected to narrow their arguments and then present the purpose of the study.

While writing the literature review section, be focused, selective, and goal-oriented. Rather than creating confusion on your research topic, provide a summary, synthesis, and critical evaluation of the topic. Carefully select studies that contribute to the conceptualization and understanding of your study, provide a logical flow and connect the studies to each other, reveal research gaps and position your paper, report conflicting and supporting literature, and finally locate your arguments based on the intellectual space you created when you formulated your literature review section.

If applicable, you can provide a theoretical or conceptual framework. Using such a framework helps you contribute to a broader understanding of the topic, build on an existing body of research, navigate among different assumptions, and provide researchers a basis for further study. When you use a theoretical or conceptual framework, you also need to explain how it relates to your research topic and report what your assumptions are. The most significant point is to bring this framework into the discussion section and interpret your findings through that lens.

Methodology

If you torture the data long enough, it [sic] will confess to anything.
Ronald Case

This section explains how you conducted your study, which methodological paradigm you adopted, and how it contributed to the exploration and explanation of the research in question. This section should be clear and concise in providing adequate details that may be needed to adopt or replicate the study. This section reports the procedures that inform how the research was conducted and the data collected and analyzed. It is, therefore, crucial to provide a rationale and justification for the methodological paradigm adopted.

It is usually helpful if the authors clearly state and articulate the methodology (qualitative, quantitative, mixed, or other emerging research method) and research model or design (e.g., survey, case study, phenomenology, experimental study, explanatory sequential mixed design) at the beginning of the methodology section. Always include sub-sections such as research sampling or research group, data collection tools, data analysis procedures, reliability and validity issues, ethical issues, and limitations of the study. Please note that the methodology section should function like a flawless machine in which each working part meaningfully contributes to the overall methodological process, because unreliable methodology undermines the overall research process as well as your findings, discussion, and conclusion.

Because methodology acts as a pillar of your research, a flaw in methodological design can quickly undermine the overall research. It is, therefore, of utmost importance to double-check your methodological procedure before conducting your research. Please also note that the design, and flow of the methodological section is already identified when the aim of the study was defined.

Findings and Discussion

Report your findings systematically and in the same order if you have more than one research aim or question. To report your findings, use figures and tables. To avoid repetition, do not provide the same data in the text that you provided in tables and figures. When you report your findings, do not manipulate data and refrain from biased judgments and interpretations that might misdirect readers.

In the discussion section, you are to interpret your findings and report any new understanding or insights that emerged from your research. One of the best strategies is to compare and contrast research findings from multiple angles by benefiting from the related literature. Make sure that you take a critical stance without overinterpreting the research findings. This section should be in line with the aim(s) of the study and should be linked to the literature review and, if applied, should use the theoretical or conceptual framework as a lens to interpret the findings.

In general, researchers exhibit their expertise in the discussion section. You can highlight the significance of your paper and show that your paper fills a gap and contributes to the related literature, discusses the findings critically, and pushes the readers to think critically. It is generally effective to develop explanations based on the findings of the study, provide a deeper understanding by synthesizing the findings, and formulate a critical discourse based on the aim(s) of the study. In simple terms, this is where you report how your findings make sense and how you support the results by citing related literature, both supporting and opposing. Note that what you argue should be subjective, scientifically robust, reliable, and valid, yet not speculative.

Conclusions, Implications, and Suggestions

The conclusions, implications, and suggestions section is where you provide a synopsis of your findings and report your conclusions. It is also where you demonstrate your contribution to the related literature by distilling solid conclusions based on your findings. Be sure that your conclusions are in line with your research purpose and in the scope of the study. Again, it is also important to report the implications of the study and how it may affect the related stakeholders and what should be taken into consideration. Finally, providing suggestions is also very helpful for future research direction. Your suggestions can be critical in terms of setting a future research agenda and shaping future research trends. In this regard, provide solid and clear suggestions that indicate specific actions. Please also remember that the conclusions, implications, and suggestions section is where most people who are not in academia may show an interest.

References

References, along with in-text citations, are crucial in terms of supporting your ideas through empirical evidence and addressing this evidence. In addition, to avoid plagiarism, you need to cite and appropriately reference your sources. Providing a systematic and complete list of references is also helpful for those who would like to snowball some key studies and also helpful to show where the scholarly arguments come from and how other researchers can locate them. You need to be certain that you cited key references and that your references are relevant, recent, and listed appropriately according to the required referencing style. It is also important that references are well-balanced and linked to the overall purpose of the study. A well-balanced reference list provides sources that include counterarguments as well as supporting references. You should cite recent references so that authors have access to a current and up-to-date outlook regarding the research in question. Please also remember that citing relevant references proves that you did an in-depth prior reading and conducted a thorough review of the related literature on your topic. Finally, clean and proper citations and references are an indicator of how meticulously you worked on your study, which will leave a good impression on editors and reviewers.

Final Remarks

This chapter reports on how I approach writing a scholarly paper and roughly explains the anatomy of one. However, these are not golden rules but, rather, strategies I have used that have worked well thus far. When you write a paper, please remember that there is no perfect output; but there is a perfect effort you can apply.

Before you submit your paper, edit and polish it so that it shines on the desk of the editors and reviewers. When you submit it, you may get desk rejections, or you may be subject to meaningless, unfair comments (never forget the Reviewer 2 phenomenon — it exists). Deal with those reviewers, defend your arguments, convince them, and provide a sound rationale if you do not choose to revise your paper as suggested. During the editorial processes, you will have defeats and victories, but remain optimistic; if you view every criticism as an opportunity to make your paper better, one day you will experience the magical moment and hear, "We are pleased to inform you that your paper is accepted for publication." Please keep your hopes high, even if you are rejected on the first submission, and always remember that every paper eventually finds its home.

References

Bozkurt, A., & Sharma, R. C. (2021). In pursuit of the right mix: Blended learning for augmenting, enhancing, and enriching flexibility. *Asian Journal of Distance Education, 16*(2), i–vi. https://doi.org/10.5281/zenodo.5827159

Bozkurt, A., & Sharma, R. C. (2022). Digital transformation and the way we (mis)interpret technology. *Asian Journal of Distance Education, 17*(1), i–viii. https://doi.org/10.5281/zenodo.6362290

Bozkurt, A., & Zawacki-Richter, O. (2021). Trends and patterns in distance education (2014–2019): A synthesis of scholarly publications and a visualization of the intellectual landscape. *The International Review of Research in Open and Distributed Learning, 22*(2), 19–45. https://doi.org/10.19173/irrodl.v22i2.5381

Bozkurt, A., Karakaya, K., Turk, M., Karakaya, Ö., & Castellanos-Reyes, D. (2022). The Impact of COVID-19 on Education: A Meta-Narrative Review. *Tech Trends, 66*, pp. 883–96. https://doi.org/10.1007/s11528-022-00759-0

Carroll, L. (1865). *Alice's Adventures in Wonderland*. Macmillan.

Dennen, V. P., & Lim, C. P. (2021). Publishing as a Collaborative Endeavour: Insights from the Editors of The Internet and Higher Education. In Hartshorne, R., Ferdig, R. E. & Bull, G. (Eds). *What Journal Editors Wish Authors Knew About Academic Publishing* (pp. 49–59). Association for the Advancement of Computing in Education (AACE). https://www.learntechlib.org/primary/p/219093/

Fozdar, S. (2022). The curse of knowledge: Why are academic papers so difficult to read? *HoniSoit*. https://honisoit.com/2022/04/the-curse-of-knowledge-why-are-academic-papers-so-difficult-to-read/

Gevin, V. (2018). How to write a first-class paper. *Nature, 555*, 129–30. https://doi.org/10.1038/d41586-018-02404-4

Hartshorne, R., Ferdig, R. E. & Bull, G. (2021). *What Journal Editors Wish Authors Knew About Academic Publishing*. Association for the Advancement of Computing in Education (AACE). https://www.learntechlib.org/primary/p/219093/

Hodges, C. B., & Curry, J. H. (2021). Publishing in TechTrends: A Journal Linking Research and Practice in Educational Technology. In Hartshorne, R., Ferdig, R. E. & Bull, G. (Eds), *What Journal Editors Wish Authors Knew About Academic Publishing* (pp. 111–17). Association for the Advancement of Computing in Education (AACE). https://www.learntechlib.org/primary/p/219093/

Jandrić, P. (2022). Alone-Time and Loneliness in the Academia. *Postdigital Science and Education*. https://doi.org/10.1007/s42438-022-00294-4

Johnson, T. E., Lin, L., Young, P. A., Ilgaz, H., Morel, G., & Spector, J. M. (2021). Thinking from Different Perspectives: Academic Publishing Strategies and Management in the Field of Educational Technology. In Hartshorne, R., Ferdig, R. E. & Bull, G. (Eds), *What Journal Editors Wish Authors Knew About Academic Publishing* (pp. 37–48). Association for the Advancement of Computing in Education (AACE). https://www.learntechlib.org/primary/p/219093/

Moore, S., & Dickson-Deane, C. (2021). Behind the Curtain: Understanding the Review and Publishing Process for a Peer-Reviewed Research Journal in Higher Education. In Hartshorne, R., Ferdig, R. E. & Bull, G. (Eds), *What Journal Editors Wish Authors Knew About Academic Publishing* (pp. 61–73). Association for the Advancement of Computing in Education (AACE). https://www.learntechlib.org/primary/p/219093/

Naidu, S. (2021). The Fate of a Submission Is Sealed Long Before Its Consideration for Publication! In Hartshorne, R., Ferdig, R. E. & Bull, G. (Eds), *What Journal Editors Wish Authors Knew About Academic Publishing* (pp. 29–35). Association for the Advancement of Computing in Education (AACE). https://www.learntechlib.org/primary/p/219093/

Perneger, T. V., & Hudelson, P. M. (2004). Writing a research article: advice to beginners. *International Journal for Quality in Health Care, 16*(3), 191–92. https://doi.org/10.1093/intqhc/mzh053

Straus, V. (2012). *A guide to writing an academic paper*. Washington Post. https://www.washingtonpost.com/blogs/answer-sheet/post/a-guide-to-writing-an-academic-paper/2012/01/18/gIQAjGCTCQ_blog.html

The Wachowskis. (1999). *The Matrix*. Warner Bros.

Warren, N. L., Farmer, M., Gu, T., & Warren, C. (2021). Marketing ideas: How to write research articles that readers understand and cite. *Journal of Marketing, 85*(5), 42–57. https://doi.org/10.1177%2F00222429211003560

9. Writing and Making the World

Catherine Cronin

> The only way to make borders meaningless is to keep insisting on crossing them... For when you cross a border, you are not only affirming its permeability, but also changing the landscape on both sides
>
> Lina Mounzer, 2016

Like many people, perhaps, I feel that my identity is a blend of multiple and often contradictory aspects. I am a born New Yorker who has made my home in the west of Ireland. I am an open education scholar, community educator, engineer, and feminist. My winding path through formal education includes mechanical and systems engineering, women's studies, and open education — BSc, MEng, MA, PhD. I have worked mostly within academia, often in the community, and for a short time in the IT industry. I am impelled to question, and often to transgress, borders and boundaries.

While writing is not my primary professional activity, I consider it to be central to my work — and even to my sense of self. Whether it is a research article, book chapter, blog post or review, writing is where the often disparate parts of "me" come together. Always and inevitably, all selves come to the writing table. At times in my career as a scholar, I tried to quieten some of these voices, but not any longer. If I were to share any advice with fellow scholars and writers it would be this: In order to say what you need to say, know the rules of your field, discipline, and genre. Follow them. Then challenge them, subvert them, extend them, and renew them — as much as your purpose requires and your situation allows.

In preparing to write this chapter, I reflected on my forty-year career, focusing specifically on research, writing and publishing. While not written as a reflective memoir, I have organized my reflections around three key periods: my formal education, early/mid-career, and completing my PhD as a mature student. I imagine these stages as moving from tilling the soil to planting, growing, flourishing, et al.

Formal Education: Tilling and Planting

As a researcher and writer who left elementary school in the 1970s, I marvel at how often I return to foundational lessons I learned in those years. I hold enormous gratitude for the teachers who helped me to develop an understanding and deep love for language, reading, and writing. As noted by other authors in this volume, I am grateful to the elementary school teachers who taught me grammar and spelling (diagramming sentences!), even though my favoured academic subjects were mathematics and science. All these years later, I continue to learn — and to break rules and make mistakes, of course. But those language foundations are firm ground on which to stand when facing any writing task, even today.

In my engineering education (BSc and MEng), writing was not a priority. The curricular focus was on mathematics and problem-solving. However, in my late twenties, I returned to education to complete a Master of Arts in women's studies. What a joy! My motive was to take a deep dive into subjects that I loved (history, sociology, literature, feminism) but had not had the opportunity to study in my engineering education. Deep reading, study, and discussion of intersectional feminist theory, histories of education, and sociological analysis were like water to a parched throat. From my lecturers and peers (all mature students), I learned much about research and academic writing, but also about the imperative of recognising and valuing the personal and political. Reading work by scholars such as bell hooks, Audre Lorde, Paolo Freire and Cynthia Cockburn revealed the raw truth of this for me. I continue to believe that neither the personal nor the political should be ignored in the interests of achieving so-called "objectivity" in academic writing. I completed a master's dissertation in the area of gender and technology, drawing on all I had learned in the women's studies course, together with my lived experience as a young woman engineer (Cronin, 1992; Cronin, 1995).

This formative experience of combining the personal, political, and academic helped to change the path of my career and my life. Thereafter, I sought work that would enable me to develop and contribute as an educator and researcher in areas with social impact and a commitment to furthering equity.

Early/mid-career: Growing, Pruning, Maturing

Throughout my career, I have worked in higher and community education, including large-scale research projects, undergraduate and postgraduate teaching and supervising, adult education, programme management, and developing and teaching community education programmes. In reflecting on these varied experiences for the purposes of this book, I identified three experiences that were instrumental in helping me to develop as a writer and to find confidence in my voice.

I worked as an associate lecturer with The Open University in Scotland for several years in the 1990s, teaching two courses: Issues in Women's Studies (U207) and Introduction to Information Technology: Social and Technological Issues (DT200). This was my first work as an open and distance educator, made doubly fascinating because DT200 included teaching online using CoSy, one of the earliest applications of online conferencing systems in higher education (Wilson & Whitelock, 1998). By far, the greatest satisfaction of working as an OU associate lecturer was teaching and learning with students — all mature students bringing their varied life experiences to their studies. Teaching with the OU also meant benefitting from outstanding professional development and support — at a distance, but no less personal and effective for that. At regular intervals, samples of my assessment feedback to students would be reviewed by a senior lecturer, who would return written feedback to me. While this helped me to develop as a teacher, it also helped me enormously as a writer, striving always to balance assessment and academic requirements with the personal development and wellbeing of each student.

I also worked for three years as a researcher for a sector-wide project funded by the Scottish Higher Education Funding Council, "Winning

Women in Science, Engineering and Technology"[1] (1995–97). Our small team of researchers explored barriers to access, participation, and progression for women in STEM fields in Scottish higher education; and highlighted global examples of good practice designed to address these challenges. This was an opportunity to undertake collaborative research and writing as part of a team of experienced researchers; to work with advisory groups across a national higher education sector; and to present research findings to funders and to the sector. Our work was published in summary form as a set of guides for Scottish higher education (described in Roger, Cronin, Duffield, Cooper, and Watt, 1998). However, our theoretical findings, including a feminist analysis of women's under-representation in STEM, were not accepted by the funders for inclusion in the guides, despite endorsement by our advisory groups. As researchers, we believed in the importance of this work. Two of us from the research team undertook to refine the work and ensure that it was published in an academic journal (Cronin & Roger, 1999). This was an important and foundational learning experience as a researcher and writer: undertaking work of value, challenging hegemonies, encountering structural resistance, and persisting in finding alternative paths to publishing.

A third early/mid-career experience that proved foundational was moving to a full-time post in an Information Technology department in higher education in the mid-2000s: coordinating a fully online master's programme and teaching in a BSc programme. At this stage, I was deeply steeped, academically and in practice, in critical and feminist pedagogies and research. I consequently found myself challenging many boundaries — particularly regarding assessment, collaboration, and community engagement. Writing was central to this work in a number of ways.

I first worked to change the assessment requirement for the undergraduate module to wholly continuous assessment, eliminating the need for a final exam. This enabled me to design new forms of continuous assessment, many with input from students. Students were asked to submit various forms of written work during the semester (e.g., annotated bibliographies, reflections, project proposals), each of which

---

1   What was called SET (Science, Engineering and Technology) is now commonly called STEM (Science, Technology, Engineering and Mathematics).

would receive feedback; this technique enabled students to refine their work as it developed. Students also were invited to choose the mode of their final digital media project, with the primary requirement being to apply what they had learned to design and develop a digital resource for a community that was meaningful to them. Students developed websites, blogs, videos, and podcasts for a range of diverse communities interested in music, dance, history, physical fitness, animal welfare, and more. Openness also played a role in this work. I supported students in publishing their work openly, if they wished. In addition, through the use of social media and open tools, our small learning community in Ireland collaborated with students and educators in the UK, Germany, Spain and New Zealand (Cochrane et al., 2013; Cronin, Cochrane & Gordon, 2016).

Alongside all these experiences as an educator and researcher, I began to blog, finding enjoyment in writing informally about teaching, assessment, and key issues such as digital literacies, digital identity, privacy, open teaching, open research and more.[2] Altogether, these research, teaching and publishing (formal and informal) experiences led me to a point in 2014 where I chose to complete a long-considered PhD.

PhD and Post-PhD: Flourishing, Still Learning

People undertake doctoral studies for myriad reasons. I began PhD research in my fifties; my motivation, at that stage, was not primarily to increase my career prospects. My motives were more complex. I was working as an active open educator/researcher, often being asked to speak with groups about digital and open education issues. I found myself sharing the experiences of my students, citing others' research, and reflecting deeply on the challenges of openness within higher education, particularly regarding the furthering of equity in education. I came to believe that by completing substantive research in this area, I could better advocate within my institution (and perhaps more broadly) for the need to develop critical digital/open capabilities and to implement supportive open education policies. In essence, I identified a research topic of value and felt that undertaking this as a

---

2   See http://catherinecronin.net/blog/

PhD researcher would enable me to do the work with the structure and support required. I cobbled together what funding I could, completing the research initially while working full-time and latterly by researching, and writing full-time.

PhD research is primarily a solitary endeavour, so collaborating wherever possible was crucial for my motivation and mental health, as well as for continuing to learn and to challenge my assumptions. GO-GN,[3] a global network of doctoral researchers in open education, was a lifeline of peer support, mentorship, and friendship. Also helpful was an informal group of researchers/writers (a mixed group of students and staff) who met regularly for "Shut Up and Write" sessions at my institution. A few of us from this group also met informally, using Wendy Belcher's (2009) *Write Your Journal Article in 12 Weeks* as a guide. We adapted the timescale to nine weeks and over the course of one summer, we supported one another in completing and submitting our respective articles. The process helped me to produce the first publication based on my PhD research (Cronin, 2017).

Completing a thesis is a huge challenge for any researcher. The deeper one studies and understands any topic, the more complex and multifaceted it becomes. When and how to draw a line under the work and submit — a gnarly question! In my case, working to a strict submission deadline (after which I would return to full-time work) proved helpful. I relied here on my IT and project management background. A year before my deadline, I created a chapter outline for the thesis, scheduled weekly deadlines for writing, review, and revisions of each, agreed these with my supervisor, and set to work. It was a demanding year and there were several setbacks. But breaking the Herculean goal of completing the thesis into (somewhat) smaller tasks helped me to get it done — submitting just three weeks later than planned. It was not the perfect thesis, but it was *my* thesis and it was done!

Career opportunities did arise after completing the PhD. I went on to work for three years at Ireland's National Forum for the Enhancement of Teaching and Learning in Higher Education, a small, academically-led team supporting all higher education institutions in Ireland. As digital and open education lead, I advocated for and supported the

---

3   See https://go-gn.net/

development of open capabilities across the national higher education sector and led the development of a sectoral guide to creating enabling policies for digital and open education (National Forum, 2021). This period of work was undertaken almost entirely during the COVID-19 pandemic. As with so many of us working in higher education during that time, it felt as if every fibre of my being was required to do the work that needed to be done, i.e., to support students, faculty, and staff. For me, that meant relying on teamwork, collaboration, communication, research, and writing; values such as prioritising care and equity; and advocating for those who were most marginalised during the crisis.

Writing our Challenging Times

I write this in summer 2022, with swirling crises all around. Climate and ecological emergencies, a continuing pandemic, deepening inequalities, rising authoritarianism, surveillance capitalism, and more. We are all embedded in this context, regardless of our disciplines or areas of expertise. My response is to make sure that my work is charged with this urgency, whatever ultimate form the work may take. I intentionally seek to engage in diverse collaborations that are committed to equity and social justice. This includes co-editing *Open at the Margins*, a collection centring marginal voices and non-dominant epistemic stances in open education (Bali et al., 2020); co-editing a special issue of *Learning, Media and Technology* focused on feminist approaches to education and technology (Atenas et al., 2022); writing and co-editing *Higher Education for Good: Teaching and Learning Futures*, a book focused on hopeful higher education futures (Czerniewicz & Cronin, forthcoming); as well as other projects (e.g., Atenas et al., 2022; Zamora et al., 2021).

As writers, each of us is unique. I wish for all writers the opportunities and confidence to bring all of yourself to your work. Returning to the advice shared at the start of this chapter: by all means know and follow the rules, but don't stop there! Challenge rules and conventions, subvert them, extend them, renew them — as much as your purpose requires and your situation allows. Our words create the world anew, each time we write. As Angela Davis et al. (2022) wrote of the brilliant Octavia Butler: "we will dream our way out; we must imagine beyond the given" (p. 16).

References

Atenas, J., Beetham, H., Bell, F., Cronin, C., Henry, J. V., & Walji, S. (2022). Feminisms, technologies and learning: continuities and contestations. *Learning, Media and Technology, 47*(1). https://doi.org/10.1080/17439884.2022.2041830

Atenas, J., Havemann, L., Cronin, C., Rodés, V., Lesko, I., Stacey, P., Feliu-Torruella, M., Buck, E., Amiel, T., Orlic, D., Stefanelli, C., & Villar Onrubia, D. (2022). *Defining and Developing 'Enabling' Open Education Policies in Higher Education*. UNESCO

Policy Brief, presented at World Higher Education Conference 2022. http://oars.uos.ac.uk/2481/

Bali, M., Cronin, C., Czerniewicz, L., DeRosa, R., & Jhangiani, R. (Eds) (2020). *Open at the Margins: Critical perspectives on open education*. CC BY-SA Rebus Community. https://press.rebus.community/openatthemargins/

Belcher, W. L. (2009). *Writing your Journal Article in Twelve Weeks: A guide to academic publishing success*. University of Chicago Press.

Cochrane, T., Buchem, I., Camacho, M., Cronin, C., Gordon, A., & Keegan, H. (2013). Building global learning communities. *Research in Learning Technology, 21*. https://doi.org/10.3402/rlt.v21i0.21955

Cronin, C. (1992). *Women in Engineering: Issues, challenges and strategies* [Master's thesis, University of Limerick].

Cronin, C. (1995). Is the 'feminine engineer' an oxymoron? Women's views and experiences of gender and engineering. In P. Byrne, J. Conroy, & A. Hayes (Eds), *U.C.G. Women's Studies Centre Review, 3* (pp. 43–52). Women's Studies Centre, University College, Galway.

Cronin, C. (2017). Openness and praxis: Exploring the use of open educational practices in higher education. *The International Review of Research in Open and Distributed Learning, 18*(5). https://doi.org/10.19173/irrodl.v18i5.3096

Cronin, C., Cochrane, T., & Gordon, A. (2016). Nurturing global collaboration and networked learning in higher education. *Research in Learning Technology, 24*. https://doi.org/10.3402/rlt.v24.26497

Cronin, C., & Roger, A. (1999). Theorizing progress: Women in science, engineering, and technology in higher education. *Journal of Research in Science Teaching, 36* (pp. 637–61). https://doi.org/10.1002/(SICI)1098-2736(199908)36:6<637::AID-TEA4>3.0.CO;2-9

Czerniewicz, L., & Cronin, C. (Eds). (2023, forthcoming). *Higher Education for Good: Teaching and Learning Futures*. https://doi.org/10.11647/OBP.0363

Davis, A., Dent, G., Meiners, E. R., & Richie, B. E. (2022). *Abolition. Feminism. Now*. London: Hamish Hamilton.

Mounzer, L. (2016, October 6). War in translation: Giving voice to the women of Syria. *Literary Hub*. https://lithub.com/war-in-translation-giving-voice-to-the-women-of-syria/

National Forum for the Enhancement of Teaching and Learning in Higher Education. (2021). *Guide to Developing Enabling Policies for Digital and Open Teaching and Learning*. https://hub.teachingandlearning.ie/resource/guide-to-developing-enabling-policies-for-digital-and-open-teaching-and-learning/

Roger, A., Cronin, C., Duffield, J., Cooper, M., & Watt, S. (1998). Winning women in science, engineering and technology in higher education in Scotland: Some epistemological and pedagogical questions. *European Education, 30*(4), 82–100. https://doi.org/10.2753/EUE1056-4934300482

Wilson, T., & Whitelock, D. (1998). Is it sustainable? A comparison of student and tutor online time across three distance-learning courses. *Research in Learning Technology, 6*(1), 25–31. https://doi.org/10.1080/0968776980060105

Zamora, M., Bali, M., Mehran, P. & Cronin, C. (2021). Equity Unbound as critical intercultural praxis. *The Journal of Applied Instructional Design, 10*(4). https://edtechbooks.org/jaid_10_4/equity_unbound_as_cr

10. A Collaborative Approach to Research and Writing

D. Randy Garrison

As I begin this chapter, I offer this caveat as it will become evident that I have little experience writing in a personal manner: I have always been told to write in the third person and be objective. As a result, in writing this chapter, I am not exactly building on my scholarly strengths. Moreover, my approach to research and writing is self-taught and developed in the crucible of scholarly critique, shaped by the focus on simplicity of communication. The strategy is to answer the research question and communicate that insight as clearly as possible. Moreover, I take a more intuitive approach to my work as opposed to following a standard plan of attack. I am always looking for new ways to think about a problem and exploring these insights. This approach means taking a systemic view of things and not getting caught up in the minutiae. This also translates into making connections and creating coherent perspectives. It should become evident that my approach to research and writing is driven by curiosity and the search for explanation. Ideally, it is a search for the key concept that provides coherence, understanding, and the means to explore further. I note this at the outset because what I have to offer here is more strategic than tactical. Therefore, my advice regarding specific writing techniques will be limited. That said, I believe my approach may be better appreciated with an understanding of my background and how I became a researcher.

My Educational Journey

I ended up in academia largely by chance. I was forty years old when I accepted a temporary university position. I never previously considered an academic career. However, I was always curious which unintentionally prepared me for a career as a researcher. My curiosity was the basis for my love of learning. However, I was never a very good student because I never much cared for being told what to learn. When I was growing up, studying was largely a memorization process which I despised. This is important to mention as I believe it had a profound impact on my learning and success as a researcher. This aversion to memorization revealed a need to understand and very much shaped my independence of thought and how I approach research and writing.

As an undergraduate, I majored in mathematics education but developed a particular interest in cognitive psychology and the learning process. This interest in learning significantly shaped my future studies. After graduation, I became interested in computer applications in education. I must note that this was in the early 1970s and before the proliferation of the microcomputer. I was offered a scholarship at the University of Calgary and went on to develop and evaluate a computer-assisted physics programme to qualify for a master's degree. After this, I continued my career in education with a move to a college setting, teaching adults. This was career-changing as it stimulated my interest in adult education and paved the way to completing a doctorate in the subject. While earning this degree was never intended as a career move, it unexpectedly opened the door to an academic career and provided the philosophical and theoretical foundation for my research interests.

Consistent with my systemic approach to research, it may be useful to note that I believe a significant reason for my success was based upon an ability to see things back to front. I attribute this to my background in statistics and being able to assess a viable means to analyze data and the best way to answer the question. This is where I felt I had an advantage as I tended to see the problem back to front. That is, I had a very good idea of the data I needed and how these could be analyzed to best inform the question at hand. This perspective expedited my graduate programme research and made my research career more productive. I have found that not seeing the research process systematically is a significant weakness of many graduate students. Too often they ask interesting questions but in a way that may make it very difficult to gather, analyze, and get good results.

My Academic Career

My university career began with a one-year temporary appointment as director of distance education at the University of Calgary in 1984. This appointment was to replace a faculty member going on academic leave. Much to my good fortune, the faculty member did not return, and I was offered a tenure-track position beginning in 1985. What was equally fortuitous was that I found myself in a field that needed fresh thinking. It was an area to which I could bring my knowledge of learning and educational technology. As a result, I wrote my first book, *Understanding distance education: A framework for the future* (Garrison, 1989). While the sub-title was a bit pretentious for a relative newcomer, I believe it was a timely critique of distance education with its dependence on independent learning. At the time, distance education was described by Otto Peters (1994) as an industrialized form of education based on the advantages of efficient mass education. While I understood the necessity of such an approach at the time, emerging technologies were mitigating the dependence on independent study. I argued that education was inherently a transaction, and I chose to emphasize the importance of interaction and collaboration for an authentic educational experience. This perspective fundamentally shaped my research direction and educational views.

Perhaps the defining characteristic of my research approach is collaboration which I had first learned through sports. I played both individual and team sports (tennis, basketball) but appreciated the camaraderie of the latter. From a research perspective, I saw that thinking and working cooperatively had numerous advantages. While we never truly work alone as we benefit indirectly from the work of others, it is enormously beneficial to be stimulated by the knowledge of others through direct and shared experiences. Collaborative discourse not only encourages deeper thinking, but I also find that it is more satisfying. It simply makes too much sense to me not to benefit from the expertise of others. The challenge is finding the most productive means to work together. Productive collaboration will require negotiations based on the personalities and abilities of the group members. A simple example is that when drafting an article, I preferred to have the first author do the initial draft (regardless how incomplete) and then allow others to contribute. The reason for this was my inability to write collaboratively in real time, which, for me, did not give me time to reflect and allow a flow of ideas.

To be clear, I developed many of my ideas individually but was never reluctant to share and work with others to refine them. The first significant work in this regard was in the field of distance education with my colleague Doug Shale. I believe we significantly reshaped the field by focusing on the educational transaction and considering distance as a constraint, not a defining characteristic. Doug had worked with Athabasca University and had important insights into the advantages and disadvantages of dedicated open distance education institutions. His brilliance was exciting, and we produced a book titled *Education at a Distance* in 1990, where we argued that distance should be considered a structural constraint and not a defining characteristic of the experience.

Collaboration, however, reached new heights when I assumed the position of Dean, Faculty of Extension, at the University of Alberta in 1996. While I had two colleagues at the university, Terry Anderson and Walter Archer, there was little expectation of collaborative research. The beginning of our collaboration was grounded in the challenge of implementing an online (actually blended) graduate programme. At that time, there were few programmes that had implemented this model and there were few examples of how to do this.

The justification for delivering a quality learning experience online was the catalyst for the Community of Inquiry framework. I had explored some of the core concepts before arriving at the University of Alberta, but the synergy of my colleagues and circumstances created the environment that allowed us to bring these ideas together. We began by meeting for lunch at least once a week to keep things moving. Sharing ideas in such a setting was inspiring. However, what moved this work forward was a research grant that Terry Anderson was awarded. This provided the funds to hire a graduate student, Liam Rourke, who proved instrumental in the literature review and testing of our concepts. This team of four coalesced in the late 1990s and was crucial to our ambitious research project.

I also regard supervising graduate students as another potential area of collaborative research in academia. With my graduate students, I followed the practice of being clear as to how we would work together and outlined the implications for any publishable work to follow. To oversimplify, I offered two approaches. The first was that students already have a good idea of what they want to do and how to proceed. In this case, I would be a resource and do all I could to expedite the development of the thesis topic. An example of this approach was with Terry Anderson, whom I supervised and with whom I had the pleasure to work after his graduation.

The second alternative was a more collaborative approach where I would offer more guidance from defining a "doable" research question to co-authoring a publishable article. The explicit understanding was that the graduate student would always be first author. Two other notable examples of this approach are Norm Vaughan and Zehra Akyol. I am proud of the fact that we also continued to collaborate on notable subsequent research projects such as blended learning and shared metacognition, respectively. Clearly both collaborative approaches can work successfully.

Collaboration has been enormously beneficial for me in another perhaps surprising manner. I must confess that I have never been comfortable giving presentations. I am a reflective person and giving presentations requires a degree of performance art with which I am not comfortable. I have always been more comfortable listening to others' perspectives and being challenged to make sense of a new idea or perspective. Leaning on my colleagues when doing presentations is where I was most at ease. This collaboration also made an inherently one-way communication at least feel like it was more of a dialogue. My fear was to bore people or be off-topic in terms of what the audience expected or wanted. Notwithstanding that an audience expects to be provided with key information, my preference is to try to make a presentation more interactive. In a dialogue, one can adjust and address the interests of the participants. Unfortunately, at research conferences this is most often impracticable.

Philosophies that Guide my Work

While collaboration had been a consistent theme in my work, this was not always the case. As an undergraduate, I was very much interested in critical thinking and the research behind it. Along with my background in math and science, individual cognition prepared me for my work in the field of computer-assisted learning. At the time, I was not fully conscious of the fact that computer-assisted learning was largely supporting independent and self-directed learning. However, as I matured as a teacher, I recognized the importance of engagement in the educational process and shifted my focus to the educational transaction.

This shift in thinking goes back to my first teaching experience where there was a crucial inflexion point in understanding education as a transaction and the importance of focusing on the activities of learners. Although I was trained in secondary mathematics education, my first teaching position was teaching an elementary class. Not having any training in this area, I stood at the blackboard (yes, this was 1969) and started basically lecturing to the class. Within minutes, I had totally lost the attention of the students. At the time, I was lost. However, it then became apparent to me that learning was based on learner engagement and not directly on teachers talking. I realized that the challenge was to engage the students in meaningful learning activities. This experience shaped my educational philosophy and led to the collaborative-constructivist approach that I use in my research.

As time went by, it became more apparent to me that I was very much in tune with the thinking of John Dewey, the American educational philosopher. Dewey (1933) emphasized the importance of experience, collaboration, and critical reflection. The unifying concept for Dewey was inquiry as reflected in the pragmatic application of the scientific method. Most importantly, he did not distinguish between the individual and the group. Personal learning and development were dependent upon the group dialogue. On a larger scale, Dewey argued that society was dependent upon the educated individual being capable of critical thinking. Therefore, personal reflection and collaborative discourse are organically and inherently connected. This unity of reflection and discourse became the foundation of my personal perspective and eventually, the core of the Community of Inquiry framework.

Notwithstanding this fundamental shift in my view of educational practice, as an academic, I was oriented to the theoretical side of the research process. I see myself as a theorist in the sense that I try to make sense of complex educational transactions and develop models that parsimoniously describe unified individual and group dynamics. Subsequent research has used these frameworks and constructs to test this understanding theoretically and pragmatically. This perspective has provided a window for researchers to develop research projects and relevant hypotheses. The final piece of this approach was to develop tools such as the Community of Inquiry survey instrument and the Shared Metacognition instrument (https://coi.athabascau.ca/coi-model/coi-survey/) to assist in the precise and efficient study of these topics.

Research for me has been driven largely by connecting ideas and making sense of complex dynamics such as teaching and learning. For this reason, I do not believe worthwhile research questions are hard to generate. I would emphasize the necessity of staying focused on the big picture and not to be distracted by shiny objects. For example, I have not spent much time addressing the latest software such as Twitter or Facebook. There was always some innovation that was supposed to transform educational practice, but it never did. Rather, the question for me was why most technological developments did not have a transformational influence. For this reason, I focused on the essence of the educational experience and contextual influences. The challenge was to ask the right question such that it could be resolved in reasonable time and effort. My research was never dependent on research grants, although a Social Sciences and Humanities Research Council of Canada (SSHRC) grant facilitated the first phase of our work validating the Community of Inquiry framework.

Writing Strategies

Writing is a test of one's thinking. Conversely, clear thinking leads to good writing. This reciprocal relationship reflects my approach to writing. My approach is a matter of clearly understanding what you want to say and then saying it as succinctly as possible. This focus on ideas requires considerable research and reflection. The key is to be grounded in viable and relevant constructs. In this regard, I am shaped by my philosophical and theoretical assumptions while still searching for and remaining open to new ideas and perspectives. This approach provides fidelity of thought and has proven to be productive in guiding my thinking and the communication of my ideas. This focused but open approach provides the means to creating coherent knowledge frameworks and reflects my minimalist writing style. In terms of my style, I have always tried to communicate my thoughts as clearly and simply as possible, sometimes at the expense of clarity. Notwithstanding this limitation, it was important for me not to embellish or digress from the theme of the manuscript: Keep the primary message in mind and bring things back to your main ideas and argument.

From a pragmatic perspective, I must admit that the greatest tool that allowed me to be a passable writer is the word processor. When I was a graduate student in the early 1980s, I got access to an early version of a word processing programme (on a mainframe computer) and thought I had gone to heaven. I could make major and minor edits with impunity. This was an absolute lifesaver that allowed me to mask my deficiencies as a writer who is not naturally gifted. I could do as many edits as needed. Moreover, the university was covering the cost of printing so I could bang out multiple draft copies of my thesis. This expedited my progress enormously. Considering the editing powers of modern word processing programmes (e.g., grammar and spell checks), there is little reason one cannot be a passable writer. The key is to know your subject and maintain focus on the topic. Do not try to cover too much content or become enamoured with a thought or phrase that does not fit.

To understand my approach to writing, it is essential to appreciate that I was not driven by outcomes. I stayed in the process of exploring and making sense of things. I believe that writing strongly depends on one's passion for and knowledge of the subject. That is, writing helped me to make specific connections and justify my arguments. Writing for me was always a journey and exploration with the goal being to make sense of a problem and offer evidence for my thinking. This approach encouraged rigorous thinking. Engage in the process and do not dwell on the outcome. It is through the flow of the writing dynamic that insight and expression emerge. While I admit it is a thrill to see your work in print, this was not my primary motivation. This elation did not last long and in short order I had trouble remembering exactly what I had published. Notwithstanding the pressure to publish, stay true to answering your research questions and find excitement and satisfaction in the process.

More specifically, the advice I offer is to establish a daily routine for writing. While this protocol is not new, it contributed greatly to my productivity, especially considering the administrative responsibilities I had throughout my career. The best way to get yourself in the zone is a regular schedule. A routine makes it easier to get started and get back into the flow. The other thing is that, at the end of a session, make a note of where you want to go when you start the next session. A routine also means you generally do not have to block off large chunks of time. In this regard, my advice is to try and do a little every day; but if this daily writing is not possible, try not to leave extended periods between sessions. Whether it is getting up early or working late at night, it is helpful to have familiar blocks of time. Not only does a routine sustain motivation, but it is surprising how much can be accomplished by doing a little every day. Finally, regarding routine, I very much valued a block of time on the weekends where I could focus on more challenging tasks such as getting started on a manuscript.

Another tactic that worked for me was not to edit my work as I went along. Just get your thoughts down and worry about how it reads later. In terms of getting started, I got my mind in the right space by doing the appropriate reading and reviewing my notes. I certainly always had an idea of where I wanted to go, notwithstanding those invariably new insights that emerged, and I often went in unexpected directions. But writing for me is a creative process, and so, as I explored ideas and how they could relate to and inform the topic at hand, I was always having to rearrange the order of ideas and passages and do more research on ideas where necessary. However, pauses and explorations for such purposes were often constructive in giving perspective and direction to the writing challenge.

Counter-intuitively, taking a step back to assess how ideas are, or are not, fitting together can expedite progress. Reflecting on the overall structure allows a check on the flow from one idea to the other. This is important when approaching writing in a more spontaneous manner that does not rely on a comprehensive outline. When approaching writing in this way, creating transitions is a constant but important challenge to maintain the flow and integrity of the manuscript. In fact, it is a check on the logical flow of the text. My approach is not the way writing is taught. I seldom make a detailed outline and follow it without question. To be clear, I do not recommend any particular approach but encourage you to find what best works for you.

A significant barrier for many academics is trying to be perfect, which, in my view, seriously restricts creativity and productivity. The burden of perfection is related to my previous comments regarding flow and editing. Do not let your ego get ahead of you. My advice is to be open and let others provide feedback — especially early in the process. The longer you wait, the harder it is to be open to feedback; as your expectations rise, the greater the fear of submitting for publication review. Be prepared to get rejected and learn from the experience. I learned this early on when I tried to publish my doctoral research. I crammed too much content into an esoteric manuscript; not surprisingly, it was rejected. I learned that I had to communicate more clearly and not try to appear smarter than I was. Most importantly, parsimony will help you to think more deeply and clearly. Because I never considered myself to be a good writer, I never had much of an ego regarding putting something out there and getting feedback. As time went by, I did get a little better at expressing myself and organizing my thoughts, but I never had excessively high expectations regarding my prose. In short, manage your expectations with humility.

Regarding writer's block, my experience is that writers block is simply not being prepared in terms of breadth and depth of knowledge. There are no shortcuts to preparing for a productive writing experience. My approach was never to force the process. I would step back and review my material and perhaps do more reading to get my mind in the right space. I strongly believe that the most important stimulus for research is to immerse oneself in the material. Reading widely in a variety of related fields is also important. This breadth of reading provides new ideas and connections that are the source of much creativity. When reading, do not get caught up in the minutiae. My approach was to keep the big picture and core principles in mind. The challenge is to create coherent cognitive structures that will in turn provide guidance to making sense of the specifics.

As noted, much of my work has entailed collaborative journeys which have been — often powerful but challenging. There are many advantages of collaboration in the creative process. Collaboration provides a powerful and immediate means to go deeper and challenge questionable ideas and reasoning. However, specific to the writing process, it can be challenging to manage input from multiple authors. In this regard, working from a shared document is essential. As noted previously, decide who will be the lead author and assign that person to provide a draft, regardless of how complete. This strategy allows others to contribute effectively and move the process forward in an efficient manner. Not only is this productive and efficient, but it can avoid the development of hard feelings.

My final comment here may sound somewhat mystical and it may be. As a science major, I did not have much formal training or practice in terms of writing. As a result, I developed a natural or intuitive approach to writing. For me, this meant putting my subconscious mind to work and trusting it. This insight came about in my first year of university when I was in the library trying to solve a physics problem. I was blocked and, somewhat out of frustration, took a break. I did not consciously think about the problem but when I got back and looked down at my notes, I immediately saw the solution. This revelation had an important influence on my creative process. There appeared to be an interplay of the conscious and subconscious mind that I could not explain but it worked for me. From that point on, I learned to rely on my subconscious mind to let things settle. After focusing on a problem, inevitably ideas will emerge, often at times you would least expect it. I try to tap into what I refer to as my subconscious mind when I write. Related to this, and when getting into the "zone," I found that writing can be enormously satisfying. I discovered the more writing I did, the more I enjoyed the process. Once I got into that mind space, I lost myself in the process.

Conclusion

The takeaway from this discussion is to follow your own path. While we certainly can learn from others and adopt various techniques, I believe that each person must discover an approach to research and writing that works for that individual. I have attempted to share how I approach research and I hope this may resonate with some of you. Writing is essential to the research process as it adds rigor to one's thinking and understanding. Not discounting the importance of independent thinking, an important aspect of my approach is to work collaboratively. On the surface, this may appear as somewhat of a contradiction as personal reflection and scepticism are essential to creative thought. However, the key is to bring the personal perspective to the collaboration and discourse. In this way, I found that I could go deeper and explore new directions of inquiry.

Finally, let me say that I worked until I was seventy. Now that I am retired, I have continued to keep updated with research associated with the Community of Inquiry framework and shared this on a regular basis on the CoI blog. On the blog, I highlight significant developments in Community of Inquiry research. Consistent with my approach to research, I focus my attention on the assumptions and essential constructs of the Community of Inquiry framework such that we are not deflected by suggestions that violate the basic principles of collaborative inquiry and theoretical parsimony. With the encouragement of my colleagues, I have tried to stay current and contribute to developments in the field. In this regard, I am particularly indebted to my colleagues, Marti Cleveland and Norm Vaughan, who keep in touch and include me in their scholarly activities — one of the lasting benefits of collaborative approaches to research.

References

Dewey, J. (1933). *How We Think: A Restatement of the Relation of Reflective Thinking to the Educative Process*. Boston: D. C. Health

Garrison, D. R. (1989). *Understanding Distance Education: A framework for the future*. Routledge.

Garrison, D. R., & Shale, D. (1990). *Education at a Distance: From issues to practice*. R. E. Krieger.

Peters, O. (1994) *Distance Education*. Edited by Desmond Keegan. London: Kogan Page.

11. Serendipity: Becoming a Specialist in Online Learning

Tony Bates

[Spoiler alert!] Writing this chapter was revealing to me as regards my writing process. As you will see from the story that I tell, my journey has been long and slightly dog-legged — which has made it all the more interesting. At present, the rambling journey has resulted in twelve books, many conference presentations and keynotes, much travel, and an ongoing blog that is hosted by Ontario's Contact North/Contact Nord. In short, I have been producing material of and about online and distance learning for a very long time without — amazingly! — really thinking about or analyzing how I am doing it. It simply has become what I do. But there are many contributing factors that have led me to this point, factors that highlight chance, good fortune, and, as the title indicates, serendipity. I am happy to tell my story here.

As the intention of this book is to pass experience and acquired knowledge on to those who may be less experienced, I think recounting my path from "then" until "now" can be both entertaining and insightful.

Beginnings

No one wakes up at fifteen years of age and says: "I want to be a specialist in online learning," particularly in 1954, when TV was still in black and white and needed cat's whiskers for aerials. So how did I get here? It is a tale of twists and turns, a huge amount of luck, and kindness from others.

I guess it started when I was sixteen. My father and mother owned a small greengrocer's shop in Ealing, West London. They were going broke. One day my father just upped and left, apparently for what was then Rhodesia, now Zimbabwe. No goodbyes. I never saw or heard from him again. My mother, who was a qualified nurse, sold the shop for a pittance, and got a job as a night nurse in a nearby mental hospital, looking after seventy-two very sick patients; and slowly paid off the debt. She insisted I stay at school and finish my high school exams, which I did.

I did reasonably well at English and French but barely passed Latin. My headmaster was disappointed. I did not have the qualifications to go to Oxford or Cambridge. "Try a couple of colleges at London University — say King's or Queen Mary's." That was the sum of his career advice. I didn't get into either.

So, I got a job. My mother and I needed the money. I started as a bank clerk at a branch in central London, but lost the keys to the front door, and resigned twenty minutes before they fired me. I then worked as a filing clerk for the Southern Railway on what would be now less than a minimum wage for another year. I was miserable: no money, no girlfriend, no future.

The Kindness of Strangers

Over a pint of beer, one of my office colleagues suggested that I might be eligible for a grant from the London County Council (LCC) to take a two-year teacher training course (you didn't need a degree in 1958). On the off chance, one lunch time I went to County Hall, an imposing building on the bank of the Thames, and eventually found the right office. A distinguished looking man emerged, ready to go to lunch. "Can I help you?" he said. I told him that I wanted to go to teachers' college, but I needed a grant. He sighed, took off his raincoat, and asked me to sit down.

> "Do you have any O-levels?"
> "Yes, ten."
> "Oh — how about A levels?"

I told him.

> "Why don't you want to go to university?"
> "I do, but can't get in."

He laughed. "Your A-levels should be good enough. If you get accepted the LCC will cover your fees and give you a modest but manageable grant for your living expenses."

Transformation at University

Six months later, I was on the train to Sheffield, the first university to accept my application for a Bachelor of Arts general degree. I was still committed to being a schoolteacher. French was my best subject at A-level. The university, though, required all first year General Arts students to take four subjects. They held a "fair" with a table for each of the subjects on offer. As well as English and French, I had to choose two more subjects. I went round the tables. I had done some economics at night school when working at both the bank and the railway, so that was easy. I knew nothing about Psychology, but it was a new and small department at Sheffield and the classes would be small, I was told. That made the fourth choice easy.

I had good work habits, so I got really good marks at the end of the year and was offered a place in both Honours Economics and Honours Psychology. After quite a bit of agonizing (for Economics clearly had better money prospects), I went for Psychology, because it seemed the most interesting area. I went on to get a Second Class Honours, First Division, good enough to get into graduate school.

More Good Advice

Just after the results came out, the Head of the Psychology Department, Harry Kay, asked to see me and asked me what I had decided what to do next year. "I'd really like to do educational research," I said, hoping he would offer me a place as a graduate student. During earlier university vacations, I had taken a job at the National Foundation for Educational Research (NFER), cranking out analyses of variance on a mechanical calculator as part of a study on the validity of IQs.

"Hmmm," said Professor Kay. "I think educational research is a good goal, but before you do research in education, I think it would be best for you to get some experience in teaching first. I suggest you go to

Goldsmiths College (part of the University of London) and get a Post Graduate Diploma in Education, then do some teaching." Which I did.

The Teaching Years

I was lucky at Goldsmiths College. My advisor, Len Marsh, was a constructivist, believing strongly in project work. It was the early 1960s, and there was a great movement towards more modern and innovative ways of teaching, which I thoroughly supported after the sterility of my own school experience.

Additionally, at university, I had been very influenced by the work of Jean Piaget (Inhelder & Piaget, 1958), who argued that learning was a developmental process that went through stages; and by Carl Rogers, who argued that we learn best within social contexts where we construct, test, and build meaning (see, for instance, Rogers, 1969). At Goldsmiths, I was encouraged to put these and other theoretical approaches to teaching and learning into practice, through group and project work and a holistic approach to learning where learning was based on broader, stimulating activities of intrinsic interest to the students. These lessons stayed with me.

Eventually, I got a job at Rashwood, a small rural primary school in Worcestershire. I had a class of forty-two students covering three age grades, from seven to ten years old, and with a range of all abilities. Len Marsh's methods had prepared me well for this situation.

However, as well as beginning to love teaching, I was still keen on doing research. At this time, the primary school curriculum was pretty flexible. My main goal was to ensure that as many as possible maintained and improved their core skills of literacy and numeracy.

Nevertheless, with a class of forty-two, I began to feel that certain kids were getting more of my attention than others. In particular, two or three of the brighter girls were always around my desk. I was getting increasingly worried that some of the quieter or less "pushy" students, especially those struggling with their learning, were not getting enough of my attention, so I hit on the idea of sound recording my lessons. I would then be able to analyse over the Christmas break how I spent my time among the pupils in the first term. Then, I could try to modify my behaviour in the following term. I bought a two-track tape recorder, and two microphones. I got permission from the Head and sent a letter to all parents asking for their permission to record my lessons for the purpose of evaluating my teaching. They all agreed.

There were two main problems, though, with this experiment. I ended up with so many hours of recording that I couldn't possibly analyze all of it. It was at this point I discovered the value of sampling. The second problem was much more serious. I did find that there were major differences in the amount of time I spent with each pupil. Indeed, I was horrified to discover two children in the class who had never had a one-on-one conversation with me. This situation was contrary to my holistic beliefs about teaching and learning.

I made a determined effort to change that the next term. However, when I analysed the tapes at the end of the second term, there was absolutely no difference — the same kids got just as much time as before, and the same kids who mostly got less time than the other ones continued to do so, although I did manage to spend a little more time with the two previously "quiet" children.

Toward the end of my second year at Rashwood, I was approached by the NFER to see if I was still interested in a research position. However, they wanted me to have some experience of teaching in a comprehensive. With great sadness, I resigned my position to take up a position as a "remedial" teacher in a newly opened, large comprehensive school in Birmingham.

All I can say about the year I spent at Shenley Court is that I learned a lot more than the kids I taught. On the first day of the school year, the Head welcomed the new students and gave a little pep talk about the need for academic excellence in all classes. The school was run on the same principle as the English Football League. As the headmistress explained in her pep talk, every child in the school could excel. The classes were streamed strictly on tests given at the end of each term, and the first-year classes were streamed based on tests at the end of their primary school year. So, at the end of each term, the top two children would "move up" a class, while the bottom two children would go down to the next class. "This way," said the headmistress, "even children who start in Class J — (my class) — can make their way into Class A by the fifth year, if they work hard enough."

The Deputy Head then read out the names of students in each class, and their teacher guided them to their classrooms. One by one, as the classes trouped out and there were just fifteen children left in the room, one of the boys looked at me, and said: "Are we the dummies, sir?" He had already worked out the system.

I was therefore hugely relieved when the NFER eventually offered me a job as a full-time researcher on a three-year contract to work on the comprehensive school project.

Researching Comprehensive Schools

I joined the NFER in September of 1966, just as the research on comprehensive schools was beginning. I was asked to examine "the patterns of school administration and organization and their effect on the teaching staff."

The overall design required me to visit in-person a sample of fifty schools across England and Wales, and conduct interviews in each school with the head, deputy head, two senior staff, two heads of department, two senior teachers and a small group of senior students, for a total of just over 450 interviews. I designed all the questions and conducted all the interviews, as well as doing the analysis and write-up.

What struck me most was how the culture of schools differed so greatly. Some schools were almost silent as you walked in (usually former grammar schools); others were noisy and boisterous (usually the large, inner-city schools in London). The huge difference between small and large schools, and rural, suburban, and inner-city schools, made me realize the importance of culture and different values on the way education is managed and organized. To this day, when I visit England, very early on after meeting a Brit for the first time, I am asked where I was "brought up." This helps the Brit to "place" me. (I tend to vary the answer to confuse the questioner). It is no fluke that thirteen of the last fifteen British Prime Ministers went to Eton or Harrow. You could conclude that it was the school that maketh the man; alternatively, you could conclude that the education system in Britain is deliberately structured to perpetuate the rule of an existing elite.

I was again fortunate to be on an excellent team of researchers at the NFER, getting advice and help on questionnaire design, statistics, qualitative data analysis, and above all, on the politics that come into play when doing public policy research. I was even more fortunate that the NFER allowed me to take the data I had collected and use them as the basis for a PhD at the University of London. Again, I had a sympathetic and helpful supervisor, George Baron. I obtained my PhD in 1971.

Lessons and Learning at The Open University

By 1969, with my contract with the NFER coming to an end, I needed another job. Between 1963 and early 1969, the idea of a "University of the Air" had developed into a proposal for an open university that would combine correspondence education and broadcasting. It was to be called an Open University (OU), and it would be open to all, with no prior qualifications required. It was sometimes called "The University of the Second Chance" for those that were not able to go to university after leaving school.

Given my own experience of leaving school and failing to get into university, the idea of the Open University really appealed to me, so when a job advertisement appeared in the summer of 1969 for a research officer at the newly created Open University, I jumped at the chance. Luck was once again on my side. Although only one post was advertised, and someone else was offered it, they decided at the interview to hire me as well. In September 1969, I was the twentieth person to be hired at OU.

The immediate task was to do research on the print and broadcast courses that the National Extension College had developed as preparatory courses for potential OU students. The mandate was broad: investigate the effectiveness of distance education in general and bring the lessons learned to the design of OU courses.

Not long after I was hired, at the formal inauguration of the Open University at the Guildhall, in the City of London, Lord Crowther, the first Chancellor of the Open University, gave a very short inaugural speech. He said the university would be open…

- to people, with its open admissions policy,
- to methods, such as broadcasting and print and "other technologies yet to come,"
- to ideas, and
- to time and place, where students could learn and where instructors could teach from anywhere at any time.

This was 1969; yet these ideas still resonate with me today and I am a strong supporter of open educational resources with a broad vision of "open-ness" which I continue to implement in my career.

In doing the analysis of the research questionnaires on the NEC courses, the responses about the print material were calm, thoughtful, and analytical, pointing out areas of difficulty or where the materials were particularly helpful. The responses, on the other hand, to the broadcasts were quite different. They tended to be much more emotional, with extremes of high praise or very emotional criticism.

I was struck by the difference. There's something here, I thought. The two different media of print and television were resulting in qualitatively quite different responses from students. Since the Open University would be spending more than a fifth of its budget on the broadcasts, I thought it might be worth spending a little time and money on evaluating the effectiveness of the programmes. In 1970, I persuaded the new head of The Institute for Educational Technology (IET) that there was a need for a specialist research team that would focus on evaluating the BBC broadcasts. I was appointed a full Lecturer in Media Research Methods in 1971 and in 1973 we were able to establish a small Audio-Visual Media Research Group (AVMRG).

Initially, audio-visual media research covered two main areas. The first was around strategic issues. For instance, there was a constant battle with the BBC in the early days about transmission times. The BBC wanted to push the OU broadcasts into times that were less popular with the public, such as 6 to 7 am, or Sunday mornings. The OU course teams wanted repeat broadcasts, so that if students missed one transmission, they could catch the second. The AVMRG collected viewing data, showing the impact on students of different transmission times and the impact of repeat broadcasts, thus making learning more accessible to learners.

When audio cassettes became available, the AVMRG collected data on cassette recorder availability and the use of audio cassette recordings. Eventually, the research indicated that learning was more efficient if audio cassettes were designed to incorporate the stop and repeat feature to embed student activities or reflection. The OU eventually created a special audio-visual library enabling students to access the recordings at any time, and the AVMRG conducted regular research on the use of cassettes.

My hunch from the NEC Gateway research proved correct. There was often a strong affective or emotional response not only to the television programmes in particular, but also to audio as well. This could have positive or negative results. A good programme could inspire and motivate learners. Some students, though, struggled with programmes that were not didactic, that did not explain in academic terms what was being shown in the programme.

The research also found that students could be taught to use open-ended or documentary style programmes for understanding, applying, or analyzing academic concepts and principles found in the printed texts. As a result of the research, the TV programmes for the re-make of the foundation social science course started with a mainly didactic approach from the main presenter but, over time, the presenter would introduce more and more video clips, initially with explanations of what to look for. In later programmes, he would show clips without guidance, then give his own interpretation afterwards. Finally, the last two programmes were almost entirely documentary-style. The evaluation of these programmes showed that not only did students enjoy these more than the programmes on the original course, but that they also learned more.

This acquired knowledge resulted in my 1984 book *Broadcasting in Education: An Evaluation*, in which I identified two distinct cultures between academics and broadcasters, as well as two different professions with different beliefs and value systems. The BBC's traditions and arrogance made it believe that it was the best broadcaster in the world, that it knew "intrinsically" what made a good programme and therefore was above criticism; academics, on the other hand, were suspicious of the lack of "seriousness" in broadcasting, and its tendency to simplify and trivialize issues. Both arguments have some validity. The important point though is that broadcasting or video can offer a different way to present knowledge that will help some students and annoy others.

Coming to Canada

I was privileged when working at the OU to be able to travel extensively for conferences and to take sabbatical leave to work on projects. I was also very active on the Open University's behalf in a number of European Commission projects, bringing several millions of euros in grant money to the university. In particular, I worked on several projects on the use of satellites for distance education.

An invitation by Jon Baggaley at Newfoundland's Memorial University to an educational television conference in 1979 really changed my life. Serendipity! I flew to St. John's and arranged with the Extension Division to spend a week visiting the small coastal communities to see and discuss the Portapak videos the communities had made about their livelihoods, based on the Fogo Island process originally developed with the National Film Board of Canada.

When I arrived in St. John's, I was asked to provide a ride to the conference in Corner Brook on the other side of the island for an Englishwoman who had no transportation. Of course, Newfoundland cast its magic spell and, amid amazing Newfoundland hospitality, the Englishwoman and I fell in love. Eventually we returned home and then married two years later.

In 1982 I received a British Council fellowship to visit Canada and research their use of educational media. It was during this trip to Vancouver that David Kaufman of Simon Fraser University invited me into his home office after dinner one evening. He had a computer linked to a modem. This was my first introduction to the internet — and it led eventually to a paper published in the first edition of the (Canadian) *Journal of Distance Education* in 1986 called "Computer assisted learning or communications: Which way for information technology in distance education?" (Bates, 1986). This was a seminal moment for me. I had never been impressed by computer-aided instruction, which seemed to me to be far too behaviourist, but connecting distance students so they could communicate with each other online seemed to me to be much more compatible with my view of learning, as it had to several other pioneer researchers before me, such as Roxanne Hiltz and Murray Turoff (1978) and Linda Harasim (Harasim & Johnson, 1986).

By 1985, my wife and I were determined to find a way to emigrate to Canada. Fortunately, at the 1988 ICDE conference in Oslo, I was approached by Glen Farrell, the President of the Open Learning Agency of British Columbia, who asked if I would be interested in a job as Executive Director, Strategic Planning, Research, and Information Technology. At the time, I felt that, after twenty years, I had done all I could at the Open University. I felt the institution had reached stasis;

I missed the energy and excitement of the early years. Also, I wanted more responsibility as a manager. I had spent too long giving research-based advice and often seeing it ignored. I wanted a piece of the action. And so, following two years of frustration with Canada's immigration process, we finally arrived at the end of 1989 with two cats and a dog.

Lessons and Learning at the University of British Columbia (UBC)

I had five good years at the Open Learning Agency, but in early 1995, I received a call from the Provost at UBC, asking me to give some advice to the university about ways to spend a $2 million grant. I did not realize that this was an informal interview for a job with Continuing Studies at UBC. I was then hired as Director of Distance Education and Technology. The goal was to move the Continuing Studies correspondence programmes online and help the university generally with innovative teaching with technology. My background and previous work in England had prepared me well for this task.

The eight years I worked at UBC were probably the most productive of my life. We moved all the existing distance education courses online, and worked with the faculties to develop wholly online, self-financing master's programmes. We established WebCT as our Learning Management System (developed at UBC by Murray Goldberg) and I was able to bring all my experience as a teacher and philosophies of learning to the design and delivery of these programmes.

However, over time, it became clear that online learning and technology-based teaching needed to be managed across the institution. In 2003, a new senior administration decided to close the Distance Education and Technology unit in Continuing Studies, since most of its activities were with the main faculties; and move its assets, such as instructional designers and funding, directly to the faculties.

This did not work out well. The smaller faculties suddenly found themselves responsible for activities that they did not have the resources or expertise to manage properly, and two years later it was decided to merge the faculty development office and the distance education unit into a new Centre for Teaching, Learning and Technology, reporting directly to the Provost.

This was the right decision as there is a continuum between face-to-face teaching and fully online; but there are also many different possibilities in between, such as blended learning. Distance education, blended learning, and lifelong learning are critical activities for all mainline faculty departments these days. It is too important to be isolated outside the mainstream programmes, but rather it needs a central home so that expertise in different areas can be shared. UBC now has a mixed model, where the larger faculties have their own learning technology support staff but can also draw on central services when needed. This model has worked well for UBC and has helped them manage the move to emergency remote learning during COVID-19 without too much pain.

Moving On... Again

However, by 2003 I was considered redundant by the new administration, especially as I was coming up to mandatory retirement a year later. Upon my termination by UBC, I wanted to stay engaged with online and distance learning. I had brought lots of research grants and consultancy work to UBC, so I set myself up as a private consultant. Since then, I have been continuously working with clients all round the world. This has allowed me to be productive well into my 80s. I now feel that I have at last become a specialist in online and digital learning.

Everyone's life is idiosyncratic; it belongs to them and no one else. But there are some lessons from my life that I would offer to those wanting to do research or to teach. Ten important lessons that I can share are listed below:

1. Follow your passion: mine was teaching and research. I spent two years after school in misery, not following my passion. I've been lucky enough since then to spend almost all my life on these two passions. Despite the ups and downs, I've never regretted this.

2. Move to where the action will be. In research, you get much further researching topics that (a) very few others have researched before, and (b) are likely to be important in the future. This may often not fit with your academic department's interests, in which case find someone or somewhere else with an interest in these topics.

3. Money matters in research. If you can bring in research grants or consultancies or persuade your administration that research and consultancies will directly benefit the organization, you will have more influence than working in isolation, and more opportunities for further research.

4. Avoid the comparison trap in educational technology research: for example, is online learning better/worse than in-person teaching? (Answer: There is no significant difference). There are many ways to teach well. It's not the technology, but how you use the technology that matters. You can teach well or badly, online or in class. Thus, it is the *conditions* that determine the effectiveness of a medium or mode of delivery.

5. Choose a topic for your PhD where the results will have value outside the actual study. Make sure it is relevant to real-world issues so that you and others care about the research and its outcomes. If your work provides access to unique data, use them for your PhD. A PhD should not be done just to get another qualification, no matter how important that is to you. A PhD is a hard and risky endeavour; make sure the end result will be worthwhile.

6. Be eclectic in your choice of research methods. In education, you need both qualitative and quantitative research. Different topics need different methods.

7. Work with others: two heads are better than one, both in teaching and in research. You not only learn more in a team, but you also get better results.

8. *Culture* — the embedded (and often unquestioned) values and beliefs within an organization or department — is a very powerful brake on change. You need to understand and lever the culture to bring about lasting and effective change.

9. Listen to your critics, no matter how dumb or misinformed they appear to be. If you don't listen to or understand their position, you will not be able to change things. If you are not teaching or doing research to make a difference, then give up and do something else.

10. The most important thing in a teacher is to care about your students and their success. This goes far beyond merely "covering the curriculum." Our students are literally our future. Learn what they need to succeed and do your damnedest to provide that. This will give you — and them — tremendous satisfaction. Otherwise, choose something else.

It has been a long and adventurous journey. Without the help of others, often strangers, and without a lot of luck, or serendipity, who knows what I may have been?

I don't envy anyone setting out today and trying to map their future. You need both persistence and flexibility — the ability to see an opportunity and go for it. Above all, you need some luck and help from others. Serendipity needs to be recognized, exploited, and built upon. So, good luck!

References

Bates, T. (1986). "Computer assisted learning or communications: Which way for information technology in distance education?" *Journal of Distance Education*, 1(1), 41–57.

Harasim, L., & Johnson, E. M. (1986). *Educational Applications of Computer Networks*. Toronto: Ontario Ministry of Education Press.

Hiltz, S. R. & Turoff, M. (1978) *The Network Nation: Human Communication via Computer*. New York: Addison-Wesley.

Inhelder, B. & Piaget, J. (1958) *The Growth of Logical Thinking from Childhood to Adolescence*. London: Routledge.

Rogers, C. (1969) *Freedom to Learn* Columbus OH: Ce. Merrill.

12. Writing in the Margins: Maintaining a Scholarly Voice as an Executive

Mark Nichols

Why Me?

It is with some trepidation that I write this chapter. After all, I'm an odd choice alongside my much more accomplished peers in this book! My career in open and distance learning spans some twenty years, yet I have only about thirty peer-reviewed publications, two books (one self-published) and, well, now *three* book chapters to my name. Though respectable, my research history is hardly prolific. There are a few keynotes and various presentations, but my work is not centre shelf. Nor is my name immediately recognizable from any journal's contents page.

Perhaps this might explain why: in 2010 I made a choice. I had two job offers open to me, two years into my PhD study. One was a fixed term academic and researching role with a top New Zealand university; the other, a permanent senior management role in New Zealand's largest dedicated open, distance, and flexible learning (ODFL) provider. I could become a researcher in my chosen field, or a decision-maker. I became a decision-maker. So, my research since 2010 has largely, though certainly not only, been in my own time and at my own instigation.

This has two implications for my work. First, seldom do I have any opportunity to take more than a few hours each month in work time to write. So, I literally write in the margins of my day. In fact, with no exaggeration, I am writing this very sentence ten minutes before my first Teams meeting early one Tuesday morning. Second, what I write needs to either be immediately useful to me or else an account of what might be useful for others seeking to make the same decisions I am concerned with. There is a rich bank of scholarship for all practices in ODFL, which managers such as me get to explore from time to time in search of scholarly insight. This research naturally informs what I am doing, which sometimes extends to my writing about it later.

So, my roles in senior ODFL management have determined my research direction and volume. I chose to manage and lead rather than teach and research. This is not problematic for me. I publish because I practice, not lest I perish; I publish for pleasure, not for promotion. The choice to manage has brought a relevant and, I like to think, practical and grounded edge to my research. Being spread across so many research areas, from student retention to the development of learning designers, from guiding the ethics of analytics to institutional transformation, from advocating on-screen reading to explaining the advantages of online theological distance education, has been a privilege every time.

Why I Research and Write

Research and writing are often motivated by curiosity. Not always, though. My PhD started out of sheer annoyance, though annoyance eventually gave way to curiosity; I simply could not understand why the received wisdom as it related to my area of practice was so far off from what I suspected.

Curiosity is based on these sorts of questions: What do scholars think about this? What evidence is there, and how good is it? How could this idea or practice be improved? How might I help people better understand the possibilities here? What further things can I learn about this? My curiosity in others' ideas and discoveries usually lead me to reflect on my own perspectives and practice. If I think my explorations could reshape the narrative and help take it forward, I start writing.

My work on reading from the screen was driven by a curiosity, in response to a workplace decision. In 2015, Open Polytechnic moved to withdraw print for its materials in favour of on-screen only materials development (for the benefits of this, see Nichols, 2020). I have found over the years that curiosity is the best, enduring channel into a research project. Not only does it provide motivation; curiosity also leads me into the literature. Before too long, what to research and write about becomes obvious.

Curiosity aside, my motivation in research and writing is threefold: for the sake of writing, to maintain relevance, and to ensure I maintain a professional profile or scholarly identity.

Writing, for me, is a journey of discovery. Entering a writing project is an opportunity to explore, to go on a long journey where I have a rough idea of the destination and look forward to the scenery en route. I begin with a sense of adventure, not of dread. I enjoy my time at the word processor. It wasn't always like this; what changed my relationship with writing was the joy of having articles accepted! Writing is no longer a test or a trial. Instead, it is a well-rehearsed path, an activity I anticipate. Writing improves both my self-expression and self-awareness. What's not to love about that?

However, the sheer volume of ODFL-related journals and forums is simply bewildering and keeping up with it requires more focus than I can typically give. Curiosity gives me an excuse to deep dive into an element of ODFL, and the ripples of that dive inevitably extend into broader ODFL themes. I learn a lot out of sheer serendipity, gaining incidental insight across all sorts of ODFL developments during a specific study. Good scholarship draws across the breadth of ODFL practice and thought. Reading literature in one specific area provides insight across others, too.

Scholarly profile is, I freely admit, important to me. Over the years, I have served as a journal reviewer, editor, and editorial board member. I have also served on the boards or executive committees of ASCILITE, EDEN, FLANZ, and the ICDE.[1] Writing and publishing is a natural and related activity for how I understand myself as an ODFL professional; I both draw from and contribute to the scholarship that drives my practice. Eventually, scholarship and professional networking bring their own opportunities. As an example, I met Dianne Conrad — editor of this book — because of the *Leaders and Legends of Online Learning* podcast. I had certainly encountered her work before, and have cited her several

---

1   ASCILITE, Australasian Society for Computers in Learning in Tertiary Education; EDEN, European Distance and e-Learning Network; FLANZ, Flexible Learning Association of New Zealand; ICDE, International Council for Open and Distance Education.

times, but I had not established a connection with her. Much of my more recent work has resulted from professional connection.

Research and writing are interconnected. Writing is like scholarly catharsis, getting things not off your chest, but rather out of your mind. Of course, seldom is an article or book chapter accepted on first submission. I have learned to respect and even enjoy peer-reviews of scholarly work; invariably I am challenged to improve my efforts, and as a bonus I gain advice as to my ongoing development as a scholar. Research is the activity by which I engage purposefully with literature, listen to the voices of others, consider evidence and perspective, and explore others' thinking as I further develop my own thinking. If I see opportunity, I also seek to contribute my own thoughts through publication.

The Process of Writing

One of the fantastic things about our digital age is that it is so easy to record, edit, and reorganise thoughts. Sourcing, citing, and playing with information has also never been easier. The simplicity of selecting, copying, pasting, and deleting text gives me confidence to think onto the page, with all its haphazardness and random insight. Capturing thoughts, be they raw, half-baked, or well-done, results in a spread-out pile of insight resembling builders' waste intermixed with dressed timber. Some of these thoughts might just be a few words; sometimes there will be complete sentences. Rarely will there be complete paragraphs. The variety is OK; from time to time, I will sort through these bits and pieces in case I see something in there that I can dust off and repaint, remodel, or otherwise bring into the final product. The digital skip bin can never be full, and it is easily sorted.

So, when it comes time to begin an article or research project, I begin by simply writing. Beginning in this way was the best PhD advice I received (a close second was learning how to paragraph). Getting on with the writing helps me to get a sense of context, to order my thoughts, to define my position. This has several benefits, including helping me to discover the gaps I have in my thinking. When I write I'm forced to bring order to my thoughts, and I often discover I have no way of bridging some of the ideas I have. Some of those things I think are connected do not *write* as if they are. Writing requires me to be more disciplined in my understanding, more logical in my associations.

So, my initial writing is very much a chaotic exercise of self-discovery. I have learned to anticipate this and not become discouraged by it. Developing a position in this way is an extremely useful starting point. My better-honed understanding helps me to better engage with the literature, and I begin to get a clearer sense of the research questions I have. I do not expect to start by writing final copy.

I tend to begin with a basic document structure that matches my sense of where an article might go. Section headings and key themes, as they occur to me at the start of the journey, are inserted in a Word document using heading styles. My free-flowing thought is captured within these headings, which might subtly change or else be radically reworked during the process. I tend do this before seriously engaging with a single article or book chapter, drawing solely on my previous knowledge and hunches. Section headings serve as buckets for ideas, themes for observations. I return to this draft document throughout my reading, until I feel confident enough to pause with the literature and start composing a first full draft. Then, it is back to the literature. The dance across full draft to literature swings with my mental rhythm, the draft changing shape as the literature and the new ideas it raises dictates.

The discipline of the literature review is foundational to gaining a valid voice. With no anchoring in literature, you have no secure way of connecting yourself to the conversation already underway. Think of publishing as inviting yourself, then being accepted, into a free-flowing conversation between a group of experts on a subject of interest to you. The conversation is already taking place. To contribute meaningfully, you need to be familiar with the ideas already shared across the group, the terms they are using, the points of reference that everyone shares. You also need to know whether the contribution you are planning to make has already been made, and how your contribution fits across agreed points of agreement and disagreement. All this activity helps you to find your place and identify your points of difference and nuance to help nudge the conversation forward. The conversation does not start with you, and it must be respectfully joined.

I prefer the metaphor of "dancing with" to "engaging with" literature. Writing drafts as part of the journey through literature is dancing with it. End-to-end reading with notetaking is engaging with it. Treat literature as a conversation partner, not a library. Engaging with scholarly literature is a slog; dancing with it is a release. The literature is the partner of ideas, challenging preconceptions and reinforcing what others have found to be of merit. The literature review is the playground of the synthesis, and the launch-pad of the primary study. Taking time to consolidate ideas through writing and note-taking through reading as intermingled steps is far better than trying to do these one after the other. A dance is dynamic; engaging is linear.

But enough of the preliminary comments in free prose. I have developed a bit of a groove in terms of how I approach a project, and I have learned quite a bit about myself in the process. Researching and writing are the two areas you are interested in as a reader of this book, so let me tell you about them in a much cleaner form: numbered lists. And, because I have taken my sweet time in drafting, writing, and re-writing this chapter, and because I have a penchant for equilibrium, I have found a way to balance two satisfying lists of ten points each. There is an explicit message in this balance, in that both are equivalent in terms of importance for maintaining a scholarly voice.

Researching

My ten points here span across three themes: subject, literature, and method.

Subject

1. **State your subject**. Your subject is the on ramp to the scholarly conversation, and without a subject, you have nothing to reign over. My research is typically motivated by that general discomfort emerging from curiosity or else by a practice need, but neither of these is a subject. Clear subjects are elusive; draft, draft, draft, and read, read, read, and eventually the subject will find you. While this step is listed first, it often takes on its final form only after steps five or six. Once I have my subject, it heads the study in my drafts from there on.

2. **Be intrinsically driven**. Starting a research project is committing to a scholarly relationship. You have got to be able to maintain interest in the subject the whole time of the study, prepared to learn from it, dwell on it, reflect on it, and spend many hours with its idiosyncrasies. Some projects are moody. Unless you are genuinely curious about it or else have some tangible connection with it, research and writing will not be fun. If a project dries up, put it aside and move on to something fresh.

3. **Interrogate your practice**. Often what inspires scholars is not necessarily what assists practitioners. Some of my more interesting work (at least for me!) began with problems my team and I were facing in our daily activity. In fact, my next two projects following this one are directly driven by practice needs: one to learn more about an approach we are applying to seek its improvement and validation, the other to explore an innovative means of doing something entirely new (and overlooked for way too long). The best projects I have worked on are those that are of interest to my immediate colleagues and relevant to my immediate challenges.

Literature

4. **Compile the resources**. There is always the risk of gathering too much or too little. My approach is the more, the better. It is easy to cull, so I cast a wide net. With research databases and tools such as Mendeley, it is no problem drawing in a vast array of work. Yes, there are various "core" journals in ODFL, but there are also multiple associated journals and publications where surprises are found. I always use Mendeley (or Zotero) to compile resources because it is too easy to lose track of everything! As with stating your subject, this is an open-ended step; as you read, you will discover more articles to add.

5. **Scan before reading**. A shortcut to reading literature is a triage, based firstly on the abstract and conclusion. I tend to make "yes/no" decisions for a full reading on this basis. Abstracts are used to determine whether an article is a priority, or even

whether it is worth reading at all. My advice: make a list of the first five articles to read and plunge in, knowing that you'll be in the rough seas for a while. Working in batches of five motivates me and takes me back into drafting with fresh ideas. I also tend to take special note from the literature reviews in those articles I decide to read. Well-written literature reviews feature prominent work and provide structure to others' ideas, and so provide navigation pointers to assist you in charting your own passage.

6. **Start by reading the authoritative, contemporary articles.** These are often those written by renowned names in the discipline (I'm assuming that these make it through your triage in step five!) Start with these sources because they will provide the best landmarks, so to speak. Any article referenced frequently also gets boosted in my reading order, which I regularly tinker with. I tend to highlight articles in Mendeley as I go, focusing on key ideas, authors, quotes, and summary points. Full text PDFs in Mendeley are easily marked up, and sub-folders can be used to sort those works you have read from those you'll read next.

Method

7. **Establish a baseline knowledge.** I was very fortunate early in my research career to be asked to prepare a series of scholarly literature reviews on subjects related to e-learning. Naturally, this required me to write about the core ideas and published studies of the early 2000s. This was invaluable to me. I found my voice, discovered the important journals, and learned which authors and theories were significant. Knowing what the subject was about, and synthesising it for others, brought a wonderful grounding and frame of reference for my subsequent work. Formal study (I did a Master of Arts in Open and Distance Education) also plugs you in to the grid.

8. **Maintain a broad baseline knowledge.** With the avalanche of ideas now available across multiple subjects within ODFL, it is entirely impossible to keep up with the intricate breadth

of progress across all areas of practice. Fortunately, there is a series of articles and books written in collaboration with Olaf Zawacki-Richter (see, for example, Zawacki-Richter and Naidu, 2016; Bond, Zawacki-Richter and Nichols, 2018; Bozkurt and Zawacki-Richter, 2021) that provide meta-analysis across key journals. I have also benefited from the annual National Institute of Distance Learning (NIDL) "Top Ten."[2] Professional bodies including the ICDE, EDEN, ASCILITE and ODLAA[3] are great for highlighting key conversations and events. Finally, subscribing to journal tables-of-contents also provides a quick way of seeing the latest articles.

9. **Know (and respect) the process**. As with finding a subject, this ought to be obvious, yet from time to time I still rush into data gathering before settling on a method. This is always to my shame, punished usually by my having to rework (I once had an article returned three times by a reviewer who thought my method section was too light; but see point ten in the next section). In preparing this chapter, I was reminded of a conference paper I wrote early in my publishing career, included as an appendix. Along with step seven above, establish a baseline knowledge, I think writing that paper was an important beginning to subsequent research papers. For my PhD, I was also required to take methodology more seriously. Reference books about the research process, and time spent in them, are well worth the investment.

10. **Consider a baseline methodology**. There are various research methodologies that might form the basis of your work. Find one that suits your situation and get to know it well. Invariably research will involve some form of literature engagement, so preparing literature reviews is a vital skill. Pan's (2008) *Preparing literature reviews* has pride of place on my bookshelf, alongside the obligatory works by Creswell (2014), Dey (1993), Merriam and Tisdell (2016), Miles and Huberman (1994),

---

2   For example, Good Reads from 2021: https://nidl.blog/2022/01/10/good-reads-from-2021-our-nidl-top-10-journal-articles-part-3/.
3   ODLAA, Open and Distance Learning Association of Australia.

and Punch and Oancea (2014). My PhD was mixed mode, so I learned how to perform inferential statistical analysis; the sort of research I get to do in the margins, though, tends more toward case study (Yin, 2018), synthesis, and primary work based on interview. Tempting though they are, I avoid simple surveys because they typically yield shallow findings that are not easily transferable.

Writing

Writing is the oft taken for granted partner in research activity. Here are ten points, again across three themes: organising, drafting, and writing for publication.

Organizing

1. **A little at a time is fine**. Discipline is what makes a scholar. I earlier mentioned having scholarly relationship with your project, and key to any relationship is spending time together. A scholar-subject relationship does not necessarily benefit from binge time. The best schedule is one that works for you, say, on a weekly basis, two, two-hour sessions late at night and a three-hour block in the weekend. Not bingeing gives you time to reflect. When you write in the margins, this sort of approach is a necessity; I think it is also a virtue.

2. **Take writing seriously**. Ideas do not sell themselves. If you cannot write, you cannot publish — and you cannot achieve a scholarly voice. Period. Writing is where I have learned the most over the last twenty years. I'm not a fabulous writer but I have worked hard to earn the style I have, and I know how much worse it could be! As a journal editor and reviewer, I have seen countless submissions where the main flaw has simply been how poorly the ideas were expressed. There is a burden of pain involved here: either you wrestle with your writing, or the reader must wrestle with what you have written. Someone must always suffer; make it you, as the writer. Learn as much

as you can about your writing and how to write better. Learn to write like an editor.

3. **Digitize deeply**. Making the most of digital tools is obvious but learning to use them effectively and build them into a workflow takes time. I have used both Zotero and Mendeley across my career and now use one over the other solely because only one is permitted on my work PC. I have ProWritingAid installed on my home PC. I purchase important reference works on Kindle. Portability, searching and highlighting — not to mention more accurate and ready referencing — are real advantages to digital research, as is having an automated writing coach critiquing your every sentence. No article is ever printed in my workflow, and I only tried physical 4 x 6 cards once before retreating (advancing?) into digital. It is not just software, though. My desk setup makes use of two external monitors: one landscape, my main monitor where Word resides showing three pages side-by-side; the other, to my right, a portrait (yes, try it!) monitor more for reference and PDF reading/annotation.

4. **Collaborate with caution**. I have been involved with multiple collaborative projects, and I have learned to approach them hesitantly. Unless you're working with people whose work ethic, process, and output are familiar to you, take care! Working with some will divide the work constructively; working with those who aren't confident writers or reliable contributors will destructively multiply the work. If you find a good partnership, though, stick with it.

Drafting

5. **Always take notes**. From the outset, just start writing, beginning with your sense of curiosity (or discontent) and where you think your work will take you. Draft some headings in a crude initial draft. Write a mix of what you know, and what you sense. At the very beginning of a project (including this one) I begin a OneNote page in my "Professional" section, open a Word document, and name a new Mendeley folder. Each of these are

like baskets ready to be filled with ideas, drafts, and articles. My OneNote page tells me about the project, Word contains my progress, and Mendeley stores references and direct notes. My multiple monitor makeup hastens attention across these baskets. Hardly any of the initial sentences or thoughts I draft initially will appear in the final published piece, and that's fine. Words store ideas well in advance of having to present them. Drafting full sentences and paragraphs in a rough draft helps me to structure my thinking.

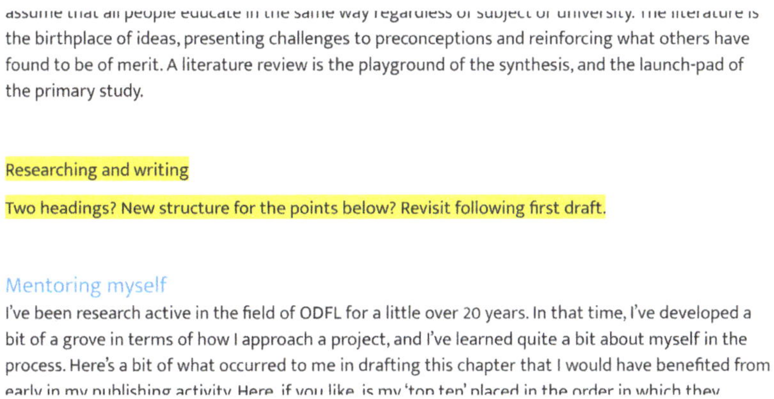

assume that all people educate in the same way regardless of subject or university. The literature is the birthplace of ideas, presenting challenges to preconceptions and reinforcing what others have found to be of merit. A literature review is the playground of the synthesis, and the launch-pad of the primary study.

<mark>Researching and writing</mark>

<mark>Two headings? New structure for the points below? Revisit following first draft.</mark>

Mentoring myself

I've been research active in the field of ODFL for a little over 20 years. In that time, I've developed a bit of a grove in terms of how I approach a project, and I've learned quite a bit about myself in the process. Here's a bit of what occurred to me in drafting this chapter that I would have benefited from early in my publishing activity. Here, if you like, is my 'top ten' placed in the order in which they

Fig. 1. Screenshot signalling structure revision

6. **Continuously revise your structure**. The process of drafting and redrafting should not be underestimated. Expect *it* and *the time* that it takes to do it. As Kidder and Todd observe, "Most problems in writing are structural, even on the scale of the page. Something isn't flowing properly. The logic or dramatic logic is off" (2013, p. 170). I expect to write and rewrite multiple times to ensure good flow. I found myself doing this at a critical juncture in my drafting process for this very chapter. In Figure 1, you'll see a note I made myself during the first draft to revise structure; you'll identify some of the final text — and note the typo. Figure 2 shows the initial heading structure I used.

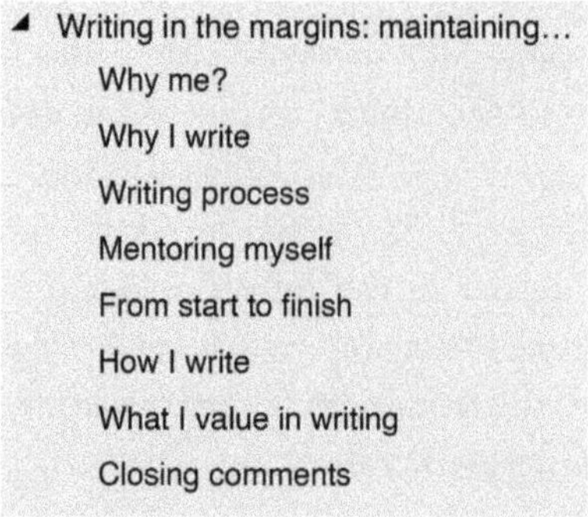

> - Writing in the margins: maintaining...
>   - Why me?
>   - Why I write
>   - Writing process
>   - Mentoring myself
>   - From start to finish
>   - How I write
>   - What I value in writing
>   - Closing comments

Fig. 2. Screenshot showing initial chapter structure

7. **It is draft right up to acceptance**. This was a late lesson for me, but it is made such a positive difference: treat everything up to galley proofs entirely as drafts. I think in fifty shades of draft, starting with the aforementioned builders' waste. Every one of my publications has undergone extensive re-writing. At one stage, I thought it was because I hadn't learned how to write effectively, but now I know it is just part of the process. Research and writing are, after all, work. The willingness to write and rewrite takes both tenacity and humility.

Writing for Publication

8. **It is never the last word**. Do not kid yourself; chances are your article will not make the incredible splash it did for you as you wrote it. Keep a sense of proportion. Expect to see scholarship move on, and for your work to perhaps raise an eyebrow or two rather than earn a standing ovation. The best you can hope for is others seeing the merit of your ideas as your work assists them in their own endeavours. Raising the tide of scholarly insight by even a drop is a contribution, as you have added to public discourse for others to draw from. I have spoken with various successful scholars who express surprise that their most-cited work is one they considered incidental! Being published is its own recognition and reward, and it is an indicator you have made a positive difference.

9. **Write for the reader — and the editor — and don't forget the reviewer**. Ultimately, you're not writing for yourself. You may get pleasure out of writing (it is something I genuinely enjoy), but you're not the centre of your piece. One of the most important ways of checking whether you have met this goal is to purposefully read your work aloud before submission. Awkward sentences suddenly come out of hiding; gaps in the narrative are suddenly revealed as incomprehensible chasms. Another important activity here is a paragraph check, whereby you note in the margin what each paragraph is saying in a few words. This is an excellent check for structural logic.

10. **Learn from the reviewers**. I'm certain every published researcher has experienced the dichotomous results of double-blind peer review: to one reviewer the work is the best thing since sliced bread, with insight that everyone's been waiting for; to the other, it is a tangled mess that adds nothing new (ironically both could be right, depending on who is reviewing it). Reviewers are not the enemy, but they are the stewards. Journals tend to be picky in who they accept as reviewers, so their views are — as it says on the tin — from academic peers, who often have different subjective views. All have the same commitment to quality scholarship. I have learned a lot from reviewers and now understand their feedback as investments in my work. If they don't understand my main points, then clearly, I haven't successfully written for them (#7 and #9 above). Believe me when I say that reviewers have your best outcomes at heart. They are the best free tutors you will ever have!

The Leisure of the Margins

I have gone for a familiar and somewhat relaxed writing style in this chapter, and I have drawn on various metaphors on the themes of activity and travelling. All of this is intentional, because ultimately research and writing are familiar and inter-related, requiring energy and journey. I love travel when I get to it. I love the new sights, the discoveries, taking photos, browsing local shops, relaxed dining, soaking in the culture, enjoying the noise. Oddly, my research and writing activity feels similar.

I'm not one for packaged tours. I have learned to not follow a strict, linear pathway. I tend to wander. If I sightsee by list, I get worried about the time spent at each destination. Sometimes a good article or thought gets me straying into another area, where I wander for a while. Perhaps this is yet another benefit of publishing for pleasure; there is no pressure to be slavish. I have learned to enjoy the journey, and plan for meandering. But perhaps that's because I research for the sheer pleasure of it, relishing the learning, reflection, and engagement it brings.

Being on the margins needn't make you marginal.

References

Bond, M., Zawacki-Richter, O., & Nichols, M. (2018). Revisiting five decades of educational technology research: A content and authorship analysis of the British Journal of Educational Technology. *British Journal of Educational Technology, 50*(1). https://doi.org/10.1111/bjet.12730

Bozkurt, A., & Zawacki-Richter, O. (2021). Trends and patterns in Distance Education (2014–2019): A synthesis of scholarly publications and a visualization of the intellectual landscape. *International Review of Research in Open and Distributed Learning, 22*(2).

Creswell, J. W. (2014). *Research design: qualitative, quantitative, and mixed methods approaches*. SAGE Publications.

Dey, I. (1993). *Qualitative data analysis: a user-friendly guide for social scientists*. Routledge.

Kidder, T., & Todd, R. (2013). *Good prose: the art of non-fiction*. Random House.

Merriam, S. B., & Tisdell, E. J. (2016). *Qualitative research: a guide to design and implementation* (4th ed.). John Wiley & Sons.

Miles, M. B., & Huberman, A. M. (1994). *Qualitative data analysis: an expanded sourcebook*. SAGE Publications.

Nichols, M. (2020). Reading and studying on the screen, and, Addendum: two articles. *Journal of Open, Flexible and Distance Learning, 24*(1), 33–60. https://www.jofdl.nz/index.php/JOFDL/article/view/421

Pan, M. L. (2008). *Preparing literature reviews: qualitative and quantitative approaches* (3rd ed.). Pyrczak Publishing.

Punch, K., & Oancea, A. (2014). *Introduction to research methods in education* (2nd ed.). SAGE Publications.

Yin, R. K. (2018). *Case study research and applications: design and methods*. SAGE Publications.

Zawacki-Richter, O., & Naidu, S. (2016). Mapping research trends from 35 years of publications in Distance Education. *Distance Education, 37*(3), 245–69. https://doi.org/10.1080/01587919.2016.1185079

Appendix: Early insight

As I reflected on this chapter, I was reminded of a conference paper I wrote almost twenty years ago as a young senior lecturer — back in the day when paper proceedings were still in vogue — for a professional body too small to consider digitizing its archives. It is a paper 3,500 words in length called *"Building a secondary research paper or literature review."* I have included a slightly adapted summary of its main points below. The paper suggests that preparing a literature review is like building a house, drawing on principles of building to describe the activity of secondary research:

Building insight	Principle	Description
1. Make sure you're a builder	The principle of Apprenticeship	Have a sense of professionalism and the basic skill set. Work with someone more experienced if you are getting started.
2. Start with an architect's plan	The principle of Setting Objectives	Set an aim, write a reason, list the issues you will explore. Have a sense of what your endpoint is: an article? Conference paper? Blog post?
3. Gather the building materials	The principle of Exhaustive Quantity	Get into the literature. Search the databases, follow the leads, draw from the best sources, organise what you find. Don't fear volume.
4. Don't blame your tools...	The principle of Research Technique	Start with abstracts and summaries. Sort your articles into themes and prioritise those sources that are clearly more important.
5. Build a firm foundation #1	The principle of Topic Immersion	There's no better word for it — immerse yourself in the flow of thinking. Start with the prioritised, follow your best sense from there. Take notes.

6. Build a firm foundation #2	The principle of Diminishing Returns	As you read, you'll find that reading more does not mean knowing more. Stop when the ratio of new ideas to new articles fades.
7. Build the framing	The principle of Structure	Draft section headings for your review. These should emerge naturally from all you have read and reflected on since your project began.
8. It needs a roof	The principle of Idea Integration	Start a fresh document, built on the frame above. This should cover everything you have learned and give final shape to the subject.
9. Don't forget to decorate	The principle of Critical Feedback and Editing	Decorating requires multiple coats of paint and makes a mess. Several drafts will likely be needed before you're done.
10. Market value	The principle of Dissemination	Meet the market, which is to say, discover and comply with the submission. requirements of your chosen channel or audience.
11. On the imperfection of analogies	The principle of Perspective	Expect that your understanding will change as you learn more. This is the treasure of the research endeavour.

You can see echoes of these insights across this chapter, and I'm happy to report that the advice I gave twenty years ago has proven itself since. Mind, what once took eleven points now takes twenty. I put that down to better Perspective (point eleven).

13. Indigenous, Settler, Diasporic, and Post-colonial: The Identities Woven Through our Academic Writing

Marguerite Koole, Michael Cottrell, Janet Mola Okoko, and Kristine Dreaver-Charles

When I was invited to contribute an article about my writing, my first thoughts were, "Really? Why me?" I was honoured to be asked, but even now I feel like I am clumsy at the craft. Having wasted several months wafting back and forth pondering what I could possibly contribute, I began talking about it to my colleagues. As I shared my writing anecdotes — successes and travesties — they shared theirs. I realized then that it would be interesting to gather our collective stories. Upon completion of the chapter, we all mused how this reflective project was both difficult and rewarding as it forced us to consider our own identities.

Some scholars argue there is a direct link between what and how individuals write and what they become (Gilmore et al., 2019). We suggest that identity and writing co-create each other: our identities are socially constructed through a "complex interweaving [of] positionings" (Ivanič, 1998, p. 10). Just as weft and warp form a woven fabric, our approaches to and perceptions of the writing experience are entangled within our cultural sensitivities. As a diverse group of colleagues, we use this chapter to reflect on our individual journeys as scholars, researchers, and writers. In this way, the chapter is polyvocal. "Polyvocality is the power of many voices to shift and sustain narrative change" (Weidinger, 2020, para. 5), and seemed an ideal fit to allow for diverse perspectives while producing novel insights through synthesis. Scholars have noted that this approach aligns with social constructionist perspectives, that it often disrupts traditional hierarchies within knowledge production, and that it provides agency to those with lesser situational power by creating a rhetorical space for "democratic debate, more hegemonic resistance and more openness and honesty among practitioner researchers" (Arnold & Brennan, 2013, p. 353). This chapter, therefore, presents the reflections of four colleagues at different career stages and from multiple cultural backgrounds, but who all share in the process of scholarly writing.

While writing, we each reflected upon our own writing practice and how our identities have been woven into and out of our writing experiences. We considered our backgrounds and training as scholars, our thoughts on identity and voice in our writing, our writing anxieties, and our reflections on our writing processes. Throughout the process, we realized how our positionality and relationships within and outside academia were integral to how we identify, struggle, learn, grow, and progress through the writing experience. It also became apparent that our voices manifest differently depending on our relationship to our readers, to our topics, to the academic world, to our socio-cultural identities, to our communities, and to the larger political processes that shape our existence.

Our reflections and analyses are not intended as a post-colonial critique in which we differentiate colonizers from colonized or raise awareness of social, economic, and material realities (Noda, 2019). Rather, this is a conceptual piece; we are attentive to our larger political and material realities which impact the academy and the writing process. We are interested in how our positionings have shaped our approaches to writing with the aim of learning how to support each other and share what we have learned. Our exploration into writing from the settler, Indigenous, diasporic, and post-colonial perspectives is also potentially useful to students and their supervisors. As scholars, we know that personal narratives of students, which attest to their struggle to write and find their identities as writers, provide strong evidence that scholars should *not only* theorize academic "identity" *but also* strategize how to better support *both* emergent writers (Ivanič, 1998) *and* each other as more or less established scholarly writers.

In discussing our identities and how they interweave through our academic writing, we organized this chapter around Ivanič's (1997) four aspects: 1) autobiographical self, 2) discoursal self, 3) self as author, and 4) possibilities for selfhood. Ivanič describes the autobiographical self as that which is shaped through one's culture and socialization. It is constantly in flux. The discoursal self is the impression that writers give of themselves through their texts. The impression can be multiple, contradictory, and consciously or unconsciously performed. The self as author refers to the way writers see themselves — that is, how they perceive the enactment of their own voice. Finally, and this might be most helpful to writers, the possibility for selfhood refer to how writers may choose from a selection of "subject positions" that are available within socio-cultural and institutional settings. Ivanič refers to these as positionings which allow and/or constrain writers to perform multiple writer identities (p. 27). Co-existence of the different selves may not be harmonious, but they can continuously negotiate boundaries allowing new perspectives to emerge; dialogical interaction across boundaries can be a space for learning (Akkerman & Bakker, 2011). Through the sharing of our own narratives as academic writers, we hope to create a collegial space that resonates with other writers.

Autobiographical Selves

As Ivanič (1997) defines it, the autobiographical self is shaped through one's culture and socialization. To better understand writing behaviours and attitudes, it is helpful to understand the writer's formative years. Writing is always situated and "multivoiced" (Castelló et al., 2009, p. 1110); it incorporates voices of one's community and prior writings. In addition, the expectation is that it, too, will be incorporated into future writings (Castelló et al., 2009). Therefore, it is a significant aspect of the writer's character.

Marguerite

Having migrated from the Netherlands, then to Iowa in the US, my great-grandfather eventually settled on a farm in Southern Alberta in 1915. It was not until I had completed several academic degrees that I became aware that I grew up on the traditional territory Blackfoot (Siksikaitsitapi) Confederacy (Treaty 7). The farm and surrounding countryside offered an idyllic setting in which to grow up. My brother and I spent our free time digging tunnels in the hills, riding motorbikes in the nearby river bottom, riding horses with my cousins from the farm across the road, constructing contraptions using parts in the wood and metal scrap piles, swimming in the muddy dugout pond, and engaging in all kinds of other creative activities and games. School, on the other hand, was unremarkable and uninteresting for me.

Academically, the turning point occurred in the second half of Grade Ten when I was in a French class. Just after we had just written our first test, the teacher decided to publicly call upon the students in the room and predict the mark each student was going to get on the test. When he got to me, he said, "Marguerite will likely get around 72%." When I heard this, I was appalled. I thought, "I'm not just average." When I received my result, it was 72%, exactly what he had predicted! My sense of my academic self was awakened. From that point forward, I began to study for tests, listen in class, and do my homework. I began to achieve high marks and was on the honour roll every year. My weakest subject was English — and it remained so during my undergraduate degree. Yet I had developed a love of languages — especially Spanish and French — which required the acquisition of some serious knowledge of grammar, sentence structures, and punctuation.

I began teaching English as a Second Language (ESL) in Spain during the 1990–1991 academic year. Returning to Canada, I then taught English for Academic Purposes at the University of Lethbridge. Working alongside supportive and knowledgeable colleagues, I developed a reputation for creativity in my teaching. At the same time, I continued to hone my knowledge of language structure. However, I was not yet "a writer" per se. My writing, really, began in graduate school where I wrote copious research papers, a thesis, and eventually a PhD dissertation. I am now an Associate Professor in Educational Technology and Design at the University of Saskatchewan. I can trace my paternal and maternal ancestors back to the mid-sixteenth century, and to the best of my knowledge, I am the first person in my lineage to earn a doctoral degree.

My academic area is educational technology. I approach this area through various perspectives such as the social construction of reality, socio-materialism, and post-humanism. Now, I tend to publish anywhere from three to eight journal articles (or book chapters) per year. My goals are always the same: to write as clearly as possible, to entice readers with a snappy title, to ensure philosophical commensurability, and to contribute something new.

Kristine

I am a member of the Mistawasis First Nation. I grew up in Prince Albert, Saskatchewan. I live and work in my Treaty 6 Territory and the homeland of the Métis. Books were always readily available, and I naturally developed a love for reading. My parents would often take me to the library and my late grandmother would read to me. I became a teacher and spent my early career teaching in Northern Saskatchewan. I have been working at the University of Saskatchewan for almost a decade. I would say that I am mid-career.

I have had many amazing opportunities in the academic world as a PhD student. I have been fortunate to travel and present at international conferences. I have a few publications and, in the past year, I was the lead author on my first peer-reviewed paper. I felt that was an especially good accomplishment. My mentors are my co-supervisors. As a first-generation graduate student, I have benefited immensely from their time and guidance — including this opportunity to share and reflect upon our writing processes.

Janet

I was born in Nairobi, Kenya to two civil servants who came from two different sub-tribes and spoke different dialects of the same tribe. We still maintain our ancestral home in Western Kenya. I come from a culture that is typically oral; my family was not different. However, I am one of those children who was sent to boarding school at a very early age (age five) because that was where "able parents" thought quality education was. It also worked well for my parents because of the transient nature of their jobs.

I went to school through a system which I consider to have been inherited from the British colonialists — by choice — because the Kenyans who were tasked with developing a new system during and after independence (known as the Ominde and Gachathi Commissions) felt it was useful to use the model that already existed (Eshiwani, 1993) with English as the official language. When I went to school, as was stipulated in the initial policy at independence, the language of the catchment was the medium of instruction in grades one to four in Kenya, which remains the policy today. This meant that besides learning my mother tongue (Luhya), I had to learn the formal and official national languages, English and Swahili. I am uncertain if the teachers were adequate in their own knowledge or if it was even formally in the curriculum. To further complicate my early years, I also had to somehow learn the native language of the places where my parents moved as well as those surrounding any new school I attended; I changed schools at least twice at every level of education. The result is that, at various points in my life, I have worked with at least four languages concurrently.

My career started with teacher training before pursuing a master's degree in educational planning. My post-graduate experience included working as a curriculum developer and research officer at Kenya Institute of Curriculum Development (KICD) and for a non-governmental education project in Eastern Africa. My work in these positions required me to write formal reports which, in many cases, were very linear, structured, and pragmatic. The purpose of my formal writing was mainly to communicate technical information aimed at influencing policy. Therefore, I approached writing from a realist — or rather, objective — premise because my professional reports were aimed at informing or influencing policy. My research agenda and scholarly work is still based on a pragmatic stance where my focus on seeking answers to practitioner-oriented questions in school leadership drives the methodology, methods, and style of my academic writing.

Michael

I grew up in a large family on a small farm in County Cork, Ireland in the 1960s. In retrospect, I found that contracting rheumatic fever at age three, an affliction which resulted in being bed-ridden for almost a year, was a pivotal event in my life. My mother, who had a great love of reading, helped me pass the time by teaching me to read. So, I cracked the code of reading early, and I revelled in the wondrous stories and exciting worlds that I was able to access through books, sparking an early fascination with Canada. In addition to inculcating a lifelong love of reading, my early exposure to and proficiency with text gave me a huge academic advantage over my peers. School, consequently, came easy to me and, despite the fear-based culture propagated within Ireland's Catholic-dominated educational system, by my mid-teens I knew that I wanted to become an educator. Thanks to a state scholarship, I was the first in my family to go to university, completing a bachelor's degree in history and literature and a higher diploma in education. I began teaching history and literature in a local secondary school. Ambitious to continue formal learning, I then completed a master's degree in history. A serendipitous connection with a supervisor, combined with a desire to come to Canada, brought me to Saskatchewan to complete a PhD in history in the late 1980s.

My research focus and writing has evolved significantly over time, motivated by changing personal interests and occupational/scholarly priorities and requirements. The original focus of my scholarship was the Irish diaspora, but my interest shifted quickly to local Indigenous circumstances as the parallels between the Ireland's colonial history and the neo-colonial dynamics of 1990s Saskatchewan became evident to me. Employment as an instructor with the Indian Teacher Education Program at the University of Saskatchewan provided an opportunity to engage with Indigenous history, especially schooling in historical contexts in Canada and beyond. The transition to the department of Educational Administration in 2007 allowed me to deepen my exploration of Indigenous education discourse in historical contexts and to interrogate strategies that might achieve more equitable outcomes for Indigenous students in local and global educational contexts. My positionality is complicated by virtue of having both Canadian settler and Irish diasporic identities and affiliations. As a citizen of Canada and a member of the White Settler group, I'm well aware of the privilege I derive from white skin and educational advantage. But retaining citizenship, family ties, and cultural affiliations with Ireland still connects me with a Third World heritage and historical experience. I therefore see myself as a member of both a colonizing and colonized group and I attempt, through personal, professional, and political actions — including my writing — to mobilize insights from these complex intersections to advance reconciliation within the academy and social justice with society at large.

Discoursal Selves

The discoursal self is the impression that writers give of themselves through their texts (Ivanič, 1997). We reflected upon how we try to portray ourselves and for whom we write.

Marguerite

Interestingly, it was only upon starting this project that I realized something: I seldom consider my "voice"; rather, my focus is always on how I might make the sentences clearer and on how to best organize the ideas. My apparent lack of voice caught me off guard. What does it mean to have a voice? It means to have a discernible perspective. To have a perspective implies positionality and relationality. Everyone must have a voice in their writing. The inability to perceive one's own voice suggests, perhaps, an affinity within the writing context. Sometimes, one only becomes aware of one's own culture when one journeys outside of it: experiencing alienation, strangeness, or a level of disconnect provides a space for reflection. Objectivity and "placelessness" are Eurocentric attributes. I identify that, in my writing, I conform to hegemonic conceptions of "appropriate" writing — that is, writing that follows the norms and constraints of academia (Kilby & Graeme, 2022) in an effort to portray myself as learned and knowledgeable. Perhaps the technology focus of my work also subconsciously puts me in a mindset that assumes that place/geography is unimportant. Somehow, my unconscious socialization as an academic has successfully eased my entry into academe and the role of writer.

This chapter is one of my few personal or semi-autobiographical pieces. It is rare for me to share personal reflections, family information, or events in my personal life. Even on social media, I limit discussion of my day-to-day life and my feelings — although I have been known to share pictures of spectacular meals as well as interesting places and events. There are times in my qualitative research where I will discuss my philosophical and professional positioning. However, anything more personal must be relevant to the context of the piece. I seldom feel anxiety about academic writing and even sharing rough drafts causes me little discomfort. The lack of discomfort may be owing to my cautiousness in terms of personal disclosures which are judicially selected and limited, thereby reducing risk of personal attacks or judgment.

Increasingly, I have been incorporating more comments on social justice and the effects of neoliberalism on the field and practice of education. I am, therefore, becoming more sensitive to the political dimensions of my positioning and the potential of my words in influencing other scholars who, in turn, may influence pre-service teachers and practitioners. On a professional level, when engaging in this type of writing, I am mindful of how I use words. I ensure that I offer sufficient support for my statements, and I attempt to maintain a mature, professional tone. On a personal level, I am mindful of potential political blowback from politicians upon me or the university. Although we have academic freedom, there are ways that governments can exert pressure to diminish such freedom. Furthermore, as a female academic, I have watched social media trolls threaten scientists, academics, and health care workers. I am acutely aware of how much power I do *not* have.

For me, readers are an abstraction; they are an unidentifiable amalgam of academics, students, and professors. When I'm writing, I want my writing to be logical and concise. I want my writing to flow from idea to idea but offer a variety in sentence structure and sentence length. As such, I want the reader to feel that I am a logical thinker with a balanced point of view. I acknowledge contradictory points of view whenever possible and ensure there is a balanced and up-to-date coverage of the literature in order to convince the reader that the arguments are sound and based upon prior literature.

As a student, I wrote for my professors. My PhD supervisor was a significant mentor who painstakingly took the time to discuss philosophy, provide feedback on my papers, indulge in recent readings and new turns in the field, and share her knowledge of how to interact in my PhD defence and with other scholars. Now, I write to resolve problems, to answer questions in my field, to explore new and emerging technologies, and to present different philosophical and theoretical perspectives. I think when I write. As each word is set down on the page, it co-constructs meaning. A sensitivity to how the words interact brings about an internal discourse in which tensions between the connotations create new meaning and new understanding. Over the years, exploring different philosophical positions — whether one of the constructivisms (social, relative, or cognitive), the social construction of meaning, socio-materialism, or postdigital thought — has helped me to think through deeper levels of meaning and to harness the possibilities of metaphor and visual depictions of concepts, principles, and theories. I use visual models and depictions heavily to guide my thinking and writing. As I continue to mature as a writer, I find that I write for myself because exploration of the world through prose has become increasingly fascinating.

Kristine

When I write, I write for my late grandmothers, for my ancestors, and for people whom I believe need to read my work and hear my stories. I write for my professors, who do their best to encourage me when I need it. As an educator, I find we are often lifelong learners. I can remember teaching in the north, wanting to take more university classes, and just not knowing what options I had or where to start. So, now that I work at a university, I feel that I am here and I should study, and this includes writing. I have the opportunity when I know there are, too often, Indigenous peoples who do not have these opportunities.

I am now a PhD student in the Cross-Departmental Program in the College of Education at the University of Saskatchewan. When I write, I am trying to convey that Indigenous peoples very much have a place within higher education and that Indigenous perspectives and ways of knowing are integral to academia. I am also really interested in space where Indigenous perspectives and ways of knowing connect with Western perspectives. These perspectives do not always weave together easily, but it is a bit mind-bending when it is possible. I like layers and finding connections.

Janet

As a writer, I see myself as a custodian of a message or knowledge that needs to be relayed to a specific audience in a way that is accessible and written concisely. But in almost all cases, I do this in a foreign language — English. In other words, I am always cognizant of my position as a foreign messenger. And based on the transient nature of my career and academic life, I have learned that language and communication is cultural-specific. I have also realized that concepts, words, and expressions could have meanings that invoke political positions. The words and expressions in a given language can have different meanings in different cultural contexts. And so, for me to communicate effectively in any language, I must learn the cultural nuances of my audience. This became even clearer to me during my doctoral programme in Canada and now, as I work with both Canadian-born (domestic) and international students as their instructor and academic supervisor. The cultural experience is compounded by the disadvantage of not having English grammar as part of my basic education curriculum.

As a doctoral student, I became aware of how my cultural socialization influenced how I structured my thoughts, organized my writing, and how it sometimes interfered with the clarity and conciseness of my communication. For instance, I noted how communication in my native language(s), which are mostly oral, differed in the sense that the main meaning of a message is often preceded with an in-depth description of the context, self-identification, and communal location. It is sandwiched between a thick introduction and a brief conclusion. On the other hand, in the Western writing tradition, I have experienced the effectiveness of writing to communicate as providing a concise statement of the "essence" of the message at the onset, followed by elaboration, and a summary in the conclusion. Fortunately, both cultural orientations (i.e., African and Canadian) are serving me well as I evolve as a scholar.

Michael

I greatly appreciate the ways in which contributing to this chapter have prompted me to think about academic writing and my own positionality as a writer more deeply and critically than I normally do and to chart an evolution over time. The disciplinary shifts I have experienced over the course of my career have obviously impacted how I approach the process of writing and have also altered my self-conceptualization as a writer. My doctoral training in history privileged a very formal humanities style, characterized by third-person voice, analytic objectivity, and the Chicago referencing system, heavy with footnotes. Because of this, my early writing, of which I was very proud at the time, now seems excessively formal, depersonalized, and neutral. Shifting from history to education caused some disciplinary dissonance but was also tremendously beneficial in terms of my growth as a researcher and writer. Since history is a largely untheoretical discipline, I was first challenged to engage with theoretical concepts of ontology and epistemology as a social sciences researcher in education. Encountering the works of Paulo Freire (1970) and Franz Fanon (1967) was transformative, enabling me to confront the political dimensions of scholarship and writing, and to articulate an identity and affiliation within my own work informed by critical theory and constructivist assumptions.

Self as Writer

The self as author refers to the way writers see themselves — that is, how they perceive the enactment of their own voice and how they attempt to actively portray themselves.

Marguerite

I am not a natural-born writer. Writing is hard work; however, the more I do it, the more I enjoy it. Writing is a means of continuous learning and honing of critical thinking skills. Although I have been told that I am creative, I see myself more as an explorer who revels in ideas and seeing theoretical connections between ideas — that is, connections that others might see as disparate. Uncovering news ways of seeing the world offers the potential to find novel solutions and different, if not better, understandings of issues in the field of educational technology. Attempting to break free of disciplinary boundaries and the constraints of conventional, orthodox thought is important for moving the field forward. Exploring new ideas and applying them to current issues would be my intellectual superpower.

Kristine

I would have to say I am a struggling writer. It is not my favourite thing to do. I overthink and procrastinate with an exorbitant amount of skill. About a year ago, I had an "aha!" moment when I realized that, as a PhD candidate, I was really trying to become an academic writer. I am not sure if that realization helped or hindered my writing. But I realize that so much of what I need to do to finish my PhD is to hone my skills as a writer.

In ethnography, there is the idea of researchers positioning themselves as either insiders or outsiders, the *emic* or the *etic*. As an Indigenous woman, I would have to say I am neither and I am both. Sometimes I struggle to find my place in academia. I am not faculty. I am a staff member and graduate student. I am an outsider. The institution is a place that can be too often hostile for Indigenous people. But then, relationality is central to Indigenous ways of knowing, and the relationships I have established through my work on campus also make me an insider. The either/or of this is a construct that does not easily fit. But I also try to focus on the importance of building good relationships through my work in higher education, and this makes me feel like an insider. When projects with faculty lead to writing and presentations I am happy to participate and further develop my skills and it supports my sense of belonging in academia.

Janet

I identify as a pragmatic scholar or writer because the practicality or purpose of what I am communicating with my writing drives the style and tone within it. As a custodian of valuable knowledge that I need to relay to an audience, I have learned to use various aspects of my cultural experiences to enrich my writing — depending on the purpose and the audience. I am learning to use the experiences from both orientations. This includes working with epistemological lenses and methodological designs that call upon my ability to provide very thick and rich descriptions of phenomena, as well as those that require my writing to be objective, structured, and concise.

Michael

Who do I try to be when I write? My primary influences are socio-cultural and political. My Irish heritage, characterized by a history of struggle against oppression, combined with a liberationist and redistributive political sensibility, position me as an ally to Indigenous peoples in Canada. The bulk of my research and writing is consequently focused on drawing attention to educational disparities which disadvantage Indigenous peoples and on delineating strategies which ensure more equitable outcomes for Indigenous learners. I believe passionately in the transformative power of learning and dialogue to create a more socially just world, and I write to amplify the multiple voices, including Indigenous and non-Indigenous students, academics, educators, policy makers, and administrators, who are also committed to this work. I continue to be inspired by Freire's (1970) insight that critical scholars do not consider themselves "the proprietor of history or of all people, or the liberator of the oppressed; but he or she does commit himself or herself, within history, to fight at their side" (p. 9). In terms of voice, I share with other critical scholars a desire to use my voice and authority to highlight the experiences of those that have been marginalized, disadvantaged, excluded or vulnerable or those who have been excluded or silenced by dominant discourses (Sawchuk, 2021).

Writing Process Challenges

In a light-hearted article about why and how academics write, Badley (2018) refers to academic writers as "rotten" and "stinky" (p. 247). While he explains his point, he suggests that there is space for exploration, faltering, and frivolity. His article ends with him accepting that he will continue to improve. Self-doubt in one's writing ability is certainly one of the challenges; however, there are additional obstacles, both perceived and real.

Marguerite

What is most troublesome for me is finding the time for writing. As my academic career has developed, it is increasingly difficult to balance committee work, teaching, research, writing, family, and outside interests. As of late, I now manage meetings by scheduling as many as possible on the same days. In this way, entire days can be freed up for thoughtful work. Those days feel luxurious as long as I can convince myself to sit in front of the keyboard. Writing requires unscheduled, flexible, and uninterrupted time. I need to be able to ignore email, hallway conversations, the refrigerator, dust bunnies, the cat, and my husband. My desk and computer desktop need to be cleared of anything unrelated to the writing project at hand. Although I orchestrate this kind of time and space, other obstacles present themselves. When fatigued or unmotivated, I relent and divert my attention to busy work such as answering emails, scheduling meetings, completing paperwork, or simply resting.

When motivated to write, I begin by formulating a strategy and articulating my goal; for some, this is called an outline and thesis statement. My outline, however, is fluid and changes as new ideas and discoveries emerge. The goal usually remains constant. In preparing to write, I gather sources. Ideally, I like to spend time reading around my subject, taking breaks to think. To begin typing, I have to feel mentally settled. I have to get comfortable. I have to have read enough to feel saturated in the topic. I highlight and annotate readings, then gather my annotations, and review them. Often, I take notes and type key sentences from books into MS Word documents. I also read electronically and export quotes that are significant to me. I like having both paper and electronic copies. Paper is easier on the eyes while electronic copies are more easily searchable. When working on complex pieces with many sources, I use Nvivo (qualitative coding software) to categorize snippets of annotations and quotes allowing me to easily locate statements of support later in the writing process.

Early in the process, I like to add the sources to my software referencing tool. The ability to write and cite while automatically updating the list of references saves time — even though, at the end of the writing project, it is still necessary to double check the formatting to correct any errors in the reference and citation formatting. I must discipline myself to complete this final review of citations and references. I sometimes combine it with something pleasurable such as going for coffee with a draft of the paper.

Writing a master's thesis certainly taught me about myself as a writer and prepared me for the PhD dissertation. It is as true now as it was then: starting a first draft is the most overwhelming while editing drafts is the most enjoyable. When I was writing my master's thesis, I lived in a small town in Alberta. There was a lovely little tea house where the proprietor made fresh scones and served them with whipped cream and a strawberry compote. In the mornings on my writing days, I would bring a draft of a chapter, go to the tea house, order a coffee and scone. It was quiet mid-week, so I could sit for a couple hours munching, sipping coffee, thinking, reading, and editing. It would prepare me to return to my keyboard to input the edits. Then, having completed the editing, I would draft the next section and return to the tea house the next morning. I still try to follow this formula when writing chapters and journal articles.

By far, the most enjoyable aspect of writing now is successfully publishing. While I still curse the reviewers under my breath, I have personally experienced tremendous growth working with my anonymous reviewers. Sometimes the learning is in the form of a sudden "aha!" moment such as when a reviewer's comment made me realize the incommensurability particular concepts, for example. At other times, my writing has benefited from working through comments on how to write more concisely or better organize a paper. I have also learned how to hold my ground with confidence in my theorizing and writing skills. Such confidence grows through both experience and, notably, discussions with supportive colleagues who remind me that my work is good. The academic community can be and should be a space of positive growth.

Kristine

I am always trying to find new ways to motivate and better focus. Earlier in the year, in trying to establish a consistent writing schedule, I gathered some jars and rocks to try and track my hourly daily writing. I had enough rocks for each day in the month. Every day when I wrote for an hour, I would move a rock into the other jar. It worked for a while, and I could see the jar fill with my many hours of writing. It created a visual of my efforts and I could see that little by little, I was making progress.

For me, sitting down and focusing is the thing that challenges me the most: I think it is the worry that I will be glued to my desk for twelve to fourteen hours a day. I know I need to put in more time writing, but I am afraid to miss out on life. Writing is isolating. It can too often feel lonely. And that is my struggle. So, I sign up for online writing classes when I can. These classes help me feel connected while I write. The Pomodoro method is another useful technique that I have found. Pomodoro videos and apps are designed to help you focus and write for twenty-five-minute blocks. When I really struggle to write, I challenge myself to do one or two Pomodoro sessions and they often help me to get started.

I like the research that goes into my writing process… finding publications, figuring out who the scholars in the field are. I love to print, curate publications, and order new books. I underline the relevant quotes in printed publications. I also have a sticky-note addiction. So, when I read a book, I put a sticky-note on the quotes that resonate. Then when I need to, I can go back and re-read the entire book in a few minutes by focusing on the flagged pieces. I love the language and how authors put together their words.

When I begin writing, I usually start with really rough ideas. Eventually I try to add some headings. I mix in some quotes and revise, revise, revise until it begins to form something that still feels terrible. It is the agony of my writing. I really wish I was confident and could enjoy writing more. I also recognize that it challenges me because academic writing is a skill that will take me in new directions offering more opportunities.

Janet

There are three aspects that cause uneasiness in my writing. The first is the ability to identify and moderate how I use my strengths, and, in some cases, how I represent the two worldviews that are part of my reality — the world view of my ancestral traditions in Kenya and that of my new academic writing culture in the Western world. I mentioned in the description of my identity that these two worlds reinforce my writing in different ways. The more exploratory, non-formal nature of communicating in my Luhya heritage allows me to take risks, be creative, and provide thick and rich narrative in my writing while the more formal concise and linear nature of Western writing is critical to my scholarly and academic work. Besides balancing the strengths form the two worldviews, being a visible minority, I struggle with the feeling that my audience expects me to engage with the critical approach to discourse. This raises the need for me to attend to any assumptions about any political or cultural views that my work may invoke.

Not having had comprehensive grammar lessons as part of English language learning in Kenya creates some self-doubt in the correctness of my expression; thus, I feel the need to engage an editor in my writing. This self-doubt is also compounded by pressure from the nature of my work as an instructor and academic supervisor of graduate students. As I write, I am consciously aware that my work will be judged by my colleagues, by reviewers, and readers in general. I have a sense of inadequacy that pursues me throughout the process.

Michael

Although I am long-established in the academy, the academic writing process still represents a highly emotional journey. The struggle to carve out time to gather data and begin the coding and writing process leads to the satisfaction of marshalling the data and completing various drafts. Multiple drafts are typically required before I feel ready to submit, and the satisfaction and excitement of submission gives way to the anxiety of knowing that my research and writing — into which I have poured countless hours and significant psychological investment — is now at the mercy of anonymous reviewers and a cold and inordinately lengthy peer-review process. The roller-coaster continues when the reviews arrive. If the reviews are positive and the recommendation is to publish, I feel a thrill of satisfaction almost equal to the very first time a piece of my writing was accepted for publication over thirty years ago. And if the recommendation from reviewers is not positive, the sting of rejection is still deeply felt. But experience over time helps in anticipating and managing the often-challenging emotional journey represented by writing for peer-reviewed publication within academia.

As with other collaborators in this chapter, the pressures of work intensification constitute some of the most immediate challenges to research and writing. Neoliberal impulses within the academy have resulted in increased class sizes and teaching loads, especially supervisory responsibilities for graduate students; additionally, a corresponding imperative to secure Tri-Council funding pushes us to prioritize research topics that are fundable rather than those for which we feel genuine passion. My role as Graduate Chair in a department with a very large number of graduate programmes and students is also time-consuming, as funding scarcity amplifies the need for advocacy on behalf of vulnerable students. Having said all that, I still feel incredibly fortunate to work in the academy, as I am aware that tenured positions are becoming increasingly scarce and my previous experience in an untenured position alerted me to the uncertainty and tenuousness of part-time lecturers. I am also challenged by the topic of my writing, as Linda Smith (2005) famously described research on Indigenous topics as stepping on "tricky ground." For non-Indigenous researchers such as myself, it is even trickier because of the risk of being accused of voice appropriation, presenting oneself as a "white saviour," or being dismissed as merely performative.

As part of the reflection on my writing prompted by the opportunity to contribute to this chapter, I also noticed very different levels of motivation for writing for publication in peer-reviewed journals and applied or advocacy research. In short, since the latter often has the potential to effect policy or mobilize resources, while it is often unclear on the impact of much peer-reviewed research beyond personal advancement, I am much more highly motivated to initiate and conduct that type of writing for applied or advocacy purposes.

Discussion and Observations

Moving from polyvocality to synthesis, our personal narratives show interesting convergences and divergences. All of us wish to convey knowledge and ideas clearly and concisely. But the most significant themes include boundary crossing, relationality, and contextualization.

All of us are the first in our families to cross (or to be crossing) the PhD degree boundary. Other boundaries were also significant in the narratives. Both Janet and Kristine shared their feelings of "insider/outsider." Janet noted that in all her writing endeavours, there are language tensions that constantly remind her that she is a foreigner. Kristine noted being simultaneously inside the institution as staff and student, yet outside faculty-level academe. With a lesser sense of tension, Michael balanced his identities of settler, diaspora, and colonized peoples. While Marguerite's sense of being a settler on Treaty land arose late in her academic journey, she expressed the least amount of self-dislocation and least liminality.

A piece of writing can be thought of as an assemblage of words. In this way of thinking, words themselves are assemblages of morphemes, connotations, and denotation. Words as assemblages with the power to shape understanding, shift policy, or mobilize emerged for both Janet and Marguerite, but for different reasons. For Marguerite, words are interesting, and she has become sensitive to their choice and positioning in order to achieve clarity. For Janet, words can suggest different meanings in different contexts. For her, words are problematic, and one must wield them carefully in both a social and political sense. Words can reveal a writer to be erudite or clumsy; they can bring on judgement. And for Michael, words are sometimes political weapons that, when marshalled appropriately, can powerfully alter systems and the individuals that inhabit them, and the way in which they are resourced.

Hyland (2002) sees academic writing as "an act of identity" that exposes our "affiliation and recognition" (p. 1092). As members of communities, writers have many socio-cultural affiliations and discourses that are available to them. Interestingly, Janet, Marguerite, and Michael's narratives suggest that they have significant control over their possibilities for selfhood as writers. As established academics, they indicated comfort over "contesting the patterns of privilege" (Ivanič,

1997, p. 33). For example, Janet explained how she has learned to draw upon her oral and Western styles for different audiences. While we can choose our subject positions, we tend to balance our work alongside current expectations for academic writing in formatting, expression, and organization. As writers, we all view writing as a source of privilege but in different ways. Whereas Marguerite is beginning to critique social structures, Michael has already established himself in that area. Janet sees herself as a "custodian" of knowledge.

Kristine, as student, expressed an underlying humbleness and commitment towards her privilege to study at the PhD level — of which writing is a central aspect. Kristine's narrative suggests she is at the precipice of important boundaries — not only between student and academic but also between cultures. Students and early-career academics may be initially reluctant to take on a strong authorial voice or to expose their autobiographical selves. Not only is there danger in making strong claims but choosing a strong authorial position may alienate the writer from his or her home community. On the other hand, taking an identifiable non-academic voice may alienate them from the academy, thereby reducing access to associated privileges. Furthermore, novice writers often lack the understanding that "the boundary... belongs to *neither one nor* the other world" (Akkerman & Bakker, 2011, p. 141). This belonging and not-belonging emerged as a strong theme in Kristine's reflections.

Relationality in writing refers to how writers position themselves among others, among communities, among issues, and even among geographic locations. Marguerite's narrative suggests that her relationality remains controlled and segmented; other than her philosophical perspective, she divulges only what is necessary. Janet now shifts between positions, relative to her intended readers. Michael's writing is heavily influenced by his perceptions of affinity to colonized communities yet remains restricted by tensions arising from boundary maintenance of these communities. For Kristine, relationality is of utmost importance. The anticipated possible impact of her work adds considerable weight of responsibility and anxiety to her writing. Our sense of who we are is highly connected to our home cultures and when this sense of self must conform to standard ways of performing within the academic community, we may experience an "acute sense of dislocation and uncertainty" (Hyland, 2002, p. 1094). For Kristine, writing is more than an individual endeavour, while Marguerite, consciously or unconsciously, shelters herself from personal harm by avoiding self-disclosure.

The need to contextualize one's work is a significant aspect of writing for Kristine and Janet. Kristine must contextualize her work in order to situate herself. Janet, on the other hand, comes from an oral tradition in which contextualization is expected. Contrary to arguments by Ergin and Alkin (2019) who suggested that non-Western writers must contextualize their writing in order for Westerners to better understand their work, Kristine and Janet's narratives indicate that contextualization is necessary depending upon one's culture and traditions. Regardless of the reason, such practices (i.e., providing robust contextual and relational information) could strengthen writing if adopted more generally in the academic community by supporting more in-depth understanding.

Conclusion

Writing can be both empowering and endangering; it exposes writers' understanding of the world and themselves in relation to it. Academic writers are judged on their writing, which explains why graduate students — and even experienced academics — can react emotionally to critiques of their work. Although academic writers must cross through the "obligatory points of passage" imposed by colleagues and anonymous reviewers to traverse the boundary into the academic community, they can still actively choose their voice(s) and actively manage the boundary between worlds.

The polyvocal approach that we took in this chapter allowed us to share and compare our attitudes, struggles with, and appreciation for writing. More importantly, we were able to expose how our personal journeys have woven into the very fabric our work. An interesting outcome of this chapter is our increased recognition of the privilege we have as writers, our motivations for engaging in the writing process, and how we each bear the weight of responsibility differently. Responsibility, privilege, gender, race, nationality, and geographic location can all become boundaries, creating tension in our writing. As Akkerman and Bakker (2011) write, "a boundary creates a possibility to look at oneself through the eyes of other worlds" (p. 144). Peering into each other's gaze, we can better see each other's struggles, strategize ways to lighten the burden, and celebrate others' contributions as scholarly writers.

References

Akkerman, S. F., & Bakker, A. (2011). Boundary crossing and boundary objects. *Review of Educational Research, 8*(2), 132–69. 10.3102/0034654311404435

Arnold, C., & Brennan, C. (2013). Polyvocal ethnography as a means of developing inter-cultural understanding of pedagogy and practice. *European Early Childhood Education Research Journal, 21*(3), 353–69.

Badley, G. F. (2018). Why and how academics write. *Qualitative Inquiry, 26*(3–4), 247–56. 10.1177/1077800418810722

Castelló, M., Iñesta, A., & Monereo, C. (2009). Towards self-regulated academic writing: An exploratory study with graduate students in a situated learning environment. *Electronic Journal of Research in Educational Psychology, 7*(3), 1107–30. http://www.eric.ed.gov/ERICWebPortal/search/detailmini.jsp?_nfpb=true&_&ERICExtSearch_SearchValue_0=EJ869206&ERICExtSearch_SearchType_0=no&accno=EJ869206

Ergin, M., & Alkan, A. (2019). Academic neo-colonialism in writing practices: Geographic markers in three journals from Japan, Turkey and the US. *Geoforum, 100*, 259–66. 10.1016/j.geoforum.2019.05.008

Eshiwani G. S. (1993). *Education in Kenya: Since independence*. East African Educational Publishers, Nairobi.

Fanon, F. (1967). *Black skin, white masks*. New York: Grove.

Freire, P. (1970). *Pedagogy of the oppressed*. New York: Seabury Press.

Gilmore, S., Harding, N., Helin, J., & Pullen, A. (2019). Writing differently. *Management Learning, 50*(1), 3–10. 10.1177/1350507618811027

Hyland, K. (2002). Options of identity in academic writing. *ELT Journal, 56*(4), 351–58. 10.1093/elt/56.4.351

Ivanič, R. (1998). *Writing and identity: The discoursal construction of identity in academic writing*. John Benjamins.

Kilby, J., & Graeme, G. (2022). Sociography: Writing differently. *The Sociological Review, 10*(4), 635–55. 10.1177/00380261221108842

Noda, O. (2019). Epistemic hegemony: The Western straitjacket and post-colonial scars in academic publishing. *Revista Brasileira de Política Internacional, 63*(1). 10.1590/0034-7329202000107

Sawchuk, S. (2021). What is critical race theory, and why is it under attack? *Education Week* [online]. 18 May 2021. https://www.edweek.org/leadership/what-is-critical-race-theory-and-why-is-it-under-attack/2021/05

Smith, L. T. (2005). On tricky ground: Researching the Native in the age of uncertainty. In N. K. Denzin & Y. S. Lincoln (Eds), *The Sage handbook of qualitative research* (pp. 85–107). Sage Publications Ltd.

Weidinger, R. (2020). Polyvocal narrative strategy: Turning many voices into durable change. Narrative Initiative. https://narrativeinitiative.org/blog/polyvocal-narrative-strategy-turning-many-voices-into-durable-change/

14. Born Curious and in Trouble: Making Sense of Writing

Paul Prinsloo

Where shall I start this reflection?

It is actually a much more difficult question than one thinks. Thinking about my writing processes — the joy, the excitement, the terror when words just don't want to come — I am not sure there ever was a *beginning*, a moment in time where I would record on a calendar, or to which people would refer when they introduce me to an eager audience who has gathered to listen to me speak — "ladies and gentleman, it all started when… " Most probably there was a beginning, but I don't want to start "in the beginning." Starting with "in the beginning" would resemble a fairy tale with witches, dragons, a range of gods — big and small (with apologies to Terry Pratchett) — a happy ending for the princess (or so we are told), and a not-so-happy ending for the slain dragons. Not to mention the forces of darkness that must re-group and wait anxiously for another author to call them forth and make them visible.

Where was I? Oh, yes, providing a rationale for not starting at the beginning.

I also do not want to start at the end — as I (hopefully) have still some years to go before I will be spoken of in the past tense. The end will be when someone will pack up my study, curse me for the amount of dust on the bookshelves, look at my books, and either browse excitedly through the shelves selecting those books to keep and those books that will find their way to a second-hand bookshop, or worse, gifted to a local library where they will remain in a storeroom — where unwanted books go and die.

So, I will not start this reflection on my writing process at the end. Not yet.

I also did not want to approach this academically, in other words, provide a scholarly, referenced account of the different elements in academic authors' writing processes. It may have been an interesting and worthwhile study, but for now, that was not how I wanted to approach this reflection on my own processes. I would rather invite you, my dear reader, to accompany me on a journey in a conversation with Rainer Maria Rilke, a German poet born in 1875 and who died, of leukaemia, on 29 December 1928.

In Conversation with Rilke

A little book that made a huge impression on me as human, writer, and researcher, is Rainer Maria Rilke's *Letters to a Young Poet*. Lewis Hyde (2011), in the Introduction, explains how the letters reflect communication between a Xaver Kappus who sent his poems to the twenty-six-year-old Rilke for feedback. Hyde provides a sub-title for the Introduction and calls it "A geography of solitude" (p. xix). Writing (poems) require(d), for Rilke, solitude, "not merely a matter of being alone: it is a territory to be entered and occupied" (Hyde, 2011, p. xxv). Being alone, for Rilke, was not only a persistent reality in his life (despite being married), but solitude was the starting point: "We are solitary. It is possible to deceive yourself and act as if it was not the case… How much better… to take it as our starting point" (Hyde, 2011, p. xxv). Interestingly, Hyde reflects on how Rilke, instead of fighting solitude and aloneness, embraced it and turned it into a tool — not only containing it, but actually enlarging it.

Loneliness and Solitude

Remember to use loneliness and solitude as tool, not fleeing from them but embracing the two, schooling them, making them serve you and your writing processes. So many writers reflect on how social media and our constant need for connection and being connected is actually a discomfort with solitude, with the emptiness of being and sitting still. The sense of being alone in the world as the only boy among three sisters, has been a constant present in my life, and a leitmotif in searching for my identity — whether referring to my gender, or professional identity or on a deeper level, searching for a reason to be, and learning how to "be."

> Solitude was for Rilke the necessary enclosure within which he could begin to form an independent identity, a sense of himself free from the callings of family and convention. Solitude is the alembic of personhood" (Hyde 2011, pp. xxvii–xxviii). Rilke advises Kappus to embrace the moments when sadness and solitude enters us, and care for these feelings as we have a 'duty' towards them — "They are like the dragons in old myth that, when approached directly, turn out not to be dragons at all but helpless royalty in need of our attention."
>
> Hyde. 2011, p. xxviii

Once we embrace solitude, we must also let go of expectations of "time": "Creative life contains its own temporality and the surest way to make it fail is to put it on an external clock. Mechanical time makes haste, as it were, but haste dissolves in solitude" (Hyde, 2011, p. xxix). Allowing oneself to descend into yourself and your solitariness, letting go of haste, and embracing patience opens a space where you "court the future. It belongs to becoming rather than being, to the unfinished rather than the completed. It is not so much suited to heroes as to invalids and convalescents, those who must wait" (Hyde, 2011, quoting Rilke, p. xxxi).

Patience

How much patience do I allow myself to have? Not only allowing myself the time to descend into solitude, but also allowing myself the luxury of not focusing on being constantly aware of the next deadline and dealing with the anxiety of the possibility that I may not reach my performance targets. While I own up to my impatience and discomfort with embracing solitude, and how my self-discipline just unravels at the slightest provocation or temptation, it will also be disingenuous not to confront and call out the madness of the quantification of scholarship, researcher rankings, and the constant hunt for funding and managing your personal "brand." There is not much allowance for being unsure and appreciation of the unfinished in the increasingly celebrity researcher culture of award ceremonies that look more like Oscars or Evenings at the Met, with "We are the champions" or "Eye of the tiger" blasting from speakers big enough to wake the dead.

Patience, solitude, and the darkness of self-doubt are not for heroes but for invalids and convalescents.

In Rilke's first letter to the young poet, Rilke (2011) advises Kappus not to compare himself, his writing processes, and poems to others, or to crave affirmation from anyone. Instead, Rilke says,

> Nobody can advise you and help you, nobody. There is only one way. *Go into yourself.* Examine the reason that bids you to write; check whether it reaches its roots into the deepest region of your heart, admit to yourself whether you would die if it should be denied you to write. (p. 7; emphasis added)

He adds:

> This above all: ask yourself in your night's quietest hour: *must* I write? Dig down into yourself for a deep answer. And if it should be in the affirmative, if it is given to you to respond to this serious question with a loud and simple 'I must', then construct your life according to this necessity; your life right into its most inconsequential and slightest hour must become a sign and witness to this urge. (pp. 7–8; emphasis in the original)

Writing from the middle of this Roman circus called academia. There, where researchers battle with themselves and with one another to increase h-indices; to win grants; to increase their impacts and rankings; to compare themselves constantly with one another; to look for affirmation or hide our jealousy when someone else gets the mention, the invitation for a keynote, and/or the grant.

I have to remind myself time and again of Rilke's advice — do not compare yourself: to not look outside of yourself, *go into yourself.*

The question is not and should not be how I compare with others, but what will happen if I don't write? The question is more loaded than it seems: *Must* I write?

The first part of the answer is the easiest. In my current position, I am contracted to do research as my main critical performance area and publish at least five articles in a three-year cycle. I can hear you saying — "that is not too bad. It is doable." Of course, it is, but when you suddenly get an editor's desk rejection for an article, it creates havoc with your timelines and deliverables. There is also the issue of co-authorship; the number of outputs is divided by the number of authors. Therefore, a single-authored paper counts for an output of one (1), while a co-authored paper with another author leaves you with 50% of the output, therefore — 0.5. If you are collaborating with three authors, then the quantification game gets even more bizarre with you being awarded with only a 0.33 output.

Reaching five full output points in three years is therefore trickier when you collaborate with others. To give you an indication of how this plays out, here is an extract of one particular year:

> Peer-reviewed conference proceeding with three authors (0.3); chapter as sole author (1); chapter with two authors (0.5); article as sole author (1); article with two authors (0.5); article with three authors (00.3); article with seven authors (0.14).

I do apologize for sharing these boring details with you, but it does illustrate the brutal reality of what it takes to reach five (5) articles in three (3) years. For the reporting cycle 2019 to 2021 I was "lucky" to have had just over ten (10) outputs. I emphasize the "lucky" because I have had five editors' desk rejections for two articles during this period. I had three, yes, *three* editors' desk rejections for one co-authored article and two editors' desk rejections for another one article. What the above quantification of *being* a researcher also hides is the fact that two of the "outputs" during this cycle took more than two years to get past the reviewers.

So, you never know which one of your efforts are going to "RETURN TO SENDER," like an unwanted child or a failed adoption.

I *must* write.

There is, however, a second part to this "must"; namely, an inner compulsion, something burning inside me. If you would wake me in the middle of the night and ask me whether I *must* write, I will, most probably curse you for waking me, and then confess that I have to write. I will simply die if I do not. My Twitter profile and all my other social media profiles have this short description of who I see myself as: I was born curious and in trouble and since then, nothing has changed.

Since childhood, I was a ferocious reader and I remember filling notebooks with essays and notes. I started journalling at a young age and have been keeping sporadic reflections inspired by what I read, a

Tarot reading or insights from the I Ching, finding love and losing love as I meandered, stumbled, cruised (in more than one way), losing and finding myself.

I *must* write.

After Rilke ensured that the young poet understands the importance of getting to the source of his own writing processes and the rationale for his being a poet, he advises Kappus to "flee general subjects and take refuge in those offered by your own day-to-day life; depict your sadnesses and desires, passing thoughts and faith in some kind of beauty" (Rilke 2011, p. 8). As if Rilke could sense a possible response from the young poet that he cannot think of something in his own life to write about, he states "If your everyday life seems to lack material, do not blame it, blame yourself, tell yourself that you are not poet enough to summon up its riches, for there is no lack for him who creates and no poor, trivial place" (p. 8).

Research and Writing

I often stand amazed when someone would ask me "but what should I write about?" In academia, we have come to provide research questions to postgraduate students, but it is not *their* questions, questions that *they* own, and have wrestled with. They sit in front of us and ask us "what should I research?" We should send them away to find their questions, to read and learn to read the field, to immerse themselves till they wake up in the middle of the night knowing what is burning inside them. Likewise, if you are teaching and you don't have a research question, I cannot help you.

When I joined my university, it was as an administrative officer and tutor. Though I had postgraduate qualifications, research and writing academic articles were not part of my job description. Every moment of every working day was filled with student experiences and journeys witnessing how students grappled with the complexities of unresponsive administrative systems, finding their way, and making sense of disciplinary epistemologies and ontologies, balancing the demands of studying while working. Looking them in their eyes, seeing their hopes and fears compelled me to start documenting what I witnessed. One of the ways I tried to cope with the limits of my own understanding and awkward sense of agency was by reading scholarly articles and making notes, small case studies of the issues students faced and finding literature that could explain what was happening. Being confronted with the complexities of distance education awakened a curiosity in me that has not left me since.

Very interestingly, Rilke claims that once verses emerge from going inward, from the different layers of solitude, "then it will not occur to you to ask anyone whether they are good verses" or to send the poems to a magazine in the hope that they would be published (Rilke 2011, p. 9). It should be enough to see the poems as "your beloved possessions, a piece, and a voice, of your life" (p. 9). The worth of the artwork (or piece of writing) should be determined not by others, but by the response to an inner compulsion to write: "The verdict on it lies in this nature of its origin: there is no other" (p, 9). The value of one's writing should not be determined by "the rewards that may come from the outside" (p. 9).

Writing as a Piece of the Self

Now, this is a difficult one. *Of course*, I would like to embrace the guidance Rilke provides for the young poet. I would love to see my academic articles as my "beloved possessions, a piece and a voice, of [my] life" (Rilke, p. 9). And they are. I think this is a given, for many, if not all researchers, that our research are pieces of ourselves. When I submit an article to a journal, or deliver a keynote, present a seminar or workshop, these are never *just* a PowerPoint, or a manuscript, or some rambling thoughts. These outputs, for whatever audience, are always, at least for me, pieces of myself. I know there may be others that see invited presentations or keynotes and workshops are "just" part of academic life where previous presentations and PowerPoints are rehashed and reworked to new audiences, almost as ready-made, from-the-shelf, drop-off-and-go, and just-in-time responses to a particular demand. These remind me of one-minute noodles or a quick cup-of-soup, where you just add water and there you have a meal.

When I write, and often it is not easy but a deeply uncomfortable process, the joy and effort in crafting a sentence, a paragraph, or a slide in a PowerPoint presentation, result in a feeling that these are not just sentences or paragraphs, or slides, but pieces of me.

In this highly competitive world of researcher rankings and reputation management, it is crucial *to return to the source* of why I write, why I love crafting sentences, paragraphs, and slides and acknowledge and affirm that these arise from an inner compulsion, that I can never cheapen to ready-mix recipes for whatever audience would be kind enough to read my work or listen to my sense-making.

Possibly this explains why critique and desk-rejections from journal articles hurt and disturb so much. Acknowledging that rejections, misunderstandings, and critique hurts and disturbs, however momentarily, because these manuscripts, drafts and presentations were more than "just," but our possessions, pieces of our lives. Acknowledging the hurt and discomfort does not for one moment deter from the immense value that these rejections and critiques add to our thinking and writing. Often, after receiving critique, rejection, or request for a major revision, the feelings of hurt and discomfort dissipate as one attends to the comments and critique as guidance. But even then, there are often remnants of feeling misunderstood, or even under-valued, if not misrecognition. Which brings me back to Rilke.

While peer review and quality criteria are inherent to academic publishing (and should be, in one form or the other), I think it is crucial for authors who publish to treasure the words of Rilke: "The verdict on it lies in this nature of its origin: there is no other" (p. 9). Often in these moments when you hesitate before you press the submit button, or when you walk onto the stage (or more likely, switch on your microphone, camera and ask for permission to share your presentation), I remind myself that what I bring, what I submit, is the result of my own sensemaking, often emerging from deep within myself, and therefore, there is none other similar to what I am about to submit or present. I have to respect, love, and honour, my own processes — they are uniquely mine. No matter the outcome of the submission or the feedback after the presentation, I shared what I had to and could share.

As such, I keep Rilke's advice very close to my heart — that the value of my thinking and writing should not be determined by "the rewards that may come from the outside" (p. 9). These words sound a warning in the context of the doxa of "publish or perish" and the ever-increasing push to apply for research funding, which, when successful, result in additional pressures; and when unsuccessful, result in feelings of resentment, depression, and a questioning of one's own sense of self.

These words, however, are also a warning against being seduced by the constant lure of considering one's h-index as an indication of the value of one's research, thinking and being an author and researcher. Equally, the applause after the keynote, the compliments and handshakes should not deceive one to think that the appreciation and/or applause are unconditional, or permanent. On the contrary. I would be disingenuous to ignore how pleasurable is a good review on a manuscript submission, or applause after a presentation is. Of course, it is amazing and cause for gratitude, and often, celebration. Rilke's words are, however, a sober reminder to never forget the reason for writing, the reason for producing art; namely, because we simply have to.

Which brings me to the second part of his advice referred to above — comparing ourselves with others. Within the context of academic publishing, and possibly publishing as a whole, comparing oneself, and being compared with others, is an inherent characteristic of the field. Submitting applications to be rated as researcher, or to be considered for a research grant, implies being compared not only to other researchers and applications, but to specified criteria that do not, necessarily, acknowledge the internal processes, sensitivities, and vulnerabilities of researchers. Often the criteria emerge from other interests, despite being good in their intentions, such as measuring impact, while many researchers will testify that achieving impact is mostly outside of the locus of control or the researcher or project, and criteria for measuring impact often misrecognizes the complexities and entangle of projects with the nexus of structural and inter-personal power-plays, context, and unforeseen circumstances. Being awarded a grant does not grant the researcher(s) superpowers, possibly to the contrary, when researchers and the project become a prized possession and claimed by various interests.

Knowing that one's work will be compared to other works and applications, knowing that comparison is an inherent characteristic of scholarship and academic publishing, means assuming "this fate and bear it, its burden and its greatness, without ever asking after the rewards that may come from the outside" (Rilke, 2011, p. 9). It is crucial to find one's inner compass and create our worlds and find the reason for being an artist, a scholar, and a writer, in ourselves.

Following through with his argument that the young poet should not find his rewards in the praises and demands of those who would read his work, Rilke states "Works of art are infinitely solitary and nothing is less likely to reach them than criticism, only love can grasp them and hold them and do them justice" (2011, p. 18). The young poet is advised to "trust yourself and your instincts; even if you go wrong in your judgement, the natural growth of your inner life will gradually, over time, lead you to other insights. Allow your verdicts their own quiet untroubled development which like all progress must come from deep within and cannot be forced or accelerated" (p. 18). Allowing time to take its course and time, itself, will not be hurried and the young poet should allow the natural maturation of his thinking and writing processes.

> Everything must be carried to term before it is born. To let every impression and the germ of every feeling come to completion inside, in the dark, in the unsayable, the unconscious, in what is unattainable to one's own intellect, and to wait with deep humility and patience for the hour when a new clarity is delivered: that alone is to live as an artist, in the understanding and in one's creative work (Rilke, 2011, p. 18).

Addressing the impatience to grow as fast as possible, and to constantly look at how time passes, Rilke advises the young poet that "ten years are nothing" (2011, p. 18). We should not measure ourselves against time, as if our processes and thinking can be hurried, but rather grow and ripen like a tree which does not hurry the flow of its sap and stands at ease in the spring gales without fearing that no summer may follow. It will come. But it comes only to those who are patient, who are simply there in their vast, quiet tranquillity, as if eternity lay before them. (p. 19).

Time

And patience. Not only patience with one's own processes and thinking, but also with how life evolves and unfolds outside of us.

Reflecting on these words, I cannot ignore the fact that I am in a hurry. While I was born curious and in trouble, I had, from the time that I became conscious of my own thinking, a deep sense that time and how my life would emerge and evolve, was, to a large extent, out of my control. I was in a hurry to discover life, to read as much as possible, to experience as much as possible, driven by and living on a daily dose of adrenaline. Combined with the curiosity and my own hurriedness, it comes as no surprised that trouble was never far away. And trouble there was, possibly more than many would experience in two lifetimes. Not that I am proud of the trouble. To the contrary. I made some really stupid decisions in my life, the consequences of many of these will accompany me for the rest of my life, until the moment I hurry and hurl myself towards the big Unknown. I had to learn that the unfolding of the effects of those stupid decisions would not be hurried up. Not only could the effects of some of my decisions not be hurried up, the understanding and forgiveness of those affected by many of my decisions was not within my control. I had to let me go of my desire for reconciliation, for understanding and absolution. "Forgive and forget," the saying goes. I am afraid that no one can demand that of anyone, even less so for myself.

While these events taught me *slowness*, if not dealing with facing the impossibility of resolution, my inherent and insatiable curiosity in my scholarship continue to inform the hurriedness in my research. My hurry is most probably informed not only by an inner drive to know more and write more, but also by the fact that I consider myself a late bloomer, in more than just my scholarship.

By the time I started to work in a university setting as a student advisor and tutor, instructional designer, and later as full-time researcher, I had a permanent sense of arriving *late*. Very early on did I realize (and accept) that I am *behind* and had to catch up. Not only did my work require of me to be conversant with educational theory and the evolution of educational technology, but there was also so much that I wanted to know. My days did not have enough hours. I was relentlessly reading and catching up. Disregarding the advice Rilke (2011) provided to the young poet, I was comparing myself to others: those who knew more, wrote more, and were cited more. In mitigation, I did not know about Rilke's advice then, but I think even if I did, it would have had no effect on me. I would have justified my drive to know more and to write more by referring to the reality that I arrived late, and that I was catching up.

Making matters worse, outside of my intrinsic curiosity and drive, was a system (both in the institution and in the field of publishing) that encouraged and rewarded quantity, often without considering quality. Very early in my current role as permanent researcher, I was made aware of researcher rankings, of its importance for the institution and my own scholarship. Needless to say, I accepted the challenge.

In retrospect, I don't regret the pace, the hunger, and the perpetual hurry. Yet, I am increasingly aware of the cost. Like someone who start long distance running relatively late in adulthood, the cost of the drive, the training routine, and competition creeps up on you in the late hours of the night and in waking up feeling as if a terrible alien has taken over your body and is consuming you slowly.

I am two years away from compulsory retirement. I am more aware than ever before of how hungry I am, how much more I want to know and write about, and how time is slipping away from me like my bank balance two weeks before the end of the month. So, when Rilke admonishes the young poet to not think about ten years as nothing, I want to cry out that I have even less than ten years. And yet, now more than ever before do I realize the wisdom in Rilke's words that trees do not "hurry the flow of its sap and stands at ease in the spring gales without fearing that no summer may follow" (2011, p. 19). Now, more than ever before, do I hear his words to embrace a "quiet tranquillity, as if eternity lay before [me]" (p. 19).

It is important to note that Rilke's (2011) advice also holds true for the process of writing or preparing a presentation. Often ideas and words will flow, impatiently, waiting to find expression on a screen, or in a PowerPoint. Writing is effortless, joyful, and experiencing this flow is a truly a gift. Most of the times, however, writing is difficult, almost as if one is looking in vain for a thought worthy to express on paper. Knowing that one cannot just walk away from the article due to having already expressed the invitation to submit the chapter or article, or just because of the external quantification of research, is not possible. You are chair-bound, staring at the screen, typing, and deleting what you have typed in a tango with self-doubt that maybe you attempted too much, should not have committed yourself, or that maybe you just have writer's block.

It is in moments like these that I need to embrace Rilke's (2011) words to trust not only the writing process like a tree trusts the sap to flow, but also to quietly wait for the season to change. This seems to be easier than done with deadlines following your every waking moment like zombies craving for whatever you have left to offer them, before you, yourself, become a zombie.

I have not found a defence against these moments of sheer panic when my fingers hover directionless above the keyboard, and I doubt my ability to ever get the writing done. I have not found the magic words to shout to the zombies that would make them return to wherever they came from. Sometimes, just when I think I have found the "cure," the cure disappears, and any intention to write a best-selling self-help book for struggling authors evaporates. At times, I would take solace in a long walk or jump into a pool of cold water and quiet down my restless spirit. Lately, I must confess, that the latter really brings me a lot of clarity, in general, and quiets down my monkey brain. When I get into the cold water, I do not get into the water with the expectation that I would be any closer to an answer afterwards. Any expectations for any possible result disappear the moment I jump in, catch my breath, and focuses on controlling my breathing. I must confess that the quietness that follows is the closest to an undefined sense of peace than I have experienced. Somehow the cold water slows down time, or at least my sense of time and hurriedness, and allows me to wait patiently for the season to change.

Other times I would go for a walk, change my focus to fix something that had been on my to-do list since I threw away my previous to-do list. Or I would attend to the thousand-and-one emails, which, most probably, include reminders for reviews, submissions, and student queries. I must confess that attending to emails often would bring back a sense of pure panic as I realize how far behind I actually am; but knowing the dangers of losing my peace, I just get them out of the way, one by one.

Maybe it is my age, of the stage of my life where I find myself while writing this chapter, but I am learning to be more caring to myself, more patient, and more forgiving. I am embracing Rilke more and more, practicing conscious eating and living, meditation and letting go of attachment... trusting the seasons.

This approach aligns well with Rilke's advice to the young poet to embrace the simple, small things that people often overlook and don't value, and not be disturbed by the unresolvedness of many of the questions that live in him.

> ... be patient towards all that is unresolved in your heart and to try to love *the questions themselves* like locked rooms, like books written in a foreign tongue. Do not now strive to uncover answers: they cannot be given to you because you have not been able to live them. And what matters is to live everything. *Live* the questions for now. (p. 23; emphasis in the original)

Embracing not knowing the answers to the many questions has the promise, according to Rilke, that one may "without noticing it, live your way into the answer, one distant day in the future" (2011, p. 24). In a later letter, Rilke again refers to the difficulty of living with questions rather than answers and states, "People have tended (with the help of conventions) to resolve everything in the direction of easiness, of the light, and on the lightest side of the light; but it is clear we must hold on to the heavy, the difficult" (p. 42). Holding on to the difficult, and knowing that we know but little, is made bearable by "a certainty that will never forsake us" (p. 42), a certainty emerging from knowing why we write. In a follow-up letter, Rilke advises Kappus to "accept our existence in as wide a sense as can be; everything, even the unheard of" and that the "only kind of courage" that is required of us to have the courage "for the oddest, the most unexpected, the most inexplicable things that we may encounter" (p. 55). Rilke compares it to being open to explore more than just our own particular spaces with which we are acquainted, "a place by the window, a little area to pace up and down" (p. 56). Such spaces, however comfortable, also holds a certain security. We should not fear the unknown and that which is foreign to us, as these may, if we embrace them, "become our most intimate and most reliable experience" (p. 57). From Rilke's letter, it seems as if the young poet shared with Rilke his loneliness, sadness, and insecurities; and Rilke responds by stating:

> Why should you want to exclude from your life all unsettling, all pain, all depression of spirit, when you don't know what work it is these states are performing within you? Why do you want to persecute yourself with the question of where it all comes from and where it is leading? (p. 58)

Instead of resisting these feelings and experiences and trying to look for reasons why something is happening, Rilke advises Kappus to allow the experience to run its course, to allow it to teach us whatever it has to teach us: "Do not draw over-rapid conclusions from what is happening to you. Simply let it happen. Otherwise, you will too readily find yourself looking on your past, which is of course not uninvolved with everything that is going in you now, reproachfully (that is, moralistically)" (pp. 58–59).

Living the Questions

Research is about questions, and we often value the answers more than the quality of the questions. This is not to say that I underestimate the continuous strive for evidence to solve some of life's most difficult questions and dilemmas, such as a cure for HIV and cancer, or to find the solution to whatever question had been baffling scientists and scholars throughout the ages. I think what Rilke advises the young poet is to embrace not knowing, as a permanent state of being an author or an artist. Rilke states that we must love questions as if they were locked rooms or books written in a foreign language. I think this is powerful. Personally, it is the questions that drive my own processes, and where I don't find the answers, or where the answers are simply not forthcoming, Rilke's advice is that I am not yet ready to "live" the answer.

I take this advice of Rilke not only to refer to questions inspiring my writing and scholarly reflections, but broader questions about my life, the serendipities that characterise much of my life, and my choices and dealing with the effects of my choices. There are many locked rooms. I am surrounded by books written in foreign tongues. Understanding Rilke, these are givens and I am not yet ready to live the answers. For now, I must live the questions.

In stark contrast, Rilke refers to individuals who "resolve everything in the direction of easiness, of the light, and on the lightest side of the light" (Rilke, 2011, p. 24). I must confess that I would have loved more easiness, to live life and to write with the "lightest side of light." And yet, reading Rilke and his comparison of living securely in a little room, "a place by the window, a little area to pace up and down" (p. 56), in contrast to living in strange and uncomfortable spaces where one will encounter "the oddest, the most unexpected, the most inexplicable things that we may encounter" (p. 55); I opt for the latter. Not because of any masochistic tendencies, but because of an openness and curiosity to embrace life to the fullest, opening myself to what the discomfort, loneliness, and depression that "these states are performing within you"

(p. 59). Why should I persecute myself asking: "Where it all comes from and where it is leading?" (p. 58).

Possibly, it is easier at this stage of my life and career to embrace Rilke's advice to embrace life in its widest sense. To embrace the locked rooms and the books written in foreign languages. And to embrace not knowing. Knowing that I may not be ready to live the answers to the questions.

In his second last letter to the young poet, Rilke advises that he should allow life to "take its course. Believe me: life is right, whatever happens" (2011, p. 62). He concludes his letter by reflecting how he spoke to the young poet about life and death "and of the greatness and splendour of both" (p. 63).

And this brings us, dear reader, to a tentative conclusion, but not the end.

Conclusion

I started this reflection by avoiding a beginning, a point of reference of where it all started. Somehow, I thought claiming a "beginning" would firstly mean that I know where it all started (which I frankly don't know), and secondly, it was, at least for me, the most boring option.

In this reflection, I used Rilke's (2011) *Letters to a Young Poet* as my point of reference and entered into a conversation with Rilke, reflecting on his view of inspiration, the challenges that artists and poets face, and although being an artist and poet are worlds away from being an academic researcher and scholar, his words and his advice to the young poet inspired and continue to inspire me.

In the end, and at the end of this reflection, I hope that my conversation with Rainer Maria Rilke allowed you some glimpses of the questions that inspire my writing, my despair and ecstasy and my living in awe of what I don't know and don't understand; and being seduced by the splendour of life and death.

References

Hyde, L. (2011). Introduction. In Rilke, R. M. *Letters to a Young Poet* (pp. xix–xxxvii). Translated by Charlie Louth. Penguin.

Rilke, R. M. (2011). *Letters to a Young Poet*. Translated by Charlie Louth. Penguin.

15. A Few Words in Conclusion

Dianne Conrad

It seemed to me that I needed to write a few succinct thoughts to conclude these amazing chapters; but I promised in the Welcome and Introduction not to try to thematize or order them. However, I think it's in our writing nature, as published authors, to try to tie things up nicely at the end. Certainly, as an editor, I've asked many authors to add something solid to the conclusion of their work, something satisfying with which to leave the reader. That said, this will be short!

In a recent publication of my own, *Opening the Online Door to Academe* (2022), I highlighted some of the various paths that academe provides for its scholars… call it, in the style of Belenky, Clinchy, Goldberger and Tarule's (1986) "ways of knowing how to be successful in a challenging and diverse field." The contributors to this book have demonstrated so articulately and thoughtfully their "ways," and I thank them for the forthrightness, clarity, and honesty that hallmark each chapter.

In the book mentioned above, I outlined scholarly, teacher-ly, and administrative routes to academic success. I share with Mark Nichols the experience of "working from the margins"; that is, wearing two hats — moonlighting, in a sense — by taking on teaching positions while employed full-time as an administrator. And while I pretty much stayed on the margins throughout a long career, some of our contributors moved from mainstream institutional life to the freedom of more independent scholarship, building on their years of institutional experience. Perhaps this is a route that is attractive to us "mature" — that is to say, old(er) — folks. Let's keep an eye on some of our younger contributors.

What can the novice, or questioning, or unsure scholar/writer/researcher/teacher take away from these stories of perseverance, experience, and perhaps just plain happenstance or good luck? I think it's important to acknowledge that, as one author wrote and others alluded to, the serendipity of being "in the right place, at the right time" can be very instrumental to the academic journey. And, on the opposite end of the spectrum, careful and methodical planning and decision-making also brings advancement and rewards. The chapters you have already read in the book have detailed some of the authors' arduous journeys either "up the ladder" or through various hardships and hurdles.

Arduous journeys are often assisted by mentors. David Starr-Glass, specifically, foregrounds the importance of mentoring; but several others, including Tony Bates, Jennifer Roberts, Junhong Ziao, and myself, tell stories that highlight the importance to a newcomer of helping hands, sage advice, or even simply kindness or a receptive ear. The lessons here are two-fold: Be a mentor when that possibility occurs and/or be open and receptive to mentoring.

Our contributing authors have broad and varied backgrounds — literature and fine arts, sociology, business, technology and science, teaching at various levels, and even the world of entertainment. This diversity is well understood in our field: as Tony Bates wrote, "No one wakes up at fifteen years of age and says: 'I want to be a specialist in online learning.'" I, too, have written much the same in stating that nobody graduating from secondary school has "adult educator" on their minds. I, myself, grew into that role, bringing with me many years of university education, all of which served me well. Similar stories are detailed throughout these chapters.

As a teacher at graduate and doctoral levels, I have relished the opportunity to introduce many adult learners from many diverse backgrounds to our field. My own education, spanning English, psychology, business administration, and adult and distance education prepared me well for the career that followed and, clearly, my author-colleagues similarly benefited from their preparatory years. Perhaps not all roads lead to open and distance learning, but, as demonstrated in these pages, the roads are wide and varied, offering myriad opportunities to those who are seeking entry to the field.

The roads that our contributors have walked have reflected history, whimsy, determination, politics, coincidence and good fortune, adversity and hardship, confidence, lack of confidence, doggedness, and commitment. Many refer to having suffered Brookfield's (1990) Imposter Syndrome, as I, myself, have done. I thank them all for their honesty and sincerity.

References

Belenky, M. F., Clinchy, B. M., Goldberger, N. R., & Tarule, J. M. (1986). *Women's ways of knowing: The development of self, voice, and mind*. Basic Books.

Brookfield, S. D. (1990). *The Skillful Teacher*. Jossey-Bass.

Conrad, D. (2022). *Opening the Online Door to Academe*. Brill.

Index

academe 13, 181, 192, 213, 215
academia 41, 87–90, 92, 95, 97, 114, 119, 130, 133, 174, 180, 182, 185, 191, 200, 202
Academia.edu 78
academic discipline 21, 31, 98
academic journals 20, 28, 95
academy 9, 92, 174, 180, 190–191, 193
Addison, Joseph 103, 154
adult education 62, 65, 121, 130
advice 9, 15–17, 23, 51, 56, 60, 68–69, 76, 78, 90, 93, 97, 102, 116, 119, 125, 129, 137–138, 142, 146, 151, 158, 162, 172, 200, 204–205, 207–208, 209, 211, 212, 214. *See also* tips
Africa 51–52, 54–56, 88, 90–92, 98–99, 178
African 90, 96, 183, 195
agency 71, 74, 80–84, 150–151, 174, 203
Akyol, Zehra 133
Alberta 60, 132, 176, 188
Alberta, University of 60, 132
American 22, 53, 56, 60, 72, 84, 134
Anderson, Terry 7, 14, 62, 132–133
Apple Notes 37–38, 51
Archer, Walter 17, 62, 66, 132
Athabasca University (AU) 45, 64–65, 132
Atlantic Ocean 52
Atwood, Margaret 10
Audio-Visual Media Research Group (AVMRG) 148
Australasian Society for Computers in Learning in Tertiary Education (ASCILITE) 157, 163
Australia 92, 163
Australian 94

authors 7–11, 14–17, 21, 23, 28–29, 32, 34–36, 40–41, 54, 61, 64, 66–67, 76, 83, 88, 101–103, 106–112, 114, 120, 132–133, 139, 162, 175, 177, 184, 189, 197–198, 201, 204–205, 209, 211, 213–214
authorship 64, 104, 169, 201

Baggaley, Jon 150
Bandura, Alfred 81–82, 84
Baron, George 147
Bates, Tony 17, 141, 150, 154, 214
Belcher, Wendy 124, 126
Belgians 22
Bermuda 59
Birmingham 145
blogs 34–35, 41–42, 117, 119, 123, 140–141, 163, 196
boundary, boundaries 39, 47, 56, 119, 122, 175, 185, 192–195
Bozkurt, Aras 16, 101, 106–109, 115, 163, 169
British 72, 146, 150, 169, 178
British Broadcasting Corporation (BBC) 72, 148–149
British Columbia, University of (UBC) 151–152
Brookfield, Stephen D. 18, 97–98, 215
Butler, Octavia 125

Calgary, University of 130–131
Cambridge, University of 142
Campbell, Katy 60
Canada 9, 64, 135, 149–151, 176, 179–180, 183, 186
Canadian 10, 16, 18, 150, 179, 183
Cape Town 52
Carroll, Lewis 108, 115

Case, Ronald 112, 170
Centre for Open Education Research (COER) 64, 94
challenge 8, 13, 22, 31, 55, 81, 83, 87, 96, 109, 119, 122–124, 126, 131–132, 134–135, 137–139, 161, 187, 189, 191, 208, 212
China 71–73, 75–81, 94
China Scholarship Council (CSC) 77
Chinese 71–73, 75, 77–80
Chomsky, Noam 72, 84
Cleveland, Marti 140
Cockburn, Cynthia 120
collaboration 66, 75, 122–126, 131–134, 139–140, 163, 201
colonialism 173–174, 179, 195
communication 9, 20–22, 24–25, 27, 29–31, 48–49, 53, 57, 62, 89, 102–103, 109, 125, 129, 133, 136, 138, 150, 178, 183, 185, 190, 198
Community of Inquiry (CoI) 60, 132, 134–135, 140
conferences 18, 42, 48–49, 57, 62, 72, 78, 85, 91–92, 94–95, 102, 133, 141, 149–150, 163, 171, 177, 201
confidence 8, 10, 28, 63, 76–78, 82, 93, 97, 109, 121, 125, 158–159, 165, 188–189, 215
Conrad, Dianne 7, 10, 13, 59, 157, 213, 215
Continuous Professional Development (CPD) 92
Cottrell, Michael 173
COVID-19 8, 106–107, 115, 125, 152
creativity 14–15, 17, 30, 47–48, 50, 55, 63, 67, 76, 83, 89, 101, 108, 137–140, 176, 184, 190, 206
criticism 8, 29, 57, 76, 83, 88, 93, 97–98, 103–104, 111–115, 122–123, 127, 134, 148–149, 152, 166, 184, 186, 190, 196, 200, 206. *See also* rejection
Cronin, Catherine 17, 119–120, 122–127
Csikszentmihalyi, Mihaly 81, 84
Cultural Revolution (China) 71–72
cultures, the importance of 21, 43–44, 79–80, 98, 146, 149, 153, 169, 175, 177, 179–180, 190, 193–194, 200
curiosity 7, 17, 62, 68, 73, 75, 77, 81, 102, 108, 110, 129–130, 156–157, 160–161, 165, 201, 203, 206–207, 211
 curiosity-driven 68

Damocles, sword of 9
Davis, Angela 125–126
DEC International Forum 79–80
Dewey, John 134, 140
Didion, Joan 33, 44
digital literacy 96
dissertation 36, 47, 55, 60–61, 63–65, 68, 120, 176, 188. *See also* PhD, thesis
distance education 9, 57, 64, 71, 74, 87–88, 91–94, 98, 106, 115, 131–132, 147, 150–151, 154, 156, 203, 214
Dreaver-Charles, Kristine 173
Dron, Jon 10, 17, 33, 39, 45
Dublin 94
Dyer, Geoff 50, 58

Easter 108–109
Edinburgh, University of 75
editing 9, 14, 34, 104, 125, 136, 138, 188
editor 10, 14, 23, 28–29, 34, 51, 61, 68–69, 75, 78, 88, 96, 102, 111, 114–115, 157, 164–165, 168, 190, 200–201, 213
Edmonton 64
education 8–10, 14–16, 18, 21, 32, 36, 45, 47, 53, 56–57, 62–65, 71–74, 76, 81, 87–88, 90–96, 98, 106–107, 115, 119–127, 130–132, 134–135, 143, 146–148, 150–154, 156, 169, 177–186, 203, 207, 214. *See also* adult education, distance education, open learning
educational technology (Edtech) 131, 153, 169, 177, 185, 207. *See also* technology
Eliot, T. S. 49, 58
England 146, 151
English 14–15, 18, 22, 28–29, 55, 61, 72, 74–75, 77–78, 81, 84, 99, 142–143, 145, 150, 176, 178, 183, 190, 214
English as a Second Language (ESL) 176

Eurocentric 180
European 22, 85, 127, 149, 157, 195
European Distance and e-Learning Network (EDEN) 94, 157, 163
Evernote 37
Facebook 135
Fanon, Franz 184, 195
Farrell, Glen 150
Flexible Learning Association of New Zealand (FLANZ) 157
Freire, Paolo 120, 184, 186, 195
French 14, 52, 142–143, 176
Garrison, Randy 17, 60, 62, 66, 129, 131, 140
Geertz, Clifford 53, 58
German 94, 198
Germany 64, 94, 123
"giving back" 16–17, 44
Goldberg, Murray 151
Google Images 95
Google Scholar 8, 40, 67
Guangzhou Institute of Foreign Languages 74
Harasim, Linda 150, 154
Haughey, Margaret 60
Hemingway, Ernest 74
higher education 9, 21, 32, 56, 62, 71–73, 81, 96, 121–127, 182, 185
high-impact journals 27, 78
Hiltz, Roxanne 150, 154
hooks, bell 120
Huang, Guowen 75, 84
Hyde, Lewis 198–199, 212
identity 10, 44, 54, 80, 91, 102, 119, 123, 157, 173–174, 184, 190, 192, 195, 199
Imposter Syndrome 7, 18, 22, 88, 97, 215. *See also* Brookfield, Stephen D.
India 92, 94
Indigeneity 173–174, 179, 182–183, 185–186, 191
Information Technology (IT) 119, 121–122, 124, 150
Institute for Educational Technology (IET) 148

Institute for Open and Distance Learning (IODL) 91
interdisciplinary 32, 56, 88–89, 98
interdisciplinarity 88–89, 92, 98
International Council for Open and Distance Education (ICDE) 94, 150, 157, 163
internet 47, 49, 53–54, 90, 111, 150
Iowa 176
Ireland 119, 123–124, 179–180
Irish 94, 179–180, 186
Istanbul 94
James, Henry 55
Jandrić, Petar 101, 116
Jerusalem 22
Jobs, Steve 105
Johannesburg 51
Joplin 38–39
journals 11, 13, 20–22, 27–30, 41–42, 57, 66, 68, 72–75, 77–79, 82, 89, 93, 95–96, 122, 126, 155, 157, 161–164, 177, 188, 191, 195, 203–204. *See also* academic journals, high-impact journals
Jung, Insung 78
Kaufman, David 150
Kay, Harry 143
Kenya 177–178, 190, 195
Kenyans 178
keynotes 41–42, 94, 141, 155, 200, 203, 205
Kindle 45, 165
knowledge 8–9, 17, 19–20, 22, 24–26, 30–32, 36, 41, 63, 73, 81, 83, 89–90, 93, 95–96, 101, 116, 131, 136, 138, 141, 149, 159, 162–163, 174, 176–178, 182–183, 185, 192–193
  new knowledge 25–26, 81
Koole, Marguerite 16, 173
Latin 14, 142
Lawrence, D. H. 50
Leaders and Legends of Online Learning 157
Learning Management System 151
Lee, Michael 104
Leicester 51
Lenz, Frederick 105

Lethbridge, University of 176
LinkedIn 41, 78
literature 13–14, 23, 28, 30, 54, 61, 65, 76–77, 102–103, 109, 111–114, 120, 132, 157–163, 169, 171, 179, 181, 203, 214
London 126, 140–142, 146–147, 154
London, University of 142, 144, 147
Lorde, Audre 120
Louis, Clarence 9
Marclay, Christian 104
MarkDown 38
Marsh, Len 144
McGreal, Rory 14
McLuhan, M. 43–45
Melbourne 94
Melville, Herman 39, 45
Memorial University 150
memory 35–36, 42, 101, 104
Mendeley 161–162, 165–166
mentor 16–17, 20, 66, 68, 75–77, 83, 90, 93, 98, 182, 214
mentoring 9, 16, 90, 214
metaphor 34, 39, 108–109, 160, 168, 182
Milner, Marion 47–48, 58
Mistawasis First Nation 177
Moleskine notebook 37
Moore, Michael 60, 110, 116
Moscow 94
motivation 10, 15, 19, 36, 65, 68, 71–73, 78, 80–84, 123–124, 136–137, 149, 157, 162, 189, 191, 194. *See also* self-directed learning
  extrinsic 73–74, 81–82, 84
  intrinsic 71, 73–74, 78, 80–84, 144, 207
Mounzer, Lina 119, 127
Nairobi 177, 195
National Extension College (NEC) 147–149
National Foundation for Educational Research (NFER) 143, 145–147
National Institute of Distance Learning (NIDL) 163
Netherlands 176
networking 62, 94, 157

Newfoundland 150
New Zealand 123, 155, 157
Nichols, Mark 18, 155–156, 163, 169, 213
Norway 57
notes 8–10, 23, 35, 37–39, 50–51, 53, 68, 77, 79, 103, 110, 112–113, 129–130, 137, 139, 160, 162, 165–166, 168, 171, 187, 189, 201, 203, 208
  note-taking 37, 53, 103, 160, 165, 187
Nvivo 187
Okoko, Janet Mola 173
OneNote 37, 165–166
open and distance education (ODE) 71, 74, 76–78, 80–83
Open and Distance Learning Association of Australia (ODLAA) 94, 163
open, distance, and flexible learning (ODFL) 155–157, 161–162
open educational resources (OER) 56, 96
Open Education Practice (OEP) 96
open learning 47, 53, 56
Open Learning Agency 150–151
open, online, and distance learning (ODL) 13, 62, 93
Open University in Scotland 121
Open University of China 77
Open University of Shantou 77
Open University (OU) 121, 147–150
Open University United Kingdom (OUUK) 72, 77
Ortega y Gasset, José 108
Oslo 150
Oxford, University of 44, 142
Palmer, Amanda 105
passion 17, 19, 31, 42, 47, 62, 69, 136, 152, 191
patience 91, 199, 206, 209–210
Perry, David 73–74
Peters, Otto 131, 140
PhD 36, 47, 55–56, 63, 75–76, 88–91, 93, 97, 109, 119–120, 123–124, 147, 153, 155–156, 158, 163–164, 176–177, 179, 182, 185, 188, 192–193
Piaget, Jean 144, 154

Plath, Sylvia 47, 54–55
polyvocality 16, 173, 192, 194, 196
Pomodoro method 189
PowerPoint 203, 208
Powers, Richard 33, 45
Pratchett, Terry 197
Prinsloo, Paul 9, 15, 197
prior learning assessment and recognition (PLAR) 62
procrastination 49–50, 52, 55, 185
ProWritingAid 165
publishers 27, 29
publishing 7–10, 13, 19, 21–23, 27–28, 30–31, 40–41, 60, 63–64, 66, 74–75, 87–88, 93, 99, 119, 122–123, 126, 137–138, 156–157, 159, 163–164, 169, 177, 188, 191, 195, 200, 204–205, 207
"publish or perish" 21, 204
rankings 32, 199–200, 204, 208
reading, the importance of 9, 11, 27, 51–53, 57, 61, 69, 72, 76–77, 91, 95, 102–103, 114, 120, 137–138, 160–162, 168, 172, 187
reflection 15–18, 20, 22, 24–25, 33, 39, 43, 48, 78, 97–98, 120–123, 134–135, 140, 148, 169, 174, 180–181, 191, 193, 197–198, 201, 211–212
reflection-in-action 15, 25
reflection-on-action 15, 25
rejection 27, 28, 68, 191, 200, 204. *See also* criticism
research 7–10, 13–15, 17, 19, 21, 27, 29, 32, 41, 47–49, 51–57, 59–65, 67, 69, 71–79, 81–83, 88–89, 91–99, 101–103, 105–107, 109, 111–114, 116–117, 119–125, 129–135, 137–140, 143–153, 155–165, 168–172, 176, 178–179, 181, 186–187, 189–191, 196, 200, 202–205, 207–208
ResearchGate 78
respect 14, 79, 83, 158, 163, 204
reviewers 7, 10, 23, 28–29, 40, 56, 62, 69, 78, 89, 93, 96, 111, 114–115, 157, 163–164, 168, 188, 190–191, 194, 201
Richard III 51
Rilke, Ranier Maria 9, 198–200, 202–212

Roberts, Jennifer 16, 87, 214
Rogers, Carl 144, 154
Rose, Ellen 15, 18
Rourke, Liam 62, 132
Ryle, Gilbert 53
Saskatchewan 16, 177, 179
Saskatchewan, University of 177, 179, 182
Savrock, Joe 60
scholarly blindness 104
scholarly paper 101–103, 105, 107–110, 115
scholarship 31–32, 55, 74–75, 77, 130, 156–157, 167–168, 179, 184, 199, 205, 207–208, 213
Schön, D. 15, 18, 25, 32
Scotland 121, 127
Scottish 121–122
Scrivener 38
self 17, 24, 176, 193–194, 205
  as author 17, 20, 119, 129, 157, 175, 184
  autobiographical 175
  discoursal 81, 105, 175, 180
  possibilities for 20, 80, 95, 98, 157, 175
self-directed learning 90, 134. *See also* motivation
self-efficacy 71, 74, 76, 78–80, 82–84, 88
settler 174, 179, 192
Shale, Doug 132, 140
Sharma, R. C. 108–109, 115
Sheffield, University of 143
Simmons University 73
Simon Fraser University 150
Slick, Grace 108
Smith, Linda 191, 196
Social Sciences and Humanities Research Council (SSHRC) 62, 135
solitude 198–200, 203
South Africa 51–52, 55–56, 88, 90–92, 98
South African 90, 96
South Africa, University of 91–92
Spain 123, 176
Spanish 14, 176
Starr-Glass, David 16, 19–20, 23, 32, 214

STEM (Science, Technology, Engineering and Mathematics) 122
St. John's 150
sub-Saharan Africa 54
success 8, 14, 53, 84, 91, 93, 95, 97, 126, 130, 154, 213
  being successful 8, 10, 19, 28, 40, 53–54, 61, 65, 82, 204, 213
Sun Yat-sen University 76
supervisor 14, 60, 64–65, 124, 147, 179, 182–183, 190
Swahili 178
technology 15, 18, 36, 38–39, 43, 45, 62, 67, 89–90, 98, 115, 120, 125–127, 131, 135, 147, 150–154, 169, 177, 180, 182, 185, 207, 214. *See also* educational technology
theory 24, 47, 57, 62, 71, 74, 77, 80, 82–84, 87–88, 91, 112–113, 120, 122, 130, 135–136, 140, 144, 162, 182, 184, 195–196, 207
thesis 17, 47, 54–55, 65, 89, 91, 93, 124, 126, 133, 136, 176, 187–188. *See also* PhD, dissertation
tips 7, 16, 52, 54–55, 68, 71, 101. *See also* advice
tools 10, 37–38, 43, 53, 112, 123, 135–136, 161, 165, 171, 188, 198
Turoff, Murray 150, 154
Twitter 41, 135, 201
United Kingdom (UK) 72, 75–77, 90, 123
United States of America (USA) 73, 176, 195
Vancouver 150
Vaughan, Norm 133, 140
Verne, Jules 109
Voice of America (VOA) 72
Wald, George 104
Wales 76, 146
Wales, Cardiff, University of 76
WebCT 151
Worcestershire 144
Word document 159, 165, 187
words as tools 43
writing, the craft of 8, 13, 20, 26, 31, 42, 109, 111, 173, 203–204
Wuhan University 73
WYSIWYG 38
Xiao, Junhong 16, 71, 73, 75, 84–85
Zawacki-Richter, Olaf 64, 78, 106, 115, 163, 169–170
Zimbabwe 142
Zotero 161, 165

About the Team

Alessandra Tosi was the managing editor for this book.

Lucy Barnes and Maria Eydmans performed the proofreading.

Lucy Barnes indexed this book.

Jeevanjot Kaur Nagpal designed the cover. The cover was produced in InDesign using the Fontin font.

Jeremy Bowman typeset the book in InDesign. The text font is Tex GyrePagella; the heading font is Californian FB.

Mihaela Buna wrote the Alt-text for the images in the book.

Cameron Craig produced the paperback, hardback, EPUB, PDF, HTML and XML editions. The conversion is performed with open source software such as pandoc (https://pandoc.org/) created by John MacFarlane and other tools freely available on our GitHub page (https://github.com/OpenBookPublishers).

Laura Rodriguez Pupo was in charge of marketing and distribution.

This book has been anonymously peer-reviewed by experts in their field. We thank them for their invaluable help.

This book need not end here...

Share

All our books — including the one you have just read — are free to access online so that students, researchers and members of the public who can't afford a printed edition will have access to the same ideas. This title will be accessed online by hundreds of readers each month across the globe: why not share the link so that someone you know is one of them?

This book and additional content is available at:

https://doi.org/10.11647/OBP.0347

Donate

Open Book Publishers is an award-winning, scholar-led, not-for-profit press making knowledge freely available one book at a time. We don't charge authors to publish with us: instead, our work is supported by our library members and by donations from people who believe that research shouldn't be locked behind paywalls.

Why not join them in freeing knowledge by supporting us:
https://www.openbookpublishers.com/support-us

Follow @OpenBookPublish

Read more at the Open Book Publishers **BLOG**

You may also be interested in:

Open Education
International Perspectives in Higher Education
Patrick Blessinger (editor)

https://doi.org/10.11647/OBP.0103

Democratising Participatory Research
Pathways to Social Justice from the South
Carmen Martinez-Vargas (author)

https://doi.org/10.11647/OBP.0273

Hanging on to the Edges
Essays on Science, Society and the Academic Life
Daniel Nettle

https://doi.org/10.11647/OBP.0155

www.ingramcontent.com/pod-product-compliance
Lightning Source LLC
Chambersburg PA
CBHW061250230426

43663CB00022B/2962